PURITAN'S PROGRESS

By MONICA FURLONG

WITH LOVE TO THE CHURCH
THE END OF OUR EXPLORING
CONTEMPLATING NOW
TRAVELLING IN
PURITAN'S PROGRESS

Puritan's Progress

Monica Furlong

Coward, McCann & Geoghegan, Inc.
New York

ACKNOWLEDGMENT: all illustrations are reproduced by permission of the Trustees of Bunyan Meeting, Bedford.

First American Edition 1975

SBN: 698-10688-1

Library of Congress Cataloging in Publication Data
Furlong, Monica.
    Puritan's progress.

    Bibliography: p.
    Includes index.
    1. Bunyan, John, 1628-1688. I. Title.
PR3331.F8   1975   828' .4'07 [B]   75-28324

Printed in the United States of America

TO CHARLOTTE AND ALEX
with very much love

Acknowledgments

———

I should like to record my particular thanks to Mr. Gordon Tibbutt of Bedford for all his help and kindness in the preparation of this book. Also to Professor Roger Sharrock of King's College, London, the librarians of the Friends' House Library and Dr. Williams's Library, Dr. Alfred Plaut, Miss Alison Webster, the Trustees of Bunyan Meeting, and to Mrs. Joan Horton, who prepared the manuscript. Also to the Arts Council of Great Britain who assisted me with a grant.

I am also grateful for the books *John Bunyan* by Richard Greaves (the Sutton Courtenay Press), and *John Bunyan in America* by David E. Smith (University of Indiana Press) which helped immeasurably in my understanding of Bunyan's theology and of his influence in America.

Contents

———

PURITAN'S PROGRESS

Introduction

———

Nearly three hundred years after his death John Bunyan is still a name known to many who are neither historians nor specialists in English literature. He is known principally as the author of *The Pilgrim's Progress*, and is paid perhaps the greatest compliment given to an author — otherwise reserved in England chiefly for Shakespeare and Dickens — that the characters and events of his masterpiece are known by name even by those who have never read his works. Bunyan transcended the cultural and religious framework from which he wrote and achieved a universal audience — the *Progress* was translated into more than 198 languages.

Bunyan's work interested many remarkable men and for several centuries was known to most educated people. References to him and to his work appear in the writings of Johnson, Pope, Swift, Cowper, and Matthew Arnold, and in the letters of Keats, Browning, Lamb and George Eliot. Sairey Gamp in *Martin Chuzzlewit* speaks of 'this Piljian's Projiss of a mortal wale' and Charlotte Brontë, Harriet Beecher Stowe, and Louisa Alcott all use imagery drawn from the *Progress*. The *Progress* even passed across the unclouded skies of Huckleberry Finn.*

* 'One (book) was Pilgrim's Progress, about a man that left his family, it didn't say why. I read considerable in it now and then. The statements was interesting, but tough.' Mark Twain, *Huckleberry Finn*.

In America Bunyan was a more important influence even than in England; in the early years because the *Progress*, with its lonely hero setting off into the unknown, reflected the struggles of the pioneers; again at the time of the Civil War when the Abolitionists identified their struggles with Bunyan's *Holy War*. His work captured better than that of any other writer the hope and religious idealism upon which the American Republic was founded.

For some writers — Nathaniel Hawthorne and e. e. cummings in America, and Bernard Shaw in England — Bunyan was a major influence that changed and shaped their thinking and their work.

Bunyan achieved fame within his own lifetime, partly as the author of the *Progress*, which within ten years of publication had gone into eleven English editions, and been published in translation in Dutch, French and German. Partly too, because he had taken a dramatic part in one of the most important conflicts of his age. He refused to 'conform' to the Church of England by attending church on a Sunday, and he took a leading part in organising and preaching at a sectarian meeting, an action which had been illegal since the reign of Queen Elizabeth and for which he was imprisoned for twelve years under Charles II.

He was claiming the right which many others of similar social background were claiming at about the same time — to think for himself on matters of religious belief. A huge class of minor tradesmen and shopkeepers — haberdashers, cordwainers, candle-makers, grocers, ostlers, buttonmakers, combmakers, braziers and many more — were emerging, in particular by way of Nonconformity, to claim a religious, and political, maturity. The educated men of the period thought them illiterate upstarts, and said so; the worst insult that was hurled at Bunyan when emotion ran high was always that he was a tinker. ('You seem to be angry with the Tinker,' Henry Denne wrote to the Professor of Arabic at Cambridge, 'because he strives to mend souls as well as Kettles and Pans.')

He might have remained a figure of minor interest to historians, like other 'mechanick preachers' of his day, but for the fact that he was also an artist. There are not many artists in England who have emerged from the working-class, perhaps because the class system, with its rigid expectations, has been so powerful. It takes rare gifts of imagination and intelligence to produce works of art against a background of poverty, hard physical work, poor education, and the possibility of ridicule.

Bunyan had rare gifts, as some of the most discerning English critics have noted.

What has carried his fame, however, as much as his art, has been the attraction his work and life held for the evangelical tradition of English Christianity. This reached its apotheosis in Victorian England; George Offor's Memoir (1860) catches the hagiographical note. Bunyan is the evangelical saint and every detail of his life — his trade, his imprisonment, his blind child, even his wife's miscarriage — is reported with breathless and uncritical admiration. Offor was not alone in this — innumerable nineteenth-century clergymen wrote in similar vein; Bunyan, at least as they imagined him to be, was the Victorian ideal — chaste, temperate, hardworking, a good family man, pious, brave. The darker, more complex sides of his personality, so truthfully and fearlessly portrayed by Bunyan in his spiritual autobiography *Grace Abounding to the Chief of Sinners*, are comfortably assimilated by them with the feeling that after all his conversion changed all that. They exaggerate the sins of his youth the better to enjoy the transformation which follows (in the established tradition of improving literature), yet because of their longing to point a moral they do not look too closely at the conflict which almost shattered Bunyan, or even give full weight to his theological beliefs. They miss the man. They see neither the agony over which his faith formed such a fine bridge, the poetry with which he searched man's condition, nor the virility with which he attacked life.

It is, I believe, the poetry of *The Pilgrim's Progress*, as well as of parts of *Grace Abounding*, which should chiefly commend Bunyan to us. He is, supremely, an artist, and as an artist has valuable things to say about man's condition which remain valuable even if we do not share his beliefs or are antipathetic to them.

He is important on other levels, too. He is particularly interesting as part of the Puritan movement, forcing us to recognise what a useful function the Puritan has performed in English, European, and American history, deeply ambivalent as we are about him. In the English mind, because of the remarkable stand made by Nonconformity against persecution, Puritanism has inescapable associations with the voice of conscience (as well as other less attractive associations). Conscience itself is not always a very welcome companion, yet we respect those who have consciences particularly if we know that, as in the case of the Nonconformists, they are prepared to undergo suffering, and if necessary,

death, sooner than submit to an alien code of values. We may dislike the
Puritan for his suspicion of the senses, or rail at him for the damage he
does to the imagination, or for the guilts and repressions he has inflicted
on his children and their descendants, yet in the end we cannot withhold
all admiration from him. I think we have to recognise that we need him.

He reached his fullest flowering in the seventeenth century in England,
in parts of Europe and in New England, yet his roots go far back, perhaps
to the Stoics or to the Roman 'gravitas'. The neo-Puritans of our own
time may or may not have religious affiliations. An Orwell, a Camus, a
Solzhenitsyn, or a fictional character like Piggy in Golding's *Lord of the
Flies*, has the traditional Puritan resolution as much as a Bonhoeffer or a
Martin Luther King.

The Puritan is, amongst other things, a man who refuses to let his
beliefs be compromised beyond a certain point, and is thereafter imper-
vious to threats and hostile opinions. It is not so much that he does not
see, and rue, the cost of standing out against established opinion or mass
opinion, as that he feels he has no choice. Like Luther he 'can do no
other'.

The Puritan movement both within and without the Church of
England took it for granted that a man would suffer all things for what
he believed was right. Many Nonconformists were fined, sent to prison,
and suffered eviction and distraint of possessions. Some were transported,
some publicly whipped or pilloried. Others chose voluntary exile in the
New World.

The courage of so many individuals marks a nation; in England it
imprinted an ideal of the good man — truthful, honest, brave, god-
fearing, hard-working and dutiful — that was to haunt the English
imagination for centuries (and deeply influence the American character),
and still has a vestigial effect, though we are impatient nowadays with the
defects of the emotions and the imagination which for us tend to
discredit the Puritans.

Opponents of the Puritans feel that they damaged something sweet,
spontaneous and natural in men, an unselfconsciousness about sexuality
and the senses that we find in Shakespeare's plays and throughout
Elizabethan lyric poetry. R. S. Thomas wrote:

> Protestantism — the adroit castrator
> Of art; the bitter negation

Of song and dance and the heart's innocent joy —
You have botched our flesh and left us only the soul's
Terrible impotence in a warm world.[1]

Ernst Gombrich has shown how Protestantism, sweeping across Europe even in its milder form, destroyed painting and decorative art wherever it crossed its path.[2] In some countries painting did not actually die, but underwent a transformation and came out in a new and beautiful form, as in the case of Dutch *genre* painting, but the glad Catholic abandon seemed to be lost for ever. It was as if an operation — not quite castration, as Thomas suggests, perhaps leucotomy would be nearer the mark — had been performed on the imagination of Europe.

Puritanism produced very little art of its own, and since it did not regard art as important, this is not surprising. In England, however, it did produce two geniuses in the persons of John Milton and John Bunyan. Of these two Bunyan was the more thorough-going Puritan. For Milton, Puritanism was put on like a garment, hiding and suppressing the colourful and sensual imagery which had revealed itself in his youth in *Comus*, and *L'Allegro*. For Bunyan, on the other hand, Puritanism was the begetter of his art, without which it would not have existed. Not only did he dramatise the intense conflict his faith imposed upon him, not only did his faith encourage him to record his experience for others; the social changes for which Protestantism was at least partly responsible at last gave men like Bunyan, members of a class hitherto depressed, a chance to speak their mind. And this Bunyan did, in a voice quintessentially English, a voice both sturdy and tender. He has the robust frankness of Chaucer, the lyricism of Elizabethan poetry, and the habit, shared by Chaucer and Shakespeare, of using imagery drawn from the common life of the people of England. Unlike the Elizabethans he uses no classical imagery since he has no classical education. Instead, his imagination and intelligence have found their nourishment in the Bible, and particularly in the Old Testament. His awareness of the Bible is so constant and so vivid that it is as if its people and events are to him contemporaries; everything that happens to him in a very eventful life has this extra dimension or projection giving it new meaning and depth.

He also harks back to an earlier England where the Renaissance had not penetrated. His imagination still plays with giants, with magic, with witches and fairies, and though there is a sensible, bluff Bunyan who doubtless knew what to make of such things, there is also the peasant, with a fresh, child-like sensibility (and this is very near the core of his art) who has changed little since medieval times. If the world of magic is close at hand, then so is the mystical world. God and the Devil are always present.

One is aware in Bunyan, more than in most artists, of the silting down and compression of many generations of human thought and art to produce the stratum of his three masterpieces — the two parts of *The Pilgrim's Progress* and *Grace Abounding to the Chief of Sinners*. F. R. Leavis called his work 'the fruit of a fine civilisation'. It came, he thought, from 'a vigorous human culture. For what is involved is not merely an idiomatic raciness of speech, expressing a strong vitality, but an art of social living, with its mature habits of valuation.'[3]

Bernard Shaw placed Bunyan among the four English artists he most admired. (The others were Blake, Turner and Hogarth.) He also compared him to Nietzsche, Wagner, Ibsen and Schopenhauer, insisting rather quixotically that the conflict between Faith and Works which interested Bunyan and his contemporaries so deeply, was none other than the conflict between 'Wille' and 'Vorstellung' (Will and Representation) which occupied Schopenhauer. What Shaw really admired about Bunyan, however, was that he was an 'artist-philosopher' — that his art was part of a passionately held view of the world for which it was incidentally propaganda. 'This is the true joy in life, the being used for a purpose recognised by yourself as a mighty one; the being thoroughly worn out before you are thrown on the scrap heap; the being a force of Nature instead of a feverish selfish little clod of ailments and grievances complaining that the world will not devote itself to making you happy.'[4] Such artists, thought Shaw, were concerned with the 'unities' of the world whereas a Shakespeare, or a Dickens, was concerned with its diversities. The latter did not strive to fit their characters and their plots into any coherent whole, whereas the work of the artists Shaw most admired shone with conviction.

Shaw's view of the artist may not commend itself very much to us and there are other aspects of Bunyan which appeal to this generation more. The most striking of these was that he was an anti-establishment figure, and that as a result of his recalcitrance he suffered extremely for his beliefs, as do so many political prisoners of our own day. Not to 'conform' religiously was, in Bunyan's day, a political act, and it was one that cost Bunyan a long imprisonment and inflicted great suffering on his family. His life, his belief, and his art are closely intertwined; sometimes, as in his trial, and in his wife's passionate appeal on his behalf, reality is more dramatic than anything in his books. He understood something of the complexity of moral choice, again like many a modern political prisoner, and was tormented by the awareness that doing what he thought was right could destroy those he loved most. 'I saw in this condition I was as a man who was pulling down his house upon the head of his wife and children; yet thought I, I must do it, I must do it.'[5]

There is another, and even more interesting, conflict underlying Bunyan's great battle with political and religious authority. As a young man in his twenties he began for the first time to think deeply about religion, to wonder what claims it should make on his life, and whether he was numbered among the saved or the damned. These were common preoccupations in his day — it was quite usual to suffer deeply from morbid fears of damnation as many Puritan accounts of conversion reveal. Yet for Bunyan with his powerful imagination, his fine mind, his strong ego, it passed into something beyond anxiety and depression, beyond even the birth-struggles of 'conversion', though it included those. It passed into the kind of confrontation between God and man which in the whole of literature is perhaps best described in the Book of Job. Bunyan, in a sense, 'takes on' God in battle, wrestling furiously with his maker in an attempt to grasp the riddle of man's existence. It takes a very strong sanity to survive such an encounter, since at times he sees God and the Devil as perhaps only the psychotic sees them nowadays, and is troubled by compulsions and fears and dark premonitions that we associate with mental illness. At times Bunyan is gripped with paranoid fears that he is singled out by God for scorn and persecution — the negative side of the belief that he is a man specially chosen and with a special vocation. 'I did now feel myself to sink into a gulf, as an house whose foundation is destroyed. I did liken myself in this condition unto the case of some Child that was fallen into a Millpit, who though it could make some shift to scrable and spraul in the water, yet because it could find neither hold for hand nor foot, therefore at last it must die in that condition.'[6]

He charts this fearful period of his life with minute precision; the years of imprisonment and political persecution which follow it directly seem by contrast almost serene. His friends and acquaintance, it is clear, see in him a man who has gone down into the dark chasm that underlies human existence and emerged more human and more whole. 'There goes the man who has been in hell,' Dante's contemporaries are supposed to have said of him when they passed him in the street; the same kind of loving respect, increased by his long term of imprisonment, is accorded to Bunyan as he moves into middle age.

Bunyan, like Dante, can tell us secret, terrible things about the human condition. As with Dante we have to accept a certain framework — that of the Christian language — not because the truth described is a peculiarly Christian truth, but because without such a framework the events would be indescribable, and the reality of the events themselves probably intolerable. Bunyan, like Dante, can be insufferably didactic, and try to browbeat us into Christian attitudes, and into sectarian Christian attitudes at that, yet at his humane best he soars far beyond such pettiness. He begins from the dilemma of every man who finds himself in 'the wilderness of this world'. 'I dreamed, and behold I saw a Man clothed with Raggs, standing in a certain place, with his face from his own House, a Book in his hand, and a great burden upon his Back . . . and he brake out with a lamentable cry, saying, what shall I do?'[7]

What shall I do? How shall I become free? are the universal human questions. The moment when the burden rolls off Christian's back is a glad one for mankind, and whatever our beliefs, or lack of them, we know why he was suddenly 'glad and lightsom' and why 'the springs that were in his head sent the waters down his cheeks.' We know, too, many of the places that Christian passes through on his journey — the Slough of Despond, the Hill Difficulty, the Valley of Humiliation, the Valley of the Shadow of Death, Vanity Fair. We also recognise many of the characters who meet the pilgrims — Mr. Worldly Wiseman, Madam Wanton, my old Lord Lechery, Mr. Smoothman, Mr. Facing Bothways, Mr. Cruelty, and Parson Two-tongues. Bunyan's humour and his insight into the way human beings resist the knowledge of their frailty, redeem the *Progress* from any charge of pious propaganda.

This cannot be said of all his work. The many tracts and sermons which he wrote and preached had no intention beyond that of instructing others, or of joining doctrinal battles, and magnificent as some of them are they do not reach the level of art. *The Holy War* (1682), despite some nice imaginative strokes in the early chapters, becomes finally boring, the allegory of Christ besieging the soul gradually crushing all imaginative interest. *The Life and Death of Mr. Badman* (1680) (sometimes claimed to be a forerunner of the novel), though lively in places, has a depressing smugness about it. Bunyan in middle age, the worst of his suffering behind him, hugely successful as pastor and preacher not only in Bedford but even in the great world of London, could slip into the priggish mould of 'improving' literature.

His interest lies in the consummate artist who wrote the two parts of the *Progress* and *Grace Abounding* and the man whose life, encapsulating the conflicts of his own time, unexpectedly touches ours.

We have less need than the Victorians to believe those whom we admire are psychologically or morally perfect; we find them more interesting as men than as saints, knowing that it is out of pathology that creative insights often emerge. We can note Bunyan's paranoid fantasies about God, his strange compulsions, his exaggeration of his parents' poverty, his excessive readiness to be arrested at Samsell, his shyness with women, his touching delight in his fame and success as preacher and author, without feeling that he is thereby diminished. On the contrary, such perceptions are windows into the soul of a great man; they increase our admiration for the breadth and stature of Bunyan, for the way he has made use of every kind of experience, and has turned his weaknesses as well as his strengths to good account.

He had a touching awareness of his own faults, particularly the fault of vanity. If he loved the success that came to him in his later years (and he was too honest and childlike to pretend he didn't) he never forgot the healing process that had led him to it. Conversion is the technical word for it, but that implies a more sudden change of heart than Bunyan's, even allowing for the careful way Puritan thought divided conversion into particular stages by which it was possible to diagnose a man's spiritual state. Bunyan achieved the stages expected of a converted man and remained — this is perhaps the most important fact about him — a man to whom something cataclysmic had happened. He was like a man healed by miracle. Whatever else he doubted in life here was a fact around which other facts had to arrange themselves. As the blind man in St. John's Gospel remarks 'One thing I know, that whereas I was blind, now I see.'[8] Bunyan is a man who knows one thing — that a particular awareness of love has saved him from deathly despair, perhaps from madness, and restored him to the world of men from which he felt exiled. This is the mainspring of all his best writing, and it is this awareness of his original poverty that saves him from Puritan self-satisfaction.

And this perhaps is why he speaks in a way that the twentieth century can hear. Collectively we know something of our poverty, something of the helpless despair of the child in the mill-pit, and like Bunyan we want to be lifted out, to be saved, and not to sink helplessly into destruction. We may not look for meaning or love in the framework that seemed proper to him; we are very different people. Nevertheless, the voice of the genius is universal if we are patient enough to listen.

NOTES

1 R. S. Thomas, *The Minister* from *Song at the Year's Turning*, Hart-Davis.
2 Ernst Gombrich, *The Story of Art*, Phaidon Press (1950).
3 F. R. Leavis, *The Common Pursuit*, Chatto and Windus (1952).
4 *Preface to Man and Superman*, Standard Edition of Works of Shaw (1903).
5 *Grace Abounding*, p. 328.
6 Ibid., p. 198.
7 *The Pilgrim's Progress*.
8 St. John 9:25.

I

The Puritans

The Puritans, in the original use of the word, were a group who came to the fore in the sixteenth century, deriving most of their inspiration from the French reformer Calvin. Forming the Presbyterian party within the Church of England they advocated radical reform, a reform which involved abolishing the episcopate and reducing ritual. Believing with Calvin that the Bible should rule the life of the state as much as the Church or the individual, they planned a theocratic state. The impression they made upon contemporaries was of a group of men of almost fanatical zeal, obsessed with pious practices, contemptuous of the delights of 'this world', suspicious of the senses, hostile to the theatre, sober and hard-working. They aroused great hostility, a hostility plainly evident in contemporary plays, but even their enemies noted their courage, their readiness to suffer for their cause.

They were, however, disappointed in their major ambition. Queen Elizabeth neither encouraged them nor made martyrs of them, nor did she bow to their demands for Church reform. They complained, in William Haller's words, that she 'did not reform the church but only swept the rubbish behind the door'.[1] This frustration spawned a new group, the Independents, who wanted to rid the Church of its dead-weight by restricting church membership to those who had proved their religious convictions — 'the saints'. It was a group of Independents who founded the colony in Massachusetts Bay. Then there were those who could not wait for the slow processes of Church reform and thought that God was calling or 'gathering' them into separatist Churches outside the established Church. The settlement at Plymouth in New England was one of these. In the seventeenth century there was a burgeoning of 'separatist' Churches. These were the 'sectarians', partly consisting of Baptist congregations, partly of more extreme groups, the Quaker, Ranter, Seeker, Millenarians and others. It was to the sectarian generation of the Puritan movement that Bunyan belonged.

The phenomenon of Puritanism, though seemingly inextricably linked to Christianity, goes far back in European history and is perhaps present to some degree in all human society. Stoicism, with its emphasis on self-control, and elements of Roman thought, particularly as found in the writings of Seneca and Plutarch, strike the Puritan note. Perhaps every civilisation depends upon a natural puritanism, since men's individual inclinations have to be pruned and controlled to accommodate them to the common good. 'I know there is wilde love and joy enough in the world,' wrote the New England divine Thomas Hooker, 'as there is wilde Thyme and other herbes, but we would have garden love and garden joy, of Gods owne planting.'[2]

The suspicion of 'wilde love and joy' and the havoc it could wreak was already present in the pre-Christian era. The Romans feared it as disruptive to the stability of the state. The Jews of Old Testament times had feared something more obscure — a helpless state of guilt and shame and alienation from God which sprang from acts of disobedience. In the Christian St. Paul both of these strains met and in the Epistle to the Romans they are intellectualised in a way that was to be of great significance for the future of religious thought. Man, says St. Paul, is a sinful creature, deeply alienated from God. Desperate as the sickness is, however, the invalid is not given up for lost. There is a remedy, or justification, and this is the remedy of faith. If a man had faith in Jesus Christ, then he could recover. It involved taking various therapeutic steps such as repentance, but if he obeyed in these particulars his state of alienation could be relieved and he could be restored to a state of love and unity with God.

This theme was to be renewed by many others but most notably by St. Augustine, who added emphases of his own which were to play an important part in Puritanism. Man, for St. Augustine, was even more depraved, more utterly devoid of all natural grace, than he was for St. Paul. Yet in this desperate state he was possessed by a terrible thirst and hunger for God. Seek whatever pleasures he might, nothing could assuage his longing. 'Thou hast made us for thyself, and our hearts are restless until they find rest in thee.'³ Yet such was human perversity that men searched everywhere but in the right place to relieve their terrible agony of wanting.

The Reformers were to rediscover the Pauline principle of justification by faith as a way to set men free from the compulsiveness of good works, and the priestly domination that went with it. They saw themselves as setting men free from fear and from a childish state of bondage to priestly authority. Men might approach God for themselves, might read the Bible and think for themselves on theological questions. They could stand upright, bold in the knowledge of their justification, instead of behaving like frightened children afraid of punishment.

The two major figures of the Reformation were Luther and Calvin. For Luther the dominating ideas of theology were wrath and grace. God in his purity, perfection and justice could not be other than angry at human sinfulness, yet man, being a fallen creature, was doomed to sin repeatedly and so invoke God's anger. Try as he would, man fell short of the requirements of the Law and was plunged into despair at his failure. 'The two fiends that torment us are Sinne and Conscience.' Yet there was an escape from this dreadful *impasse*. It was not by way of the struggle to 'be good' and obey the Law, wherein man had failed so many times already; the soul must abandon that battlefield and instead 'apprehend' Christ by faith. The tormented spirit was then eased since 'grace releaseth sinne, and peace maketh the conscience quiet'. Whereas God, the all-righteous judge, was acutely aware of man's faults, Christ had a different relationship to the soul. 'Christ . . . is not a Tyrant or Judge, which will condemn us for our sinnes, hee is no caster down of the afflicted, but a raiser up of those that are fallen, a mercifull releiver and comforter, of the heavy and broken-hearted.' Luther offered a warm assurance, which Bunyan among so many others seized upon with thankfulness, that anyone who believed in Christ was saved. 'There is no damnation to them that are in Christ Jesus.'⁴

Calvin, the other Colossus of the Reformation, placed less emphasis on the wrath/grace problem than on the omnipotence and divine will of

God. In his writings the might and majesty of God were contrasted continually with the depravity of man. 'The majesty of God is too high for us to say that mortal men could attain to it, seeing that they can do no more than crawl over the earth like little worms.'⁵ For the followers of Calvin there was also an escape route, at least for some; a happy few would experience regeneration. Grace would work in them, gradually changing them from the corrupt creatures they were by nature to sanctified beings. Those who did not attain election — that is the state in which grace worked in them — must expect the opposite fate, that of reprobation, the condition in which a man was inevitably damned.

What decided the outcome for each individual soul was nothing that he did, or did not do. God, exercising his Prerogative Royal, had already made his choice before a man was born at all. As so often, Calvin emphasised the absolute power of God, the right to make arbitrary and unquestioned choice, and the duty of man to submit himself utterly. The Arminians, and others, disagreed and thought that election might happen to a man as a result of his faith, but Calvin and the strictest of his followers thought that, on the contrary, faith only happened as a result of election.

Like so much of Calvin's theology it has a sort of wooden logicality. If God knew all, controlled all, in the future as well as in the past, then he already knew the outcome for each individual soul. In that sense a man *was* already saved or damned from the moment he came into the world since the God's eye view made the end simultaneous with the beginning. Given Calvin's way of thinking about God it was only a short step to fatalist thinking. This view of man saw him as almost helpless, caught either in the groove of irresistible grace or irresistible damnation. However much he struggled it could make no difference.

The fatalism of this belief might have led to a *laisser-faire* attitude to life, and Bunyan is only one among many who at one stage told themselves they might as well be hung for a sheep as a lamb and sin to their heart's content, but few people who were influenced by Calvinist thought felt able to rest for long in that position, if only because their belief was such that no one was ever quite sure whether they were numbered among the elect or the reprobate. Many must have tortured themselves as Bunyan did fearing themselves excluded from the most desirable of groups, that of the saved.

Mercies gate is locked,
Yea, up that way is block'd;
Yea some that there have knocked,
God at their cryes hath mocked.

Thus I have sin committed
And so my self out-witted
Yea, and my Soul unfitted
To be to heaven admitted.[6]

A man could not *know* that he was numbered among the elect, but there were clues which indicated that he might be. If he found the signs of grace appearing in his behaviour he might begin to hope. In practice, according to one authority, this meant that the passivity inherent in the predestinarian philosophy 'was replaced by a fervent activism rooted in the psychological need of proving oneself a member of the elect'.[7] The Calvinist was thus always held in a 'double bind' of not being sure that he was included in the company of the elect while trying to live as if he was.

If the Calvinist ever could feel certain that he was among the elect (as no doubt men of self-satisfied temperaments sometimes managed to do) then he could enjoy a boundless security, since the strict Calvinists believed, unlike the more flexible Arminians, that a true believer *could* not fall out of God's favour, that he was bound to persevere to salvation. If they wandered a little God pursued them; as Bunyan says, God was sometimes obliged 'to whip souls to Jesus Christ'.[8] Free will was not part of Calvinist belief, though the more moderate Calvinists sometimes spoke of the importance of man co-operating with the divine will.

Salvation, even of the few, was only possible because of the death of Christ. God the all-righteous Judge needed satisfaction for the crimes (sins) committed by man and it was the death of Christ that provided that satisfaction and brought about the state of Atonement, bringing God and man back into relationship. The elect could ally themselves (as a result of the working of grace) with the perfect righteousness of Christ; by faith they could take on, as it were, the colouring of Christ. This imputed righteousness allowed them to escape the wrath of God.

They also experienced forgiveness and a release from guilt and it is this experience that Puritans, including Bunyan, loved to describe. Their guilt, they felt, following St. Paul, came from 'the Law', an abstraction which, in Bunyan's writing achieves an almost persecutory force.* Guilt led to despair, the Giant who imprisoned Christian and Hopeful, but the promise of Christ unlocked the dungeon and liberated the prisoner.

Bunyan, like most Calvinists, thought of Atonement in terms of a 'covenant'. In its simplest form this was a covenant between God and man. This idea had first appeared in the Old Testament, in the covenant between God and Adam (before the Fall), and again, between God and Moses. Calvinists called this the 'covenant of works', which they believed had been superseded by the 'covenant of grace', the gracious promise of the forgiveness of sins which man had received by way of Christ.

Much controversy in the seventeenth century centred upon 'the covenant' and what it meant. The Quakers, with their belief in the Inner Light, had no need for it in their system of theology, and the Arminians only developed the idea to a limited extent. Calvinist theology, however, made the idea very much its own and introduced refinements. Many thought that the elect only continued in grace because of the intercession of Christ, and this depended in turn on a covenant between Christ and God the Father. Their intense curiosity about *how* men were saved led them into extraordinary by-paths of discussion and argument. Gradually, too, 'the covenant of grace' came to mean not only 'the Promise' of which Bunyan speaks so gratefully, but the growing into sanctification through the many stages that succeeded 'calling'.

The passionate arguments that surrounded Calvinist doctrine could only occur because men, rich and poor alike, were passionately interested in the issue of salvation. In the Elizabethan period the Puritans were mostly middle-class and gentry. As the movement spread far from its original namesakes it gradually embraced men lower down the social scale. It also appeared in many surprising, and scarcely recognisable forms, as in the case of the Ranters who held that they were saved and sinless and so permitted all things, including total sexual license, the Family of Love who interpreted the Fall allegorically, and the Quakers who felt that Christ was to be found within each man. For centuries

---

* 'I took the Law to be a person of malignant temper from whose cruel bondage, and from whose intolerable tyranny and unfairness, some excellent person was crying to be delivered. I wished to hit Law with my fist, for being so mean and unreasonable.' *Father and Son*, Edmund Gosse, Heinemann (1907).

monks and priests had regarded theological and moral discussion as their private preserve from which the laity were excluded, except to receive instruction. The tables were now turned with a vengeance and theological discussion was the preoccupation of the masses.

Men divided into those who hated and despised the Puritans, and those who admired them. Shakespeare's Malvolio who thought that because he was virtuous there should be no more cakes and ale reveals that Puritans were regarded (by their enemies) as pompous, humourless, snobbish, concerned with getting on in the world and opposed to the simple delights of the flesh. An even more cruel portrait is painted by Ben Jonson in *Bartholomew Fair* in the character of Zeale-of-the-land-Busy (satirically known as Rabbi Busy because of his devotion to the Old Testament scriptures). Busy is not only, as his name implies, a zealous busy-body, he is also a hypocrite and a glutton. He is caught secretly stuffing himself, 'fast by the teeth, i' the cold Turkey-pye . . . with a great white loafe on his left hand, and a glasse of Malmsey on his right'. He is tedious and sententious, given to railing about the sinfulness of the times and to making long prayers and graces 'as long as thy Tablecloth, and droan'd out . . . till all the meat of thy board has forgot it was that day i' the Kitchin'. Perhaps most damning of all, he loves the idea of martyrdom, and is delighted when he is arrested, begging to be put in the stocks.

Actors and playwrights like Shakespeare and Jonson had particular reason to detest a movement which despised the stage, but their audiences undoubtedly recognised and enjoyed their caricatures of Puritan behaviour. Far from withering and dying under public scorn, however, Puritanism advanced and flourished. As the Civil War approached the Parliamentary Army became a seed-bed of Puritan ideas. Many young men, John Bunyan possibly among them, who were conscripted for the Army, heard, for the first time, magnificent Puritan preaching and endless private discussion of the Bible. The Geneva Bible was widely available — it could be bought for a few shillings.

In the troubled and excited period which led to the arrest of Charles I and his eventual execution, Puritanism was inevitably a political doctrine. Men of all sects believed that they were experiencing in their own times a great outpouring of the Holy Spirit, comparable perhaps to that experienced by the Apostles at the time of Acts. Some, the Millenarians, thought that the Second Coming would occur in their lifetime and that the death of King Charles would make way for the coming of King Jesus. Other sects, such as the Levellers and the Diggers, strove for a purely political solution, holding communistic doctrine about the sharing of land and property.

All this ferment was increased by the acute economic problems of the middle decades of the seventeenth century. In 1620 there had been a slump in the cloth industry. In the late forties there were sharp increases in the price of food, and hungry peasants lay in wait on the road and ambushed carts of produce bound for market. Many starved. The forties were one of the worst periods of economic hardship in the history of England. In the period immediately following the Civil War discharged soldiers who could not find employment begged in the towns.

It was a period of unrest in other ways. The old feudal system had finally broken down and one of the signs of the times was the many men who took to the roads and had no settled address. Some were travelling craftsmen, like Bunyan and his father, others were salesmen (as his grandfather had been), some were entertainers, some quacks. Among the craftsmen in particular were many who held strong religious convictions and who used their calling as an opportunity to preach what they believed in the farms and cottages where they worked or on village greens. Such was the hunger for religious knowledge and discussion, particularly among the poor, that the 'mechanick preachers' were immensely popular. In contrast to the clergy of the Established Church, who in any case suffered great popular contempt about this time, they talked in the accents of the people and with a deep, personal knowledge of the hardships and setbacks they endured. Christopher Hill thinks that the 'masterless men' as these travelling Puritans were also called summed up in their own persons the peculiar achievements of Puritanism.[9] Freed from the particular discipline of a settled life, the discipline of home and community, they had to find an inner discipline, an inner conviction to give their life direction and meaning. Just so did the Puritan, freed from the old Church authority and discipline, need to establish his own personal conviction and code of conduct.

Not surprisingly, the 'mechanick preachers' aroused hostility in the educated sections of the population. The Puritan emphasis on personal experience of God as the touchstone of one's Christian status seemed to imply that inspiration was all that mattered, and the poor and uneducated were quick to grasp the democratic implications of this and to insist that, in the Kingdom of God at least, they were any man's equal. The opportunity to read and study the Bible for themselves completed this sense of new riches and they acquired a vast knowledge of texts. Bunyan's literary English seems derived from the cadences of the Bible; his prose is intoxicated with its poetry, and his emotions are deeply involved with its characters. The Bible was for him, as for many of his contemporaries, the world of books, plays, poetry, learning, which his poverty and lack of education denied him.

Yet it was inevitable that the Bible, read in isolation from any body of language or literature, should be taken too literally. The mechanick preachers had no knowledge of the problems of translation, nor of literary devices which sought to convey symbolic rather than literal truth. The conviction that the Bible was inspired in its least particular led them to use texts as weapons; the more sensitive and morbid used them, as Bunyan did, as instruments of torture upon themselves. It was inevitable too that more educated men should find them ridiculous, laughing at their accents, their sententiousness, their long-windedness and their passion for texts. There were rhymes at their expense as in this one about a cobbler named How:

> Belike he thinkes the difference is but small
> Between the sword o' th' Spirit and the Awle.
> And that he can as dexterously divide
> The word of truth, as he can cut an Hide.[10]

Yet for all their absurdity the 'mechanick preachers' and the sects which mushroomed in the middle of the seventeenth century played an important part in the democratisation of England. Their beliefs gave a whole class a new confidence, and a new identity. They were no longer just the uneducated poor of no importance to anyone outside their immediate neighbours; they were part of a bigger and more important movement.

Hill suggests that the doctrine of Predestination encouraged a relative democratisation since it did not identify the elect with the worldly aristocracy. It taught that what mattered was a spiritual aristocracy which had nothing to do with class but rather with understanding and co-operating with God's purposes. It was the spiritual aristocracy that constituted the elect, and a tinker or a cobbler was as likely to belong as anyone else.

Men felt free: free from hell, free from priests, free from fear of worldly authority, free from the blind forces of nature, free from magic. The freedom might be illusory: an inner psychological self-deception. Or it might correspond to outer reality, in that it was likely to be felt by men who were economically independent. But even an illusory freedom might give a man the power to win real freedom, just as mimetic magic did help primitive man to grow his crops.[11]

Difficult as it is to believe in retrospect the Puritans saw the whole movement as a marvellous liberation of men. No longer would they live in craven fear of priests, bidden to do this or that and prepared to obey for fear of hell-fire. Salvation was not a prize for a good child; they *were* saved, regenerate, here and now by the sacrifice of Christ. They lived in a joyful time.

Unfortunately human gloom and morbidity are not so easily circumvented. It became important to men to be certain of their regeneration, and a whole body of teaching, almost an industry, grew up which told people how they could know whether they were saved or not. A favourite textbook of this kind was *The Plaine Man's Path-way to Heaven* by Arthur Dent (1601), 'Wherein every man may clearly see, whether he shall be saved or damned.' It begins by showing 'man's misery in nature, with the means of recovery'. Then 'it sharply inveigheth against the iniquitie of the time, and the common corruptions of the world'.

Then, and this must have been the part that readers leafed through with the most interest, it gave the signs of salvation and damnation. It gave eight signs of salvation, signs which, if you noticed them in yourself, could give you comfortable assurance that you were among the elect. They were:

1. A love to children of God.
2. A delight in his word.
3. Often and fervent praier.
4. Zeale of Gods glorie.
5. Deniall of our selves.
6. Patient bearing of the crosse, with profit and comfort.

7. Faithfulnesse in our calling.
8. Honest, just and conscientious dealing in all our actions among men.

The signs of damnation tended to be the obverse of these, including such things as 'seldome and cold prayer' and 'Trusting to our selves'. In addition there were nine 'cleare and manifest signs of a man's condemnation', i.e. Pride, Whoredome, Covetousness, Contempt of the Gospel, Swearing, Lying, Drunkennesse, Idleness, and Oppression (depression). They were, said Dent, like plague-sores on a man. If he revealed them, he knew what his fate was likely to be. It must have made alarming reading for a young man. Dent felt particularly strongly about swearing (a compulsion of Bunyan's in his youth), and said that it was 'an evident demonstration of a reprobate', even though he believed children often got the habit from copying their parents. (Perhaps because of these words Bunyan was later to blame his father for his swearing.)

If you suffered from the 'plague-sores' that Dent described you were certain you were not among the elect, but even if you had overcome some of the grosser sins, as was the case of Bunyan in his middle twenties, you could still suffer from coldness in prayer, or 'oppression', or impatience, and have reason to doubt your place among the elect. And if you were not among the elect then your end was certain. Devils came to you on your death-bed (and seventeenth-century writers are strikingly united about the details of damnation) and carried you away 'into that lake which burneth with fire and brimstone'. Puritanism, intending to give men joyful certainty that would deliver them from the domination of the priests, in practice kept them for long periods in a lather of uncertainty about their true condition.

Men became extraordinarily introspective about themselves, examining the motions of their minds as carefully as, in a different context, psycho-analysis does today. Preachers and writers were admired for their ability to assist men in this process, for their 'scientificall' or 'surgical' skill with the human soul. The growth of grace within was reminiscent of another profound human experience; men knew that they were justified and moving towards sanctification 'as a woman that is breeding a Child feels such qualmes and distempers, that shee knows thereby shee is with Child'.[12]

What is striking about Puritan spirituality is the way they attempted to apply scientific principles to the human soul. They thought in terms of proof and certainty, of meticulous observation, and above all of method. The Bible was used as a textbook, a statement of methodology. The sermon was a plain, logical structure, stripped of the euphuisms, the quotations, the classical allusions, the poetry, which had made the Anglican sermon an almost theatrical experience. Puritan sermons, and thinking, had a laboratory air about them. Men were being delivered from superstitious, magical, arbitrary beliefs by the light of practical experiment, reason and commonsense. Yet reason by itself was not enough, since even this was corrupted by the foulness of man's heart. The way to correct this bias, or malformation, was for man to co-operate with God and his purposes, and this had to be done by a recognition of the bias (penitence) and by an awareness that only the love and sacrifice of Christ could make this therapeutic process possible. So was grace born in the soul, and by continual effort and encouragement, like fanning a spark of fire, it gradually flared up into the splendours of sanctification.

This process of 'watching' the soul was not entirely new in Christianity — monasticism, in some of its forms, had shown some of the same meticulousness and the same curiosity about the workings of the soul. Some commentators on the Puritans see the movement as an attempt to apply monastic ideals in the framework of ordinary business and family life.

The strain of all this 'watching' of oneself and others was considerable. The first quality that was inevitably lost by it was spontaneity. If mind and body must be watched continually, rather like a criminal or a madman, in case the corruption of the heart betrayed itself, you could not afford to act or speak impulsively. Words must be weighed, conduct must be, in retrospect, analysed, sifted to see what it revealed about one's spiritual health. Puritans fell into the habit of, as it were, totting up their spiritual balance at the end of each day. They kept painful diaries of their struggles and mishaps. In some families they practised mutual confession — humiliation it was called — in which individuals not only confessed their own sins, but drew attention to the sins of others, a practice borrowed directly from monasticism. This habit survived in pockets of English life at least into the nineteenth century; Elizabeth Barrett Browning's father, kneeling at her bedside, used this oblique method of expressing displeasure to his daughter.

The reason for this very costly scrupulosity was intense suspicion of 'nature' and of 'natural man'. Since nature was corrupt, permanently distorted by the Fall, its wicked insinuation must be combated by intense vigilance; any crack, or crevice or cranny through which it might creep into a man's life and undermine it, must be stopped up. The Puritan was surrounded by enemies — Nature, the World, even his own body — it is not surprising that Puritan writing often has a paranoid ring. When, as was to happen under Charles II, the Puritans suffered real and terrible persecution, it was, in one sense, and one sense only, a gratifying fulfilment of what they had always believed about life.

A favourite way of keeping nature at bay was busyness. The Puritans believed passionately in activity and in hard work, a fact which, as time went on, was to stand them to excellent commercial advantage. 'God sent you not into this world as into a Play-house, but a Work-house' wrote one. Play, like spontaneity, like an unashamed delight in the senses, was childish, and therefore to be deplored. It was perhaps this activism which prevented any mystical flowering among the seventeenth-century Puritans. When the Puritan stood before God it was not to lose himself in love; he felt rather like a naughty child about to receive a beating, and much of his piety seemed directed at trying to reach a grown-up state where he could be beyond such humiliation, his 'lower' tendencies with all the shame associated with them, being finally and forever suppressed.

Sometimes they seem like children dressed up and playing the part of grown-ups, over-playing the solemnity and the self-control because it does not come easily to them. The elaborate pietistic practices, the morning and evening prayers, long graces, confessions; the perpetual study of the Bible and of other pious books; the Saturday afternoons spent instructing children and servants in the catechism; the interminable Sundays, in which church-going was only relieved by pious discussion; there is a note of caricature about such exaggerated behaviour especially when it is seen over against the extreme randiness of sections of Elizabethan and Restoration society.

Individuals also practised extremes of behaviour, as in the case of Puritans who would not stroke their dogs for fear of delighting the senses or who suffered agonies about whether it was right to wear colours. Continental historians sometimes suggest that Puritan rigour was particularly congenial to the English character and that it was not by chance that the observance of Sunday set in with such zeal in England. Calvin, by contrast, played skittles on Sundays, and used to visit his friends. It does seem likely that the practicality, the activism, and the independence of Puritanism made a particular appeal in England, together with the romantic appeal of heroism. You cannot get to heaven, said the Catholic Sir Thomas More, upon a feather-bed.

It comes as a surprise to discover that the Puritans had a regard for the importance of the sexual instinct. They were too practical to admire celibacy as the Middle Ages had done, and too steeped in the Old Testament not to respect marriage, though they drew the line, rather arbitrarily, at polygamy, despite the example of Moses and David. They felt that the point of marriage was a fusing of spiritual and sensual experience, and this new approach to sex was important for the change in thinking about women that it introduced. The medieval woman had been the temptress who kept men from God. The Puritan woman was an individual with a soul to be saved, and a moral and religious personality of her own. She also played a key role in the religion of the family (like the Jewish mother) and so deserved at least enough education to read the Bible and understand spiritual truths. She was, of course, expected to be obedient to her husband, believing, with the author of Ephesians, that 'man is the head', and there were Puritan husbands who expected to be spoken to with the utmost formality (like William Gouge, who insisted on being called 'Master Gouge' by his wife and forbad all terms of endearment), yet Puritan writing about women often reveals a shy tenderness that is particularly moving in a religion so lacking in tenderness. Bunyan in particular reveals a real affection and perception.

The sexual instinct was (within its 'garden' bounds) approved by the Puritans as their huge families might suggest, because its exercise did not consist merely of enjoyment but had an obvious practical value. It was enjoyment that was the real enemy. Writing of a nineteenth-century Puritan Edmund Gosse wrote, 'My mother, underneath an exquisite amenity of manner, concealed a rigour of spirit which took the form of a constant self-denial. For it to dawn upon her consciousness that she wished for something, was definitely to renounce that wish, or, more exactly, to subject it in every thing to what she conceived to be the will of God.'[13]

Some Puritans could look upon enjoyment calmly and sensibly, observing that moderation was all right, it was only excess that was sinful. As the New Englander Increase Mather observed 'the wine is from God, but the Drunkard is from the Devil'. Bunyan's pilgrims drink wine, make music and even dance on the course of their journey without anyone apparently being offended by the fact. Nearly all Puritans, however, were offended by the theatre, by card-playing and by gambling. Professor Perry Miller claims that all forms of gambling were offensive to Puritans not because of their enjoyableness but because prediction pre-empted the Providential purpose of God. If every happening, every action, was, as they believed 'meant' in the inscrutable purposes of God, then it seemed blasphemous to bet on the fall of a dice or the outcome of a game of cards.

The Puritan believed that it was his task to wean himself of the affections of this world, since this world was perishable and corrupt. Giving up pleasure was often an unbearable struggle in the beginning. 'It was a year' Bunyan says pitiably 'before I could quite give up my dancing.'[14] (The dancing in the second part of *Pilgrim's Progress* seems to suggest a later change of heart.) Gosse describes where his father's searching self-examinations led him.

> In those brooding tramps round and round the garden, his soul was on its knees searching the corners of his conscience for some sin of omission or commission, and one by one every pleasure, every recreation, every trifle scraped out of the dust of past experience, was magnified into a huge offence. He thought that the smallest evidence of levity, the least unbending to human instinct, might be seized by those around him as evidence of inconsistency, and might lead the weaker brethren into offence ... Act after act became taboo, not because each was sinful in itself, but because it might lead others into sin.[15]

This may not always have been the reason. Scrupulosity seems to take on a momentum of its own. As each act is scrutinised sin is seen to lie in even the most normal actions so that everyday life becomes filled with painful hurdles. Guilt invests every deed with inner anxiety until the joy in life is darkened. At the beginning of his period of religious crisis Bunyan surrendered one pleasure after another — playing games on a Sunday, bell-ringing, dancing. Giving up bell-ringing initiated a neurotic condition in which he feared the steeple of the church would fall on him, or the bell would fall out of the belfry, rebound on the wall, and strike him dead.

Scrupulosity, and the continual 'watching' of the self that accompanies it, has all kinds of side-effects. It leads into (though it might also be said to spring from) a kind of split, or alienation between man and his desires. A man finds himself divided into two — a sensible, responsible, righteous self which must keep unsleeping watch on an irresponsible, dangerous and instinctual self. No integration of the two is thought possible or desirable. One half of the self must be repressed to ensure the ascendancy of the other.*

This could not be other than a violent process, and not surprisingly violence had great fascination for the Puritans and often appeared in their imagery. It found expression in their descriptions of what the unrighteous must suffer in Hell, descriptions which inadvertently tell us what their own inner sufferings were like. 'Set the case you should take a man' wrote Bunyan in his sermon A Few Sighs from Hell (1658) 'and tie him to the stake, and with red-hot pinchers, pinch off his flesh by little pieces for two or three years together, and at last, when the poor man cries out for ease and help, the tormentors answer, Nay, but beside all this, you must be handled worse. We will serve you thus these twenty years, and after that we will fill your mangled body full of scalding lead, or run you through with a red hot spit . . . this is but a flea-bite to the sorrows of those that go to hell.' Bunyan forestalls any simple-minded objection on the grounds that 'the poor man' would die many times over, with the reply, common to fantasies of cruelty, that he would never be 'quite dead'. Only thus, after all, can the fantasies continue.

Another outlet for fantasies of violence for the Puritan was the Martyrology. A favourite book, even in poor households, was Foxe's Book of Martyrs. Another favourite was Clark's Martyrology which, on page after page, depicted in step-by-step woodcuts the way Protestant martyrs under Queen Mary had come to their deaths. Beatings, burnings, gougings, disembowellings, hangings, maimings and castrations were drawn in the most precise detail. Sunday afternoons were enlivened for Puritans and their children by a careful study of these horrors. In this case the cruelty was projected not on to the Devil but (to what was, in their minds, very nearly the same thing) on to Catholicism.

In other situations cruelty was projected on to 'the World', which assumed different guises at different times — the Anglican clergy, the

---

* Brearley of the Grindletonians described himself as in a state of 'Self Civill War' a phrase recalling St. Paul's plaint in Romans 7,19 'For the good that I would I do not: but the evil which I would not, that I do.'

Church of England, King Charles II and the magistrates and gaolers who did his bidding.

In daily practice the Puritans were not generally cruel, except to themselves, but they could be hard and appallingly insensitive, especially to children. Children have never perhaps had a harder time than under the Puritan regime — the length and tedium of Puritan religious practices, the strong emphasis on decorum and self-control, the shameless way in which fear was used as a spur to secure good behaviour, the enthusiastic use of the cane (which the child was expected to kiss after being beaten), all helped to make their lives miserable. Some of these practices, along with a belief in 'breaking the child's will' were common to most seventeenth-century households, in fact Continental observers had long commented unfavourably on the harshness which the English showed to their children. Edmund Gosse graphically describes the boredom and sense of restriction that afflicted such children, the utter exhaustion of the Sunday services, and the strain of continual exhortation to a zeal that did not always come naturally to them. As a child he was never allowed to read stories, with the exception of those in the Bible, which were read without a trace of feeling for their symbolic or allegorical meaning.

Thoughts of death and of hell must have been particularly terrifying since no details were spared. Bunyan, brought up in a household that was certainly less arduous spiritually than that of a family of 'saints', never forgot his childhood sufferings over the idea of devils and hell. With childish logic he decided that he would rather be a devil than a human being so that he could torment rather than be tormented; but unhappily he knew that he would not be given the choice.

The constant note of exhortation, of pointing the moral, of being 'improved' must have been especially tiresome for children. Even at the age of seventeen Gosse, living away from home, was subject to continual cross-questionings from his father by letter about the state of his soul; he never saw a letter from his father lying on the breakfast-table without a sinking of the heart and the contents often made him cry. He was expected to reply to all the parental questions in detail.

Such questioning comes very close to a kind of mental bullying, a form of which we find, rarely for Bunyan, in the incident in the *Progress* where Christian confronts, and defeats, Ignorance in argument. Children, ignorant almost by definition, had to endure near-perpetual instruction and admonition. Levin Schücking writes that, in the attempt to make faith penetrate the core of the personality and permeate the whole man, the Puritans felt that it was their duty to see that 'pressure was brought to bear from all sides and brought to bear continuously. Only the family could supply the leverage by which the process of self-reform was to be set in motion.'[16]

From the moment that a child could understand anything at all the process began. It was taught 'holy' words parrot-fashion, rather as we teach a child to say 'Daddy' or 'Mummy' or 'Pussy', in the pious hope that its first utterance would be 'Jesus', or 'God' or 'Faith' or 'Love'. By the same method little children were taught to lisp such sentences as 'God alone can save me', 'Christ is my righteousness', 'Abominate pride', 'Learn to die' in the hope, presumably, of a kind of subliminal effect.

Childhood, with its spontaneity, its lack of repressions, and its strong instinctual life was, in one sense, exactly what Puritanism was fighting against, the nearest thing to 'natural' man that ever came within their orbit. Harshly punishing 'the child' in themselves, they cannot often have shown much sympathy or understanding to the real children in their care.

Not surprisingly, the Puritans suffered a good deal from depression, or melancholia, as the medieval monks had notoriously suffered *accidie*. The continual stretching of their minds to sermons and long extempore prayers, and of their emotions to feelings of love and warmth towards God, combined with hard work and lack of play, inevitably drove them to moods of dullness and boredom, and to far worse states of gloom, anxiety and despair. Bunyan experienced all these states to the full, together with appalling fears of rejection by God ending in perpetual damnation.

Despite so much misery and hardship in the present, however, Puritans comforted themselves with the thought that their real delights were to come. This world, with its dreadful evils and corruptions, was a wilderness, but, as Bunyan reminded the Meeting at Bedford, 'the Milk and Honey is beyond this Wilderness'. Bunyan is fond of using the Exodus of the Jews from Egypt as a metaphor for the life of the Christian struggling with this world. When he became a pastor he thought of himself as Moses leading his flock to the Promised Land. Bishop Edmund King was once told by a labourer with whom he got into conversation 'Yours is a yon-side religion', meaning a religion which concentrated on the delights of Paradise rather than the happiness of this world. Similarly the religion of the Puritans was a 'yon-side' religion and nothing illustrates this better than Bunyan's Pilgrim, setting out from the City of Destruction in search of the life that only the New Jerusalem can offer him. This world is a kind of maze of illusions in which a man can all too easily lose himself. Obtaining what help and advice he can by the wayside, like a hero in a fairy-tale, the Pilgrim must do his best to find the right path and stick to it, picking himself up and dusting himself down when he makes foolish, or near-fatal errors, but also cheered by hints that he is going the right way, or will obtain joy at the end of his journey.

Joy is never *now*, but always in some future state. Christian sees the Celestial City from afar and perpetually sighs towards its beauty and security. 'The thoughts of what I am going to, and of the conduct that waits for me on the other side, doth lie as a glowing coal at my heart. I see myself now at the end of my journey, my toilsome days are ended. I am going now to see that head that was crowned with thorns, and that face that was spit upon, for me. I have formerly lived by hear-say and faith, but now I go where I shall live by sight, and shall be with him, in whose company I delight myself.'

The pilgrim cannot afford to get too attached to this world, since it distracts him from his journey, and at no point must he collude with it in its wicked ways. At Vanity Fair, Evangelist tells Christian, everything is for sale 'as Houses, Lands, Trades, Places, Honours, Preferments, Titles, Countreys, Kingdoms, Lusts, Pleasures, and Delights of all sorts, as Whores, Bauds, Wives, Husbands, Children, Masters, Servants, Lives, Blood, Bodies, Souls, Silver, Gold, Pearls, Precious Stones, and what not . . . Here are to be seen too, and that for nothing, Thefts, Murders, Adultries, False-swearers, and that of a blood-red colour.'[17]

Deeply alienated from the world and from instinctual life the Puritan compensates himself by an heroic and romantic vision. He sees himself as the central figure in a drama, a drama in which he, the champion of righteousness, fights the dragon of evil. To make the action more exciting the dangers are heightened. If he fails in his quest for salvation then the ghastly fate of everlasting torment lies in store for him. If he succeeds he does even better than marrying the princess and living happy ever after. He is guaranteed a bliss that no princess could afford him. The story is an old one, far older than Christianity; Bunyan was deeply enough rooted in the peasant life of his country to turn the archetypal theme to Calvinist advantage.

Such a romantic vision of oneself undoubtedly makes life more exciting; a man is never just his ordinary self but is the champion of truth, and the representative of Christ. The Puritans were notably sensitive about keeping up a good front to the world. It was this which led to Bunyan's arrest at Samsell, and when Bunyan considered the possibility of dying on the gallows his chief worry was whether he would let his cause down by showing his terror. Bedford Meeting, very often kindly and forgiving about one another's lapses, could not bring themselves to forgive John Rush who had got so drunk one night at the Swan that it took three men to get him home. Their remedy was to expel him from membership of the Meeting.

One of the favourite metaphors of the Puritans was that of the soldier, a metaphor originally used of the Christian by St. Paul. The Puritan liked to feel he was 'under orders', enjoined to live by a strict discipline, ready at a moment's notice to take up arms on behalf of Christ. He liked to think of himself as hardy, brave and obedient.

The romantic device had practical consequences. When the Puritans began to endure persecution after the Act of Uniformity they behaved with admirable heroism. In order to worship according to their own beliefs the sectarians had to live a surreptitious existence. 'The Baptists,' said William Penn, 'used to meet in garrets, cheese-lofts, coal-holes, and such like mice walks.' They met also by night in the woods, and carried out illegal baptism rites by night on lonely stretches of river. They suffered fines, lengthy periods of imprisonment, and every kind of public humiliation and punishment. They maintained, from their charity, the dependants of those of the brethren who were in prison or unemployed as a result of their beliefs. They spoke up, as bravely as the apostles, to hostile judges. They suffered an immense amount of public ridicule, and were betrayed by neighbours. A few of them, a very few, could not endure the tensions of life lived, as it were, waiting for a knock on the door, and 'conformed'. The majority of them, people of modest means and education, not accustomed to defy authority, stood firm through the terrible decade of the 1660s. Jonson and Shakespeare had jeered at the Puritans as hypocrites, and no doubt there was some justice in the charge, but in the hour of testing the 'Nonconformists' gave one of the most remarkable displays of courage in the whole of English history.

Some of the determination needed for this *tour de force* came from the strong community sense of the sects. If the individual Puritan was a soldier under Christ's banner, the sect was a battalion of crack troops. The same sense of specialness that upheld the individual in his lonely struggle against the world also gave direction and purpose to the sect. They were 'gathered' people, communities called into being by the will of God, tiny outposts of the Kingdom of God upon earth. Part of the penalty of specialness was to be persecuted, and the sects were not surprised by their fate.

In Bedford, the separatist church had come together in 1650. Eleven citizens, mostly small tradesmen, formed the church to begin with, people who had, in their own words 'in some measure separated themselves from the prelaticall superstition, and had agreed to search after the non-conforming men, such as in those days did bear the name of Puritans.' Mr. John Grew and his wife, Mr. John Eston the elder, Anthony Harrington and his wife, sister Coventon, sister Bosworth, sister Munnes, sister Fenne and sister Norton and sister Spencer 'all antient (long-standing) and grave Christians well knowne to one another, sister Norton being the youngest' began to meet regularly to read the Bible, to pray, to listen to sermons and discuss them as was the custom of the 'gathered' churches. It is notable that there were eight women in this small community — the records of the church show that women were to be important in the congregation both in numbers and influence. Bunyan attributed his conversion to a conversation he overheard among 'the poor women of Bedford', and it was they (almost certainly some of the women mentioned above) who introduced him to the Bedford Meeting.

One of the most remarkable personalities of the meeting was John Gifford who became their first minister. Unlike the rest of them he was an educated man, a 'gentleman' who had been a Major in the Royalist Army. He had led a life of debauchery and gambling, until one night he lost a large sum of money at cards, cursed God, and felt in himself the first pangs of conversion. For him, like his pupil Bunyan, there was a fierce struggle. He already knew members of the Bedford Meeting, but quarrelled violently with them, even wanting to kill one of them. Gradually, however, his character changed, he began to preach, and the meeting was unanimous in choosing him as their first pastor.

In 1653 (about the time Bunyan came into contact with him) he was presented with the living of St. John's Church, Bedford, so that for several years his sectarian congregation met within the walls of the established Church, a practice not uncommon during the Commonwealth. The Commonwealth years were good years for this zealous little group, vowed to 'holiness of life'. They met regularly to listen to the Word, and hear it expounded and discussed. Their sense of fellowship was particularly strong; the circumstance of their 'separation' from the established Church, of being 'called out', gave them a sense both of importance and of shared experience. Like other meetings they carried out a form of social welfare, as the Bunyan family were to know during their years of hardship. Discipline, in such congregations, was exercised by the congregation itself. The Church Book of Bedford Meeting (the record — a sort of minute book — of their meetings and discussions) gives many accounts of the deliberations of the congregation. They could be hard on members who were careless about attendance or who sinned openly, but nevertheless a real love and sense of fellowship emerges from the pages and it is not hard to see why, in a period of so much social unrest and movement of population, many found a new family for themselves, in separatist churches. And they could be more generous to outsiders than one might expect. 'Salute the brethren who walke not in fellowship with you' Gifford urged his flock in his dying letter to them (written in 1655) 'with the same love and name of brother or sister as those who do.'

With the end of the Commonwealth and anticipation of the Restoration of the monarchy, fear of intolerance began to spread among the separatists. In the case of the church at Bedford, as of so many others, the fear was well-justified. More than one of their little community was imprisoned and with the Act of Uniformity darkness was to fall upon them for nearly a decade. The Church Book has no entries for five years. In addition they were turned out of St. John's Church. The era of Nonconformist persecution had begun.

The Puritans tend to be thought of as a gloomy people, but it seems unlikely that this was usually the case. Their writings suggest an extraordinary intellectual vitality (in Bunyan's work this is matched by an imaginative vitality), a thrilling sense of purpose, and a genuine delight in the fellowship of fellow-believers. Isolation was not possible for this sort of Christian; he had to be engaged in continual interchange with the other 'saints'.

He enjoyed, too, an extraordinary simplification of life. All his actions, his decisions, had to be arranged around a central issue — what theologians call 'the soteriological journey' — that is to say the steps by which a man achieved salvation. Many of the problems which beset mankind — poverty, illness, death — when seen in the context of an individual's salvation seem less alarming. In the context of God's purpose they were seen as having meaning; they did not have to be fought against, only accepted. And with the overwhelming belief in the workings of almighty Providence that is so characteristic of Puritan thought, they were accepted. Edmund Gosse has described the way his Puritan mother accepted a lingering death from cancer, remembering 'the extraordinary tranquillity, the serene and sensible resignation, with which at length my parents faced the awful hour. Language cannot utter what they suffered, but there was no rebellion, no repining; in their case even an atheist might admit that the overpowering miracle of grace was mightily efficient.'[18]

In happier times there was a gaiety in the Puritan family which sprang directly from their beliefs.

My parents were playful with one another, and there were certain stock family jests which seldom failed to enliven the breakfast table. My Father and Mother lived so completely in the atmosphere of faith, and were so utterly convinced of their intercourse with God, that, so long as that intercourse was not clouded by sin, to which they were delicately sensitive, they could afford to take the passing hour very lightly. They would even, to a certain extent, treat the surroundings of their religion as a subject of jest, joking very mildly and gently about such things as an attitude at prayer or the nature of a supplication. They were absolutely indifferent to forms. They prayed, seated in their chairs, as willingly as, reversed, upon their knees; no ritual having any significance for them. My Mother was sometimes extremely gay, laughing with a soft, merry sound. What I have since been told of the guileless mirth of nuns in a convent has reminded me of the gaiety of my parents during my early childhood.[19]

Cheerful, vigorous, literal-minded, self-analytical, hard-working, convinced — there is something deeply formidable about the Puritan. Not the least formidable thing about him is his rigid honesty. Gosse's mother, urged on her death-bed to admit, in the pious phrase, that she felt 'joy in the Lord', insisted that though she felt peace, she did not actually feel joy, and could not go into eternity with a lie in her mouth. The spirit of English Nonconformity, meticulous in its regard for truth, spoke through her dying words. We may not always like the Puritan, but it is difficult not to admire him.

Such rigid truthfulness, however, made for a 'hard-edged' religion. It was impossible to tolerate those for whom truth is contradictory, belief uncertain, or emotions luke-warm; despite the charity of John Gifford's dying words you were included or excluded, and if you were included then your contempt for 'the World' and its corrupted ways was boundless. Images of inclusion and exclusion dominate Puritan writing; for Bunyan they were to be of crucial importance.

NOTES

1 William Haller, *The Rise of Puritanism*, Columbia University Press (1938).
2 Thomas Hooker, *The Application of Redemption* (1569).
3 St. Augustine, *Confessions* (c. 397).
4 Luther, *An Abstract Commentarie on the Epistle to the Galathians* (1635).
5 J. Calvin, *Institutes* II, 6,4 (1536).
6 John Bunyan, *A Book for Boys and Girls* (1686).
7 R. L. Greaves, *John Bunyan*, Sutton Courtenay Press (1969).
8 John Bunyan, *Doctrine of the Law* (1659).
9 Christopher Hill, *The World Turned Upside Down*, Temple Smith (1972).
10 Thomas Hall, *Vindiciae Literatum* (1655).
11 *The World Turned Upside Down*.
12 William Ames, *The Marrow of Sacred Divinity* (1643).
13 Edmund Gosse, *Father and Son*.
14 *Grace Abounding*.
15 *Father and Son*.
16 Levin Schücking, *The Puritan Family*, Routledge (1969).
17 *The Pilgrim's Progress*, Part I.
18 *Father and Son*.
19 Ibid.

2

John Bunyan's Life
1628–1659

John Bunyan was born at Harrowden in Bedfordshire at some time
during 1628. The cottage stood in an isolated position on nine acres of
land, with a view across the flat fields to Elstow church. Though not
born in the parish of Elstow, Bunyan was baptised in Elstow parish
church — where his parents had been married — on 30th November.

Almost nothing is known of his mother Mary or Margaret Bentley,
except that she was the second wife of his father, Thomas Bunyan, a
brazier or tinker by trade. Like many tradesmen of his period he kept his
family partly by his trade, partly by working the few acres of land he
owned. A working brazier travelled a good deal, visiting villages and
farms, taking work where he could find it. John Bunyan's grandfather
had been a 'pettie chapman', that is a travelling salesman, who sold
among other things the tales of adventure known as 'chap-books'. He
was sufficiently prosperous to make a will, and when he died John
Bunyan, aged thirteen, inherited 6d.

With such a pedigree Bunyan was automatically excluded from the
ranks of the educated, but he was spared abject poverty. W. G. Hoskins
has investigated the life of the cottager at around this period in nearby
Leicestershire and it is one of modest comfort, if of unremitting hard
work.[1]

Bunyan, however, was to complain bitterly in later life of the poverty and 'meanness' of his parents. 'For my descent . . . was, as is well known by many, of a low and inconsiderable generation, my father's house being of that rank that is the meanest and most despised of all the families in the Land.'[2] 'True, may that man say, I was taken out of the dunghill. I was born in a base and low estate.'[3] Finally, and most painfully, he declared (in controversy with the Strict Baptists), 'You closely disdain my person because of my low descent among men, stigmatising me for a person of *that* rank that need not be heeded or attended to.'[4]

It is true that tinkers were generally despised, as a drunken and shiftless race, often of gipsy descent, and it is possible that Bunyan as a child suffered under this prejudice, despite his petty bourgeois background. At one point he wonders about his descent and makes a note to ask his father 'Whether we were of the Israelites or no?' There seems to be a confusion in his mind here between the Jews and the Egyptians, that is the forerunners of the gipsies from whom tinkers were thought to descend.

But whatever the Bunyans' standing, or lack of it, in their own community, Bunyan was later looked down on, as so many of the sectaries were, by the educated people who engaged in religious controversy. Sneering at a man's parentage and occupation was sometimes an effective way of discounting the value of his thought. Two hundred years later Keats was to suffer rather similarly from being called an 'apothecary poet'.

Bunyan had a sister less than a year younger than himself, Margaret, and a brother William born in 1633. With his father often away the domestic work must have fallen heavily on his mother and the children.

A typical cottage of the time, according to Hoskins, would have consisted of house, barn and stable, a yard with 'hovels' where dried peas, crops, implements, wood and coals were stored. There was usually a garden where herbs were grown, and a small orchard, as well as a 'croft' or enclosed pasture. The cottager with several acres would annually devote one field to peas and beans, another to wheat, rye and barley. He would grow hemp and flax for clothing and domestic linen, he would keep chickens, and pigs, possibly a few sheep and cattle or a horse. He would generally keep bees — in those days the only source of sugar. The house would have had wattle-and-daub walls and wheat-straw thatch. Wills of the period, made by people with very modest means, mention wall hangings, pewter and brass pots, flaxen sheets and towels.

Old villagers in that part of Bedfordshire remember that until a generation ago flooding was an annual problem, so that in winter the Bunyans may well have floundered in a sea of mud.

In one of his apologetic references to his parents Bunyan says that 'it pleased God to put it into their heart to put me to School to learn both to Read and Write'.[5] There was a charity, as a result of a bequest from a former Lord Mayor of London that took care of the education of the poor around Bedford, and from this beneficence Bunyan would have learned to read and to know the catechism. C. V. Wedgwood, writing of a period ten years later says that among country folk at this time women were usually illiterate, but most intelligent men could read.

They could read, but they lacked books. Most 'decent' families owned the Bible and often Foxe's *Book of Martyrs*, as well as a cheap catechism, and chap-books bought from travelling salesmen. Few people of this class owned much more, and it is significant that when Bunyan eventually married, two books came with his bride as her dowry, and these, though intensely tedious by modern standards, were avidly, almost reverently, read by the couple, Bunyan probably reading aloud. In these circumstances, the influence of the Bible was supreme. 'The Old Testament was commonly better known to these people than the New' writes C. V. Wedgwood 'and unconsciously they acquired the outlook, because they acquired the words, of the Chosen People. To the confident, self-reliant and assertive characteristics of the Anglo-Saxons were added tenacious Jewish fatalism and an unyielding confidence in a God who was theirs against the world.'[6]

There is plenty of evidence in Bunyan's work and in his whole literary style that the spring of his imagination was the Bible. If he had enjoyed what was, in his day a 'good' education then he would have been influenced by classical and pagan authors, as Shakespeare so clearly was, and the unity and intensity of his vision would have been subtly different. Some commentators, presumably finding it hard to believe that a virtually uneducated man wrote Bunyan's works, try to argue that Bunyan must have been to a grammar school, and mention the school at Houghton Conquest, but Bunyan is adamant that he does not know Latin, that 'I never went to school to Aristotle or Plato' and there seems no good reason to doubt his word. It is difficult to believe that a child with such a powerful mind, with such amazing verbal facility, and with so few literary resources could have 'forgotten' Latin as some writers claim.

This theory, however, probably owes its origin to a Victorian wish to present Bunyan as a wild, ungovernable and rebellious child and youth, not amenable to authority and discipline. Bunyan himself fostered this view (one common to many other Puritan writers).

The few glimpses he gives us of his childhood suggest, to the modern mind, not wickedness, but insecurity and repression. 'The Lord, even in my childhood, did scare and affright me with fearful dreams, and did terrify me with dreadful visions.' 'I should often wish either that there had been no Hell, or that I had been a Devil; . . . that if it must needs be . . . that I might be rather a tormenter than tormented myself.' And 'from a Childe I had but few Equals . . . both for cursing, swearing, lying and blaspheming the holy Name of God'.[7]

A child of such vivid imagination and intelligence could not fail to be affected by the preaching and widespread interest in hell-fire. James Joyce in *Portrait of the Artist as a Young Man* has described the effect that similar preaching had upon an imaginative boy in Catholic Ireland. Many children must have suffered similarly, but learned at last to acquire a protective coating of cynicism. Bunyan, however, never grew out of his terror; it was to lead to the major crisis of his life.

He says nothing of his mother before her death when he was sixteen. He was to claim later in his life (in defence against a charge of unchastity put about by his detractors) that he was shy of women, yet the loving insight with which he describes the women in the second half of the *Pilgrim's Progress*, and the sense of a close relationship which emerges from his scant descriptions of his two marriages, show that he associated women with tenderness, happiness, even gaiety. It is likely that his mother was illiterate, certain that she was extremely hard-worked, and quite probably a weak figure in the household.

His father emerges more strongly, partly by direct reference as when Bunyan says, speaking of himself as a young man 'I wished with all my heart that I might be a little childe again, that my Father might learn me to speak without this wicked way of swearing',[8] partly through Bunyan's view of God the father, mightily powerful, fearfully exacting, occasionally cruel, sometimes sneering at the weakness and badness of the soul standing before him.

When Bunyan was sixteen, in 1644, his life underwent a sudden and radical change. His mother died in June, his sister in July, the two deaths in such quick succession suggesting that an epidemic may have been

responsible. In August his father married again. At this distance in history
it is difficult to know how this action appeared at the time. At a period
when marriages were not commonly for love, and when women were
regarded as both inferior and subordinate to their menfolk, there may
have been little more emotion connected with a third marriage than with
hiring a servant. The household had to continue in its exhausting
routines, .and could not do so without a woman. Yet even so the
marriage seems to have been contracted with astonishing speed, suggesting either gross insensitivity in Bunyan's father, or a liaison of long-
standing which he was eager to make legal.

Whatever others may have thought about it, the effect on a sixteen-
year-old boy who had scarcely had time to mourn his mother and sister
must have been considerable. He did not have to endure life with a
stepmother for long, however. In November he was mustered for the
Army. Much speculation upon whether Bunyan served in the King's
Army or the Parliamentary Army does not yield very fruitful results. A
John Bunyan served in the latter army in the Company of Colonel
Richard Cockayne, and in June 1647 served in the Newport Pagnell
garrison in Colonel Charles O'Hara's Company, but there were three
Bunyan families in the neighbourhood and there is nothing to prove that
this soldier is the famous John Bunyan. The King had passed through St.
Neots and Bedford in 1645, after the Battle of Naseby, and conscripted
there so that Bunyan might have been caught up on the Royalist side of
the conflict.

The war between King and Parliament had been going on for two
years when Bunyan joined the army and it was usual for young men to
be 'imprested'. Not all welcomed it; a contemporary report states that
eighty men ran away from one such muster 'before they were cloathed
and armed'. For Bunyan, however, it proved a chance not only to get
away from home at a painful time, but also to see more of life than he
could hope to do in a tiny village. The military rituals and hierarchies, as
well as a boyish pleasure in battles, manoeuvres and strategies, were to
emerge almost naively in *The Holy War* which he wrote nearly forty
years later. There is no evidence that he actually saw any action, though
he was later to recall, as evidence of the grace of God, how nearly he did
so. 'When I was a Souldier I, with others were drawn out to go to such a
place to besiege it; but when I was just ready to go, one of the company
desired to go in my room, to which, when I had consented he took my

place; and coming to the siege, as he stood Sentinel, he was shot into the head with a Musket bullet and died.'[9]

It is difficult to believe that if Bunyan served in the New Model Army, he would not have arrived at his religious crisis sooner. The Army seethed with political and religious debate. Religion, and the discussion of the meaning of Biblical prophecies (usually with Millenialist inter- pretations) was a matter of topical interest and heated argument. Many Army chaplains, such as Hugh Peter, were using their position to preach revolutionary attitudes. The common soldiers also took up preaching, with the same confidence as the itinerant mechanic preachers.

Previous British armies had often been composed largely of gaolbirds. The rank and file of the Parliamentary army were sons of yeomen, tradesmen, and craftsmen.

They represented that part of the people of England who had rarely, until now, raised their voices in politics . . . Since the Parliamentary forces had been reformed into the New Model Army in the spring of 1645, these soldiers — many of them still at the most formative and suggestible age — had been exposed to moral, spiritual and intellectual influences which had given them not only discipline as a body, but confidence and enlightenment as men. The sermons which they had heard convinced them that they were fighting for a righteous cause. The victories which they had won proved that their watchword, God with us, expressed an undoubted truth. Free exposition of the Bible and free discussion taught the more intelligent to exercise and to trust their own powers of reasoning. They grew to value themselves more highly as Christians and as citizens.[10]

If Bunyan at a formative age shared this stimulating life, it seems strange it left so little mark upon him. Not until after his marriage does he seem to have given religion serious thought.

Bunyan was demobilised from the Army in the late summer of 1647 in common with many others, and took up his father's trade of tinker and brazier. This meant making, as well as repairing, household pans and kettles, as well as work on farm implements and harness. The Church of Bedford Meeting has in its possession the stake anvil of Bunyan (an anvil with a spike in the bottom enabling it to be hammered into the ground) with the words 'Helstowe 1647 J. Bunyan' engraved on it, a touching memento of a nineteen-year-old setting up in business. The anvil, which a travelling tinker would carry on his back along with other tools, weights 60 lb. It is not surprising that Bunyan's metaphor for sin was a great weight or 'burden' on the back.

Images of the traveller occur constantly in Bunyan's work. Christian and Faithful in *The Pilgrim's Progress* take a forbidden route because 'the way from the River was rough, and their feet tender by reason of their Travels'. The women in the second part of *The Pilgrim's Progress* have the alarming experience of being attacked by a fierce dog when they try to knock at the wicket-gate. Mud on the road, boggy ground, sweat, physical exhaustion, the comfort of good lodgings, the sight of men hanging on a gibbet, encounter with a harlot, encounter with footpads, are all mentioned in Bunyan's writings and suggest some of the practical hardships of the life of a travelling tradesman or 'mechanick'.

At some time within the two years after he left the Army Bunyan married. The name of his wife is not known, but since it was the common custom to call the first daughter after her mother and since a daughter Mary was baptised in 1650, it is likely that this was her name.

In after life Bunyan was pleased that he had a wife who came from a god-fearing background, and she brought with her when she married the legacy her father had left her on his death, two pious but popular books, *The Plaine Man's Path-way to Heaven* by Arthur Dent, and *The Practice of Piety* by Lewis Bayly. She and Bunyan set up home together in a state of extreme penury. 'This Woman and I . . . came together as poor as poor might be, (not having so much household-stuff as a Dish or Spoon betwixt us both).'[11]

Perhaps because they had so little, though also because books were such treasured possessions, they read together. At this stage of his life Bunyan did not see himself as a religious man, but he found things in the books which 'were somewhat pleasing to me'. He was not only interested by the books, but also by his wife's conversation. 'She would be often telling me of what a godly man her Father was, and how he would reprove and correct Vice, both in his house, and amongst his neighbours; what a strict and holy life he lived in his day, both in word and deed.'

Bunyan did not take offence at this as he might have done. With his settled habit of swearing, and his roisterous young man's habits, he might have jeered at this simple girl and her pious father. But on the contrary, she 'did beget within me some desire to Religion'. It suggests that this relationship was precious to him, probably the first real security he had known since the death of his mother. It was ironic, however, that these quiet, humdrum readings, and gentle conversations, were the first steps on a journey, a 'progress' in which Bunyan was to question everything, over and over again, and very nearly to lose his reason.

His character was a mixture of hearty commonsense and acute sensitivity that sometimes fell into morbidity. Portraits of him, most of them drawn in middle-age, make him look like a bluff Englishman with a full beef-eating face and a large moustache. Many things in his writing and his character suggest immense physical energy. His physique was good. He was, according to an anonymous biographer, 'Tall of Stature, strong boned, though not corpulent, somewhat of a Ruddy Face, with sparkling eyes . . . his Hair Reddish . . .'[12] He loved dancing, playing games, and bell-ringing, this last not such a pious exercise as it sounds, since the bell-ringers often did not attend church services, and were notorious for regaling themselves at work with strong drink. He was musical, and played the violin and the flute, though it was common in his day for people of all classes to play musical instruments. He seems to have been a man who enjoyed human company, to have been quick of tongue and of wit, and to have had friends who loved him.

Yet he was a man who also felt himself imprisoned at times by fits of the most terrible despair, moods which he was to compare to being in an iron cage. At such times he would experience himself not only as worthless, but worse, as contemptible, disgusting, an offence in the sight of God and all decent people. Words, phrases, texts, would run through his mind till they drove him almost demented; blasphemous and probably obscene phrases rose to his lips.

What precipitated the worst of these attacks is not at all clear. A baby, Mary, was born in 1650 and baptised in Elstow church. Mary was blind, a circumstance Bunyan mentions later with intense love and pity, and it may well have preyed upon his mind. The extreme poverty in which the Bunyans lived, together with the responsibility of a wife and child at the age of twenty-two, must have placed considerable stress on Bunyan, especially as his income was variable and depended entirely upon his own exhausting efforts.

The first indication that a profound change was taking place in Bunyan came one Sunday when he was playing tipcat, a game played with a cudgel and 'cat' (a small projectile), with friends on Elstow village green.

The green lies to this day beside the parish church, and was the annual scene of a great fair with all the usual peddlers and quacks. To those who had grown up in Elstow and nearby parishes it was the setting of sports and gaieties. In this place, with all its happy associations, Bunyan had just struck the 'cat' and was about to do so again when

> a voice did suddenly dart from Heaven into my Soul, which said, Wilt thou leave thy sins, and go to Heaven? or have thy sins, and go to Hell? At this I was put to an exceeding maze; wherefore, leaving my Cat upon the ground, I looked up to Heaven, and was as if I had with the eyes of my understanding, seen the Lord Jesus looking down upon me, as being very hotly displeased with me, and as if he did severely threaten me with some grievous punishment for these, and other my ungodly practices.[13]

Bunyan felt at once that he had sinned terribly, and that for his sins he could hope for no forgiveness. Wretched at this belief, he decided with the childlike directness that marked so many of his inner struggles, that he might as well be hung for a sheep as a lamb. 'I resolved in my mind that I would go on in sin: for thought I, if the case be thus, my state is surely miserable; miserable if I leave my sins; and but miserable if I follow them: I can but be damned for a few.'[14]

It was a despairing decision, made on the spur of the moment on Elstow Green. Having made it, 'I returned desperately to my sport again.'

The ostensible cause of Bunyan's guilt on this occasion was not far to seek. With his wife's encouragement Bunyan had begun to take an interest in the Church, and without feeling the need to enquire very deeply into its beliefs he had begun to enjoy its ceremonial. Writing *Grace Abounding* from the stance of one who has broken with the established Church he is scornful of his youthful enthusiasm, but what he seems to be describing is the sort of romantic attachment to religion common to many adolescents and young adults, an attachment which has some of the features of a 'crush' though not necessarily personally directed.

> I adored, and that with great devotion, even all things (both the High-Place, Priest, Clerk, Vestments, Service, and what else) belonging to the Church; counting all things holy that were therein

contained; and especially the Priest and Clerk most happy, and without doubt greatly blessed, because they were the Servants, as I then thought, of God, and were principal in the Holy Temple, to do his work there in. This conceit grew so strong in little time upon my spirit, that had I but seen a Priest (though never so sordid and debauched in his life) I should find my spirit fall under him, reverence him, and knit unto him; yea, I thought for the love I did bear unto them, (supposing they were the Ministers of God) I could have layn down at their feet, and have been trampled upon by them; their Name, their Garb, and Work, did so intoxicate and bewitch me.[15]

Bunyan was reaching out beyond the confines of tinkering and poverty-stricken domesticity, trying to find a vehicle for his sublime imagination, some beauty and meaning to which he could give himself.

On the day of the game of tip-cat he had gone to church as usual in the morning and had heard the Vicar Christopher Hall, whom he so much revered, preach against Sabbath breaking, either by physical labour or by playing games. This was a severe blow to Bunyan. Hitherto, he tells us, it had not occurred to him that his romantic attachment to religion should affect the way he conducted his life. He was quite content that he should 'devoutly both say and sing' in church 'yet retaining my wicked life'. He was in the habit of playing games on a Sunday, and indeed in his hard-worked and poor existence it was probably the only chance in the week to relax with others of his own age.

He felt the sermon was aimed at him personally, and having sat miserably through it, he went home in deepest gloom, feeling laden with guilt. For the moment he found it difficult to imagine why he had even *wanted* to play games on the Sabbath. The familiar sights and comforts of home, however, soon soothed him for 'before I had well dined, the trouble began to go off my minde, and my heart returned to its old course'.[16] Comforted by his dinner he went cheerfully off to his afternoon game of Cat, the game at which he was to believe himself personally accused by Christ.

This conflict was not an unfamiliar one at the time. *The Book of Sports*, first published under King James in 1618 in order to end argument on the subject, had declared that dancing, vaulting, archery and a variety of games were permissible on Sundays after church. Charles I had reissued the book in 1633 with instructions that the vicar of each parish should make its advice known. Bunyan and his contemporaries had grown up under this dispensation and the new Puritan requirements asked them to go against the custom of their childhood. In many parishes, such as Elstow, those with tougher consciences continued to do as they pleased.

For all his bravado Bunyan could not forget the voice that had threatened him with hell on account of his sins and for about a month after his vision he says that he went on in a state of despair.

Unconsciously he was working on a method to save himself, even though consciously he had decided that was impossible. A tiny incident brought the conflict into the open and produced a startling change in him. He was standing by a neighbour's shop-window (Bunyan's drama is a small town drama. Like the characters in Dostoievski, he finds that the great challenges of heaven and hell, of good and evil, take place in 'ordinary' settings.) He was, he says, 'cursing and swearing, and playing the Mad-man, after my wonted manner', when the woman of the house came out and told him 'that I was the ungodliest Fellow for swearing that ever she heard in all her life; and that I, by thus doing, was able to spoile all the Youth in a whole Town, if they came in my company'.[17]

With typical truthfulness Bunyan tells us how utterly abashed he was. 'I stood there, and hanging down my head, I wished with all my heart that I might be a little childe again, that my Father might learn me to speak without this wicked way of swearing.' It *is* a hurt child that speaks; the dignity and self-respect of manhood is suddenly ripped away leaving him small and naked.

It is not altogether clear why he was so shaken by this incident. The woman, he tells us, was 'a loose and ungodly Wretch', and he was accustomed to swearing freely in his speech. Perhaps it was the shock of finding himself overheard by her, perhaps it was because she was a woman, and swearing seemed to belong to the province of men. Whatever the reason, the shock broke him of the compulsive habit of swearing. It was a great wonder to him to discover that he could break himself of such a habit, and it put new heart into him. Perhaps he *could* change before damnation overtook him? He began to read the Bible and to enjoy talking about religion with friends and he hit on a scheme of self-improvement, thinking that if he tried hard he was bound to win God's approval. This made him feel much better, and he confesses that he secretly believed about this time that 'I pleased God as well as any man in England'. The crisis seemed to be over.

The neighbours, he says, were much impressed at his reformation, and he was delighted to have won the approval of others. 'I was proud of my Godliness' he says. There is something of adolescence in the enthusiasm with which he throws himself into being good, apparently with faith that it could be achieved by an act of will. By self-help he feels he has saved himself from spiritual ruin.

But the mental disturbance which underlay this remarkable change was not so easily solved, and the neurotic aspect of his religious struggles began to appear when, in deference to his new-found virtue, he decided to give up bell-ringing. Bunyan loved bell-ringing. (Ronald Blythe in *Akenfield* has described how, less than a hundred years ago, this hobby assumed enormous significance in the lives of young men.) He could force himself to give up being a ringer, but he could not lose his interest in the art. He thought he would go and watch the ringers at work. Hardly had he done that, however, than he conceived a neurotic fear that one of the bells might fall on him, and in order to quiet his fear he stood under a main beam. Then he thought that the falling bell might hit the wall, bounce back, and so strike him dead. He solved this by standing in the steeple doorway where he could slip out of danger should one of the bells fall. But even this would not do. Suppose the steeple itself should fall upon him?

If bell-ringing was a frivolity, then so was dancing. Bunyan also loved dancing, but in spite of this, or perhaps because of it, the God whom he was desperately trying to placate put it into his mind to give it up. 'I was a full year before I could quite leave it,' Bunyan says. But after each of these painful sacrifices he felt better for a while, thinking to himself, as a child might think about its parents, 'God cannot chuse but be now pleased with me'.

In his state of inner turmoil, Bunyan was vulnerable to new solutions. What followed was his first clue in finding an answer to his spiritual problem, though he had a long and desperate journey still before him. Going to Bedford in connection with his work he came upon a group of poor women sitting on a doorstep in the sun and talking about religion. These women were to become well known to him in the sect to which he was to devote his life, but at the moment all that mattered was the conversation he overheard. They talked of new birth, of the love of Christ, of their own wretchedness without this love. 'Me thought,' says

Bunyan, 'they spake as if joy did make them speak . . . they were to me as if they had found a new world.'[18]

At once he recognised a vitality and a freedom in them which was missing from his own compulsive and anxiety-ridden religion. These women talked of new birth and of comfort, of the Promise of God, and their words made all his attempts at being good suddenly appear ridiculous and self-regarding. He went back again and again to talk to them, filled with a kind of hopeful envy. He knew that they had something that he had not, that he lacked 'the true tokens of a truly godly man', yet he preferred this insatiable hunger that filled him to his previous self-satisfaction. His mind, he says, 'lay like a Horseleach at the vein . . . still crying out, Give, give'.

Having come so near to what he was seeking and, unconsciously at least, knowing what a costly choice it would be for him, he was assailed by the temptation of an easier solution. The Ranters were enjoying a phenomenal success from preaching that those who were in a state of perfection might do anything they liked and still be free from sin. 'These temptations were suitable to my flesh,' says Bunyan honestly, 'I being but a young man and my nature in its prime.' If he had followed the Ranter doctrine he would not only have been free of the frustrations of a young man in his prime, but of the whole conflict which was tearing him apart. If you were a Ranter you *were* saved; no need for the agonising uncertainties and the fierce inner struggles. 'Lord' prayed Bunyan, 'I lay my Soul, in this matter, only at thy foot, let me not be deceived, I humbly beseech thee.' The solution was too easy; Bunyan turned away from the Ranters.

In his need for guidance he began to turn more and more to the Bible, and although reading it gave him great pleasure, it made him aware of a new problem, namely whether or not he had faith. Like many intelligent men of his class and time he came to the Bible with little formal education either to guide his understanding or to deaden his reactions. Like a child in its early excursions among books and pictures, he was unprotected. A sentence could seethe in his mind for days, sometimes bringing hope and comfort, more often bringing pain and fear. Learning from the Book of Corinthians that faith is given to some as a gift, he at once began to doubt that he was among the lucky few. Yet if not he felt he was irretrievably lost, and this uncertainty was so tormenting that he hit upon the idea of putting himself (and God) to the test.

Travelling between Elstow and Bedford he decided to try to perform a miracle. He would say to the puddles among the horse-pads on the road 'Be dry!' and if he had faith then, as it says in the Bible, they would be dry. He decided that before making this major effort he had better go under the hedge and pray, but when he had done so he lost his nerve. Suppose he told the puddles to dry up and they didn't, that would prove that he did not have faith, and that in turn would prove that he was a lost man. He could not bear to take the risk of obtaining such information, and perhaps felt there was something absurd about the experiment.

Deeply perplexed and troubled Bunyan then had a vision which is perhaps the most important key to his whole conflict. In his mind he saw the poor women of Bedford 'as if they were set on the Sunny side of some high Mountain, there refreshing themselves with the pleasant beams of the Sun, while I was shivering and shrinking in the cold, afflicted with frost, snow, and dark clouds; methought also betwixt me and them I saw a wall that did compass about this Mountain'. He is filled with longing to join this happy company and enjoy the warmth of the sun and searches desperately for a way to do so. After much effort he finds a tiny gap in the wall and tries, time after time, to squeeze through it. Nearing exhaustion he finds he can just get his head through, then, with difficulty, his shoulders, and finally his whole body. 'Then I was exceeding glad, and went and sat down in the midst of them, and so was comforted with the light and heat of their Sun.'[19]

This vision, with its dream-like motif of searching, made Bunyan more conscious of the sense of exclusion he had had ever since he set eyes on the poor women of Bedford. He says he knew that what it signified was that he must leave this wicked world behind him 'for here was only roome for Body and Soul, but not for Body and Soul, and Sin'. Bunyan's overwhelming feeling was one of hunger, hunger to feel himself securely numbered among those 'that did sit in the Sun-shine'. So a cruder man might have looked upon those who were born into wealth and luxury and longed to be one of them.

From wondering whether he had the gift of faith, Bunyan next began to wonder whether he was elected. Suppose the whole matter of his salvation had long ago been settled in the inscrutable purposes of God? The religion of the times could work cruelly upon human compulsions, at once beckoning a man on to seek for certainties, and offering an ntolerable prospect to those who could not obtain them. The more

Bunyan doubted his election, the more frantic he became, and the more determined he was that the wholeness he longed for should not be denied to him. 'I was in a flame to find the way to Heaven and Glory.' But the agony of his uncertainty affected his physical health and he was haunted by texts which reminded a man that his salvation was not in his own power, but depended on the mercy of God. And Bunyan could not easily believe that mercy was likely to be shown to him.

His old temptation to sin as much as he liked, since if he was not elected there was nothing to be done about it, once again assailed him.

The loneliness of Bunyan's life, with the long walks between one village and another, gave him ample opportunity to debate these tormenting questions in his mind. Sometimes, he says, when he was walking he was 'ready to sink where I went with faintness in my mind'. For weeks on end he was deeply depressed as well as physically weakened. He was struggling with a major spiritual and psychological crisis and every part of him was concentrated on the conflict. As was often to happen to him in the next few years, a text floated into his mind out of nowhere, and he went eagerly home to look it up in his Bible. 'Look at the generations of old, and see, did ever any trust in God and were confounded?' Warmed by this encouraging text he hits on the idea of reading straight through the Bible to see whether any man ever had trusted in God and been confounded. The grandeur and humanity of the Bible reached and comforted him in his terrible isolation. It was, he says, 'as if it talked to me'.

It puzzled him that he could not find the comforting text in the Bible at all, and when he did so he was 'daunted' to find that it occurred not in the canonical books but in the Apocrypha. To a man in Bunyan's condition, ready to read portents into anything, this seemed a depressing sign that what had seemed like a way out of his desperate predicament was not a way out at all. Gradually, his sick fears that 'the day of grace should be past and gone' overwhelmed him again and once more he was plunged into near-despair. Part of his agony came from the feeling that if only he had realised the importance of salvation earlier in his life he might have 'been in time' for the day of grace and so saved his soul for all eternity. His anger turned upon himself. He could not understand how he could have been so stupid as to 'trifle away my time till my Soul and Heaven were lost'.

He became more and more fascinated by Bible texts and was continually matching 'good' ones against 'bad' ones, ones that seemed to hold out some chance of salvation to him, however remote, against ones that made him feel that all depended on God's caprice. He had no confidence that God's caprice would be in his favour. The texts he did examine, he began to shred for tiny particles of meaning until their original sense was entirely lost. For example, he took Moses' division of animals into those which are clean and unclean, according to whether they chew the cud or part the hoof, and tried to apply it to men, desperately afraid that he might find himself among the swine. In our own day we would suspect madness in anyone who pursued such speculations, yet Bunyan shared them with large numbers of his fellow countrymen, preachers in particular building up these strange structures by wrenching Biblical texts from their context.

It now occurred to Bunyan that men knew of their election because they were 'called'. So that if only God would 'call' him his whole torment would be at an end. All he would have to do would be to respond, as he longed to do. Once again he felt deeply envious of the converted; he even felt envious of characters in the Bible who had been called without any doubt of the matter. He thought, 'Would I had been in their cloaths, would I had been born Peter, would I had been born John.' Pitifully, he says, that if he had been standing by when Peter and John were summoned he would have said, 'O Lord, call me also!'[20] No call came, however.

Months passed in which Bunyan seemed to get no further with his problem, and one wonders how long his sanity could have withstood these batterings of rival texts and the deep waters of despair, if he had not enjoyed the friendship of 'the poor people of Bedford' and been introduced by them to their Minister, John Gifford. Because he was at his wits' end he knew that he needed help, yet given his fears that he was incurably and disgustingly wicked it must have taken courage, as well as a remarkable trust in their goodwill, to take this step. Mr. Gifford, Vicar of the parish church as well as minister of the independent congregation, listened to him, invited him to his house, and drew him into general discussions about the dealings of God with the human soul.

But now, mentally and physically worn out, Bunyan reached the lowest point. Perhaps because, for the first time, there were others to hold him and comfort him, he could bear to look at the core of his suffering. It was that he was utterly polluted and sinful, deserving nothing but damnation. 'I was more loathsom in mine own eyes than was a toad, and I thought I was so in Gods eyes too: Sin and corruption I said, would as naturally bubble out of my heart, as water would bubble out of a fountain. I thought now that every one had a better heart than I had.'[21] The poor people of Bedford, whom he now calls 'the people of God' did their best to comfort him. They pitied him and told him of 'the Promises'. Accustomed as the sectaries were to the most terrible inner questionings, it seems likely that they may have felt a bit out of their depth with Bunyan's refusal to take any kind of comfort they offered. They might as well have told him, he says, that he must 'reach the Sun with my finger, as have bidden me receive or relie upon the Promise'. His sinfulness was not to be so lightly resolved. He talks of the intolerable tenderness of his conscience at this time. It smarted at every touch.

With the envy that was typical of Bunyan at this period he even envies the beasts, birds and fishes. 'They had not a sinful nature, they were not obnoxious in the sight of God; they were not to go to Hell fire after death.' The voice of Bunyan's self-pity speaks — you can almost hear him formulating in his mind the unfair distinction between the animals and himself. Yet the suffering behind the self-pity was genuine enough.

Suddenly a change comes over the whole conflict, or as Bunyan puts it 'comforting time was come'. For the first time the word 'love' enters his mind, when he is listening to a sermon based on the Song of Songs. 'Behold thou art fair, my love, behold thou art fair.' The preacher, in traditional fashion, elaborated the text in the context of the love of Christ for the soul. Bunyan listened to it indifferently until the speaker began to talk about the love of Christ for the individual soul. 'Then poor tempted Soul, when thou art assaulted and afflicted with temptation, and the hidings of Gods Face, yet think on these two words, My Love, still.' On the way home he could not get the words out of his head, and gradually the joyful sentence, repeated over and over again 'Thou art my Love, thou art my Love' began to play on his mind. For the first time, since the fateful game of tipcat, Bunyan began to feel joyful and full of hope, and to know that he was not perpetually doomed to grief and despair. The sense of liberation and excitement was so great that he says he hardly knew how to contain himself until he got home. He wanted to talk of the love of God 'to the very Crows that sat upon the plow'd lands before me'. He longed to have a pen in his hand to write an account of the incident, which he felt he would not have forgotten in forty years.

It was the first glimpse of light. He was to lose it again, and that fairly quickly, yet he was to discover, over and over again, that it was the awareness of love that could lift him out of his inner hell and into peace and joy.

He could only learn such a lesson by repetition, however. First, as so often with Bunyan, he had to experience the antithesis of love. It began with hearing the scriptural text 'Simon, Simon, behold Satan hath desired to have you' ringing in his head so loudly that Bunyan kept turning round thinking a man was calling after him. It was, Bunyan thought later, God's way of telling him to prepare for battle. The battle came. About a month after the blissful experience of Christ's love Bunyan was struck by a 'very great storm . . . which handled me twenty times worse than all I had met with before: it came stealing upon me, now by one piece, then by another; first of all my comfort was taken from me, then darkness seized upon me; after which whole flouds of Blasphemies, both against God, Christ and the Scriptures, was poured upon my spirit, to my great confusion and astonishment'.[22]

To add to his suffering he began to doubt the existence of God, to think that the Muslims or the Jews were just as likely to be right in their views as the Christians. His mind was filled with curses against God and Christ.

To Bunyan this seemed no less than possession. He did not want to think such thoughts, in fact they filled him with terror since he took them as signs that he was not counted among the elect. He felt himself weak, taken by force, and movingly, compares himself to a child kidnapped by a gipsy and carried far from family and friends. 'Kick sometimes I did, and also scream and cry.' The longing to blaspheme was a particular torture, and also to commit 'the sin against the Holy Ghost' even though he was not quite sure what it was. He knew that if he did know what it was he would not be able to refrain from committing it, and once again envied the simple life of other living creatures ignorant of these terrible problems.

In this condition of, as we should think, near-psychosis, Bunyan continued for about a year. Yet his hold on sanity was strong. Writing about it he had a remarkable knowledge that the conflict was in his own mind, and seems protected by this from extremes of hallucination. It is always 'as if' voices are calling him, 'as if' the Devil was in his room tormenting him, pulling at his clothes. 'Sometimes I have thought I should see the Devil.' But with characteristic precision he does not record having done so. All the same, the experience was a genuine and terrible one, having some of the characteristics of trial by torture. However long Bunyan resists, Satan tells him in his mind, he will be too exhausted to do so in the end; he will yield just as (and it is a cruel metaphor in the circumstances) 'continual rocking will lull a crying Child asleep'.

Even more terrible were his ideas about God at this period. He would imagine that in response to his pleas for mercy God would jeer at him, pointing him out to the angels as a poor presumptuous fool with a laughable conceit of himself. It is a paranoid concept both in its fear of persecution and its inverted sense of 'specialness'.

Bunyan continued to endure swings of mood between joy and despair. He had a kind of dogged determination about his salvation like the widow in the New Testament who wanted justice. If salvation was going he did not intend to miss it, and he continued to hunt for hints and clues which seemed to make it more likely and to be cast down by anything which suggested otherwise. The idea of the Blood of Christ making peace between God and the soul was a comforting one. The time he first thought seriously about that was, he says, 'a good day to me'. Mr. Gifford was just the friend and pastor he needed. He encouraged his congregation not to take 'any truth upon trust'; Bunyan scarcely needed this advice, yet the acknowledgement that truth has to be battled over and made one's own must have comforted the acute loneliness which he mentions. Mr. Gifford's words came upon him like rain, he says, and were 'much for my stability'. As always he speaks of Mr. Gifford with great respect, as of a kindly father, and with the finding of this father he describes himself as 'led from truth to truth'. An awareness of the love of God as expressed in the person of Christ seems to replace, at least for a time, the torturing ruminations, though he continues to arrange texts in his mind almost as if they were solid objects to be tried in different positions like articles of furniture.

This side of Bunyan found expression in following the debate with the Quakers which was now raging. The keen pleasure of this kind of dispute to those who knew their Bibles well was rather like a football match, each side attacking and defending, weaving and tackling, with consummate skill. It must have been a welcome relief from Bunyan's own troubles, as well as cementing his sense of unity with 'the people of God'. He was also helped by his discovery of Luther's commentary on the Book of Galatians, in fact he claimed to have preferred it to all other books he had read, except the Bible. It is not hard to see why. Luther, like himself, had suffered appalling fears of damnation, and through that experience had achieved a hard-won conviction of the mercy of God. 'The two fiends that torment us are Sinne and Conscience,' said Luther, but 'grace releaseth sinne, and peace maketh the conscience quiet.' More comforting still — 'The Lord knowes to change his sentence, if thou knowest to amend thy life.'[23]

Feelings of love and joy overcame Bunyan, but then, as before, this seemed to be the signal for the conflict to be renewed in violent form. Once again the words in his mind returned, this time with the clear and dreadful message 'Sell him.' The 'him' was Christ. 'Sometimes it would run in my thoughts not so little as a hundred times together, Sell him, sell him, sell him; against which . . . for whole hours together I have been forced to stand as continually leaning and forcing my spirit against it.' Once again Bunyan was a man under torture, and once again he knew that his adversary could hold out longer than he could. Agitation became intense, so that he could not sit still and eat, or pray, or do anything at all, without feeling that he must get up and do something else.

To the ceaseless injunction to 'sell him', like the invitation of a torturer to betray a friend or lover, Bunyan had replied 'No'. Suddenly he caught himself thinking 'Let him go if he will' and knew that this was his instant of betrayal.

> Now was the battel won, and down I fell, as a Bird that is shot from the top of a Tree, into great guilt and fearful despair; thus getting out of my Bed, I went moping into the field; but God knows with as heavy a heart as mortal man, I think, could bear; where for the space of two hours, I was like a man bereft of life, and as now past all recovery, and bound over to eternal punishment.[24]

For two years after this he tells us, he believed himself a damned man. He was deeply weary of life, yet terrified of death. He had occasional spasms of hope when he thought of the blood of Christ, yet he seemed to himself quite simply worse than anyone else with whom God had to deal. He thought of David committing adultery and causing murder, of

Peter denying his master, and finally of Judas. Even Judas's sin he could see that God might pardon, but not John Bunyan's.

Once again the old miseries of exclusion and envy returned. 'How safely did I see them walk, whom God had hedged in! they were within his care, protection, and special providence: though they were full as bad as I by nature, yet because he loved them, he would not suffer them to fall without range of Mercy: but as for me, I was gone . . . he would not preserve me, nor keep me . . . because I was a Reprobate . . .'[25]

'Specialness' and persecution at God's hands had once again taken over Bunyan's inner life. He was troubled by violent fits of trembling that continued for hours, and body and mind seemed to be breaking down beneath their intolerable stresses. He had digestive troubles, and felt at times as if his breast-bone were about to split; it was as if his body was trying to find its own exact expression of what he was undergoing.

At times he seems to have been near to suicide, as Christian and Hopeful were in the dungeon of Giant Despair. Yet like them, he was to find answer in the key Promise.

'My grace is sufficient' was the text that eventually, after interminable heart-searchings, seemed to hold out a chance of life to him. As often with Bunyan the good image is of being held by loving arms (as the bad image is of being snatched away from them into desolation). It was 'as if it had arms of grace so wide that it could not onely inclose me, but many more besides'.

He was like a man on the scales now, alternately comforted and at peace, and ripped by fear and guilt, balanced between good and evil, between God and 'the Tempter' as he often called the Devil. In one good moment it was 'as though' the Lord Jesus looked down from Heaven through the tiles upon him. Gradually, very gradually, the scales came down upon the side of goodness, of peace rather than terror. The texts which held out promise of love and forgiveness began to outnumber the others, and as his confidence in his acceptance began, very tentatively, to grow, he found he could look again at the 'terrible' texts without being overcome by them.

At about this time, his wife gave birth to another child. This may have been his second daughter, Elizabeth, who was baptised at Elstow parish church, as Mary had been, but it is not clear how long Bunyan's crisis lasted, though at the very least a period of four or five years. Some time between 1654 and 1658 John and Thomas were born to Bunyan and his wife. In 1655 the family moved from Elstow to Bedford, very probably to be nearer to the Bedford Meeting and the 'poor people' who, along with Mr. Gifford, had become the most important group in Bunyan's life outside his family. In 1656 he published *Some Gospel Truths Opened* and disputed with the Quakers, and if this is the disputation already mentioned, then the incident of childbirth he describes must have been that of John or Thomas.

What he describes is his wife, late at night, going into premature labour. They are lying in bed together, his wife 'crying by me' and he prays that her 'affliction' may be removed and that if it is removed he will know that God knows the secret thoughts of the heart. The pangs of his wife ceased, she fell asleep and Bunyan was delighted and amazed to find God as powerful as he had hoped.

The worst of Bunyan's crisis was over. Step by step he stumbled towards some confidence in himself as a person lovable in the sight of God, comparing himself to a horse in the mire desperately struggling towards a sound footing. The memory of the ordeal would never leave him, but his genius took the raw experience and turned it into the masterpiece of *The Pilgrim's Progress*.

Meanwhile his first wife died leaving four children under the age of nine and in 1659 Bunyan married his second wife Elizabeth. He was thirty-one, she probably seventeen or eighteen. Two years later the judge before whom she was to plead her husband's cause could not understand how such a young woman could be the mother of four children until she explained she was their stepmother.

The Bunyan family lived at St. Cuthbert Street in the heart of Bedford, and unless Bunyan's inner crises had seriously disrupted his work (and he very often mentioned going into the country in connection with his calling) then he must have built up a reasonable business connection by this time. Possibly the move into Bedford was an indication of greater prosperity. He says that one spring he was taken so ill that he thought he had a consumption and wondered if he was going to die, but he never again mentions this weakness, even in the long years of imprisonment, so it seems likely the illness was wrongly diagnosed. No doubt any illness which produced rapid wasting tended to be classified in this way.

The move certainly enabled him to take a fuller part in the life of the Bedford Meeting. He had begun to attend its meetings in about 1653, and the Church Book comments that he began to preach occasionally in the year 1656.

This was the year of the dispute with the Quakers and the year that he wrote his first tract — perhaps the excitement of the intellectual debate pulled him out of his depression and his isolation. He was invited to 'speak a word of Exhortation' as they put it at one of the meetings. It was the strength of the sects that they encouraged each of the members to play an active part in their community life, but Bunyan was touchingly glad to have been asked, and years later remembered the occasion. The request, he says,

did much dash and abash my spirit, yet being still by them desired and intreated, I consented to their request, and did twice at two several Assemblies (but in private) though with much weakness and infirmity, discover my Gift amongst them; at which they not onely seemed to be, but did solemnly protest, as in the sight of the great God, they were both affected and comforted, and gave thanks to the Father of Mercies for the grace bestowed on me.[26]

Bunyan was still struggling with his spiritual crisis — he goes on to report occasions when he was tempted to pour out streams of blasphemy in his preaching — yet it is impossible not to note the pleasure he takes in his newfound gift, and he continues for pages telling in much the same style how he knows he ought to be modest about it, yet he really is extremely successful at it. And successful he was, as the brethren at once acknowledged. They began to take him around the countryside to speak at meetings in nearby villages, and they gave him more and more opportunity to speak at his own meeting.

It is not difficult to see why his preaching was admired. His gift for using words is apparent in nearly everything he ever wrote, and his particular gift was a sensitive rhetoric that fired the imagination while retaining a pungent earthiness. The words he used were those in common English usage, the imagery was often drawn from the life of the family, the home, the farm, the fields. Apart from his literary genius, he obviously enjoyed talking to an audience. He had an extrovert side to his character, and liked the excitement of performing, the cut and thrust of argument, and all the human exchanges open to a travelling preacher.

It meant a great deal to him that what he preached came out of his own experience. However he dressed the argument up, and in time he became very skilled at wielding all the preaching devices of his day, he was always concerned to tell the same story — how a man who believed himself lost could be found and lifted out of despair by a loving Christ. They doubted it? But it had happened to the preacher.

It was his particular pride that he spoke to the poor and the uneducated. A few years later when he was on trial one of the justices sneered that the only people who came to hear him were 'a company of poor simple ignorant people'. Bunyan took it as an accolade, pointing out with satisfaction that it was the poor and ignorant who needed teaching and information.

The almost child-like enjoyment with which Bunyan tells of his triumphs and struggles as a preacher shows how deeply the discovery of his gift affected him. He was no longer an illiterate tinker. His fine intelligence had found a vehicle that suited it, he was praised and admired, he could see that his preaching was valuable to others, he had gained identity. Perhaps more important in view of his terror of dam-nation was that the gift seemed to offer some proof of the favour of God; the Lord would hardly trouble to endow a man so richly to preach the Word if he was bound for hell. Bunyan had not dared to ask for a miracle to dry up the puddles on the road, but without his hoping or expecting it a miracle had happened to him, and he had found a spiritual home and a modicum of peace.

He was, of course, subjected to the mockery of better-educated men. When he first began to preach he says that 'the Doctors and Priests of the Countrey did open wide against me; but I was perswaded of this, not to render rayling for rayling'. He was not so meek as he makes himself sound, as his firm answers to the justices later showed.

Nothing was likely to make any impression on the prejudices of class and education; all he could do was to continue on his own course, gradually discovering that his gift and his sincerity could sometimes leap over barriers. William Dell, the Rector of Yelden, who had been a chaplain in the New Model Army and who was well known as a Puritan, asked him to preach in his church on Christmas Day, 1659. He was the first of many to recognise that Bunyan had gifts of heart and mind and spirit that made him any man's equal.

NOTES

1 W. G. Hoskins, *The Midland Peasant.*
2 *Grace Abounding*, p. 2.
3 John Bunyan, *A Few Signs from Hell* (1658).
4 John Bunyan, *The Fear of God* (1679).
5 *Grace Abounding*, p. 3.
6 C. V. Wedgwood, *The King's Peace*, Collins (1955).
7 *Grace Abounding.*
8 Ibid.
9 Ibid., p. 13.
10 C. V. Wedgwood, *The Trial of Charles I*, Collins (1964).
11 *Grace Abounding*, p. 15.
12 *The Continuation of Mr. Bunyan's Life.*
13 *Grace Abounding*, p. 22.
14 Ibid., p. 23.
15 Ibid., pp. 16–17.
16 Ibid., p. 21.
17 Ibid., pp. 26–7.
18 Ibid., p. 38.
19 Ibid., pp. 53–4.
20 Ibid., p. 75.
21 Ibid., p. 84.
22 Ibid., p. 96.
23 *Commentarie on the Galathians.*
24 *Grace Abounding*, pp. 136, 140.
25 Ibid., p. 156.
26 Ibid., p. 266.

3

John Bunyan's Life
1660–1688

The decade of the 1650s had taken Bunyan through intense personal storms and brought him to a kind of harbour. But another kind of storm was about to strike him and many like him. Cromwell had died in 1658 and had been succeeded by his son Richard as Protector. The talk was of Restoration of the Monarchy, a move which the Nonconformists knew they would have reason to fear. Charles II came to the throne in May, 1660. It was a black year for the Bedford Meeting. After Gifford had died in 1655, he had been succeeded both as Minister of the Independent congregation and as Rector of St. Johns by John Burton, Cromwell's own nominee. But though young, he was a sick man, and he died in 1660.

The Bedford Meeting were turned out of the church, so that, just as dread for the future was beginning to overtake them, they lost at one blow their pastor and their meeting place. Far worse was to follow.

In November, 1660, Bunyan went to preach at Samsell, near Harlington, at a private house. He arrived an hour or so before the meeting to find the friend whose house it was in a nervous state. He said that he had heard that the authorities wanted to arrest Bunyan, and that there was a warrant out for him. Bunyan does not say how the friend had obtained the information, but it later proved to be correct. Francis Wingate, the local justice, had already issued a warrant for Bunyan's arrest, and knew enough of his movements to instruct the town constable to keep a watch on the house. Bunyan and his friend debated whether or not to hold the meeting, and Bunyan says that afterwards he 'walked into the close' on his own to think the matter out. He knew that he was in danger of being sent to prison, a very frightening prospect to a man with four young children and a wife, herself very young, whom he had only recently married. It seemed to him a matter of honour that he should continue with his preaching, to strengthen the weak and newly converted brethren, who might have hard times ahead of them, and to show the world what a Christian was made of.

The meeting had scarcely begun with a prayer, and Bunyan had not even started to preach, when the constable and the Justice's man entered the room, finding us, says Bunyan, 'with our Bibles in our hands'. They took Bunyan to Justice Wingate's house, but not before he had had time to encourage the little congregation by reminding them that if they had to suffer it was for a good cause. When they got to Wingate's house he was not at home, so Bunyan was allowed to leave, on the undertaking of a friend that he would return the next morning.

It seems likely that he returned to his wife on that night; it was as well that neither of them knew how many years would pass before he would sleep again in his own home.

The next morning Bunyan and his friend presented themselves to the constable who took them in turn to Justice Wingate. Professor Sharrock suggests that Wingate's estate had suffered losses in the war and that he had therefore a quarrel with the dissenters; there certainly seems an excess of zeal in his determination to take Bunyan. He asked the constable to describe the circumstances of the meeting, seemingly hoping that the dissenters were armed, and he seemed disappointed when the constable said that 'there was only a few of them met together to preach and hear the word'. They did not sound like dangerous men, and at this point Wingate changed his ground a little and asked Bunyan why he did not stick to his calling. Bunyan replied that he had no difficulty in pursuing his calling and preaching the gospel simultaneously and that he felt it his duty to help people to find Christ.

At this Wingate became very annoyed, and threatened to 'break the neck' of the dissenters' meetings. He then said that unless Bunyan could get sureties to undertake that he would not preach, he must send him to gaol. Bunyan had friends outside waiting to act as 'sureties' but he would not undertake not to preach. This meant that a 'mittimus' had to be drawn up to send him to gaol in Bedford.

There followed one of those long delays familiar to all prisoners from Bunyan's day to this in which Bunyan had to sit and wait while the legal niceties were observed. There was a wounding little incident in which an old acquaintance of Bunyan's, Dr. Lindale, 'an old enemy to the truth' Bunyan calls him, happened to come in, and jeered at Bunyan for supposing he could preach. Cruelly he reminded Bunyan of Alexander the coppersmith, a man who had been a great nuisance to the Apostles, and sensitive as always, Bunyan notes and remembers that he was 'getting at him' for being a tinker.

At which point the mittimus was ready and Bunyan was sent with the constable to Bedford gaol. It is generally thought now that this first term of imprisonment was served in the county gaol on the corner of Silver Street and the High Street, only a street away from Bunyan's home. Over a hundred years later John Howard, the prison reformer, was to visit this prison and to describe it as follows: 'The men and women felons associated together; their night-rooms are two dungeons. Only one court for debtors and felons; and no apartment for the gaoler.' In happier times Bunyan and other members of the Bedford Meeting had visited the inmates of the prison as an act of Christian love; now he was to share their fate.

The first three weeks in prison between his arrest and the quarter sessions must have been a dark time. Others have described the psychological bruising that follows the realisation that one is no longer free to move wherever one wishes. Bunyan was a man in his early thirties, accustomed to performing a job which took great physical strength and to walking long distances in the open air. Suddenly, brutally, his world had shrunk to a day-room which he shared with an assortment of criminals and political prisoners like himself, and a dungeon which he shared at night with the rest of the male prisoners. Some of the prisoners were probably people we would consider mad; later in his imprisonment one of the inmates was to be Elizabeth Pratt, a woman charged with witchcraft who exhibited symptoms we would probably ascribe to schizophrenia.

Imprisonment was bad enough, but to make things worse his wife Elizabeth went into premature labour. She was later to describe the event with moving simplicity. 'I was with child when my husband was first apprehended: but being young and unaccustomed to such things, I being smayed at the news, fell into labour, and so continued for eight days, and then was delivered, but my child died.'[1] Bunyan's stand for conscience's sake was directly responsible for the loss of his child. Perhaps it was because of concern for Elizabeth that after he had been in prison for six days some of Bunyan's friends made a determined attempt to get him out on bail. They went to the Justice, Mr. Crompton, at Elstow, who presumably knew Bunyan, and asked if he would act as 'bondsman'. Crompton asked to see the mittimus, saw that Bunyan was to be charged under the old Elizabethan Conventicle Act, and took fright. Bunyan swallowed this, the first of many disappointments and frustrations in his imprisonment, bravely. 'I begged of God, that if I might do more good by being at liberty than in prison, that then I might be set at liberty: but if not, his will be done.'

After seven weeks in prison Bunyan appeared at the quarter sessions in front of Justices Kelyng, Chester, Blundell, Beecher and Snagg, two of whom, Kelyng and Blundell, were well known as Royalist sympathisers. A bill of indictment was brought against Bunyan 'That John Bunyan of the town of Bedford, labourer, being a person of such and such conditions, he hath (since such a time), devilishly and perniciously abstained from coming to church to hear divine service, and is a common upholder of several unlawful meetings and conventicles, to the great disturbance and distraction of the good subjects of this kingdom, contrary to the laws of our sovereign lord the king.'

Asked what he had to say about this, Bunyan replied ambiguously that he frequently attended 'the church of God'. Kelyng insisted on a precise answer.

Do you come to church (you know what I mean) to the parish church, to hear divine service?
Bun. I answered, no, I did not.
Kel. He asked me, why?
Bun. I said, because I did not find it commanded in the word of God.
Kel. He said, we were commanded to pray.
Bun. I said, but not by the Common Prayer-book.
Kel. He said, how then?
Bun. I said with the spirit.[2]

There follows a fair and careful examination by the justices of Bunyan's objections to the practices of the established Church and of his own beliefs about the need for prayer to be inspired. At one point Justice Kelyng warns to 'take heed of speaking irreverently about the Book of Common Prayer. For if you do so, you will bring great damage upon yourself.' The Prayer Book had become of great political significance in the England of the 1660s; it was easy for simple souls like Bunyan to stumble unwittingly into trouble.

Nothing would prevent Bunyan from having his say, however. He went on to imply that the Book of Common Prayer is contrary to God's wishes. At once the judges began to take alarm. 'One of them said, he will do harm; let him speak no further. Justice Kelyng said, 'No, no, never fear him, we are better established than so; he can do no harm, we know the Common Prayer-book hath been ever since the Apostles times, and is lawful to be used in the church.'[3]

It is the ludicrous over-statement of a man who feels personally threatened, but Bunyan did not take warning, and cheekily asked where in the epistles or anywhere in scripture there was any mention of the book of Common Prayer.

From this moment the judges turned against him, sneering that he was deluded, possessed, a canting peddler. Inevitably, mention of tinkering appeared. 'If any man have received a gift of tinkering, as thou hast done, let him follow his tinkering.'[4]

Bunyan continued to argue until Kelyng said that really the court could not waste any more time upon him.

'You confess the indictment, do you not?'

'Now [says Bunyan] and not till now, I saw I was indicted. I said, this I confess, we have had many meetings together, both to pray to God, and to exhort one another, and that we had the sweet comforting presence of the Lord among us for our encouragement . . . I confessed myself guilty no otherwise.'

Justice Kelyng had had enough argument and proceeded to his judgment. 'You must be had back again to prison, and there lie for three months following; at three months end, if you do not submit to go to church to hear divine service, and leave your preaching, you must be banished the realm: And if, after such a day as shall be appointed you to be gone, you shall be found in this realm, or be found to come over again without special licence from the King, you must stretch by the neck for it, I tell you plainly; and so he bid my gaoler have me away.'[6]

Bunyan began to say that he had no intention of giving up preaching and one of the judges made some reply but Bunyan was pulled so abruptly out of the room by the gaoler that he did not hear what was said.

Was Bunyan justly convicted? The statute under which he was tried (and which was to be reenacted under Charles II) was that:

if any person, above sixteen years of age, shall forbear coming to church for one month, or persuade any other person to abstain from hearing divine service, or receiving the communion according to law, or come to any unlawful assembly, conventicle or meeting — every such person shall be imprisoned, without bail, until he conform and do in some church make submission, etc. . . . And for the third offence he shall be sent to the gaol or house of correction, there to remain until the next session or assizes, and then to be indicted; and being thereupon found guilty, the court shall enter judgment of transportation against such offenders, to some of the foreign plantations, there to remain seven years; and warrants shall issue to sequester the profits of their lands, and to distrain and sell their goods to defray the charges of their transportation; and for want of such charges being paid, the sheriff may contract with any master of a ship or merchant to transport them; and then such prisoner shall be a servant to the transporter or his assigns; that is whoever he will sell him or her to, for five years. And if under any such judgment of transportation shall escape, or being transported, return into any part of England, shall suffer death as felons, without benefit of clergy.[7]

There was no doubt that Bunyan was guilty of staying away from the parish church and attending 'an unlawful assembly', though the justices' method of ascertaining this (at least as Bunyan remembers it) seems a little vague. On the other hand the processes of law seem to have speeded up in Bunyan's case so that his first offence is treated as if it were his third. Maybe he was already notorious as a dissenter and the justices decided they might assume his repeated guilt; they clearly considered him a dangerous, if ignorant and misguided, man, and wanted him out of harm's way as soon as possible.

They certainly gave him ample opportunity to speak in his own defence, though it is clear that they resented a man of Bunyan's back-ground talking to them as an equal. If he had been a gentleman they would have been less annoyed, and probably been less rude to him, but it is likely that the outcome would have been the same.

It was a fearful outlook for the prisoner. Three months to cool his heels in prison, while his family became progressively poorer, and then, if he still stood by his conscience, transportation, the eviction of his family, and the selling of his possessions. And if they did not suffice to pay for his journey, then he could be sold into a kind of slavery to repay the ship-owner when the ship docked in a foreign port. Bunyan vividly portrays the frightful attacks of anxiety which overcame him. His imagination readily pictures the sufferings of banishment, of what it would mean to be 'exposed to hunger, to cold, to perils, to nakedness, to enemies, and a thousand calamities; and at last it may be to die in a ditch like a poor forlorn and desolate sheep'.[8]

In his darkest moments he thought of going to the gallows, and worried whether he would there show himself as a coward. 'Methought I was ashamed to die with a pale face, and tottering knees, for such a Cause as this.'[9] In his imagination he was, he says 'oft on the Ladder, with the Rope about my neck'. He feared the refinements of suffering which might accompany his sentence, more particularly a public beating or the pillory.

As painful as his fears for himself were his fears and longings for his family. His family were allowed to visit him in the prison, and to send in one meal a day. Tradition has it that his blind daughter Mary came every day with a jug of soup for him, and the jug has been lovingly preserved in the Bunyan museum. Maybe evangelical convictions have had a hand in this story; at a period when prisoners' water was very likely to be contaminated it seems more likely that his wife might have sent him home-brewed ale.

But the wound of separation from his wife and children could not close. He says pitiably,

> I found myself a man and compassed with infirmities; the parting with my Wife and poor Children hath oft been to me in this place as the pulling the flesh from my bones; and that not onely because I am somewhat too fond these great mercies, but also because I should have often brought to my mind the many hardships, miseries and wants that

my poor family was like to meet with, should I be taken from them, especially my poor blind Child, who lay nearer my heart than all I had besides; O the thoughts of the hardship I thought my blind one might go under, would break my heart to pieces.

The closeness of his identification with this disabled child emerges in the way he pictures the same suffering for her as for himself in his imaginary exile. 'Poor Child! thought I, what sorrow art thou like to have for thy portion in this world? Thou must be beaten, must beg, suffer hunger, cold, nakedness, and a thousand calamities, though I cannot now endure the wind should blow upon thee.'[10] In his fear and helplessness he too was a lost and terrified child.

He was tortured by the feeling of responsibility for the suffering he must bring upon those dearest to him. 'O I saw in this condition I was as a man who was pulling down his house upon the head of his Wife and Children; yet thought I, I must do it, I must do it.'[11] As so often with Bunyan he turned to scripture for comfort and for a precedent, and found an image of maternal love 'I thought of those two milch kine that were to carry the Ark of God into another Country, and to leave their Calves behind them.'[12]

At other moments, however, the conflict was unbearable, and he felt obliged to attempt to deny it by telling himself that he must as it were pass a sentence of death on everything 'to reckon ... my Wife, my Children, my health, my enjoyments, and all, as dead to me, and my self as dead to them'.[13]

For all his courage, and his strong religious faith, Bunyan was in terrible distress. Cooped up night and day with criminals, having no outlet for his physical and sexual energies, it must have been a temptation to brood continually upon the legal aspects of his case, and on how he might get off without denying his conscience. Like many prisoners he gradually became more sophisticated in his understanding of the processes of law, discovering which of his fears were grounded in fact and which in fantasy.

After three months in prison, Bunyan was visited by Paul Cobb, the clerk to the justices, to see whether he had decided to 'submit' to the Church of England. After enquiring after Bunyan's health, the clerk began by telling him that he must either submit to the laws of the land or, at the next sessions, stand to be transported 'or else worse than that'.

Bunyan, rather less *naïf* than at his previous legal examination, sug-gested that the law was not really aimed at peaceable citizens like himself, but with those who met with revolutionary intent. 'My end in meeting with others is simply to do as much good as I can, by exhortation and counsel, according to that small measure of light which God hath given me, and not to disturb the peace of the nation.'[14]

Cobb replied that that was just what all revolutionaries claimed. 'You see the late insurrection at London, under what glorious pretences they went, and yet indeed they intended no less than the ruin of the kingdom and the commonwealth.'[15] He was referring to an outbreak of Fifth Monarchy supporters under Thomas Venner in January 1661.

Bunyan protested that he meant the king no harm and that if he was allowed to exhort one neighbour in private discourse, which the law did not object to, why not two or four or eight?

'Or a hundred?' Cobb asked sarcastically. 'Yes sir,' said Bunyan in his most serious vein, 'I think I should not be forbid to do as much good as I can.'[16]

There was then a good deal of discussion of how public and private meetings should be defined, whether it was really necessary for Bunyan to preach in the present climate of opinion. Cobb seems really concerned for Bunyan and eager to persuade him to behave sensibly. 'What if you should forbear awhile; and sit still, till you see further, how things will go?'[17] Bunyan felt that this would be an act of disloyalty to God. They talked at length of a man's duty to obey, Bunyan offering at one point to issue advanced notes of his sermons to show that he was not preaching sedition, but inevitably the clerk could only finish on a note of warning, given with a degree of fatherly concern which suggests the liking he had for the prisoner.

'Well, neighbour Bunyan . . . I would wish you seriously to consider of these things, between this and the quarter-sessions, and to submit yourself. You may do much good if you continue still in the land: But alas, what benefit will it be to your friends, or what good can you do to them, if you should be sent away beyond the seas into Spain, or Constantinople, or some other part of the world? Pray be ruled'.[18] At which point the gaoler could not resist giving his opinion and adds, 'Indeed, Sir, I hope he will be ruled.'

The voice of commonsense has spoken. A prisoner is in no position to avoid being patronised by those who are free. No one in authority is likely to comprehend the dilemma by which Bunyan is tormented; instead they treat him as a simple-minded peasant, too stupid to grasp the potential consequences of his action. Even so did Pilate extend a certain courtesy to Christ.

Bunyan responded with dignity to the well-meant but insufferable advice.

'Sir', he told the clerk finally, 'the law hath provided two ways of obeying: The one to do that which I in my conscience do believe that I am bound to do, actively; and where I cannot obey actively, there I am willing to lie down, and to suffer what they shall do unto me.'[19]

At this point it seemed unlikely that anything would save Bunyan from transportation and the loss of everything he possessed. A new hope dawned, however, nearly three weeks later when Charles II was crowned. It was the tradition for a number of prisoners to be released at a coronation in a general amnesty, and according to Bunyan 'thousands' were so released on this occasion. The method of the amnesty seems to have been that those released were prisoners awaiting trial, whereas those already convicted had the opportunity to sue for pardon in a period of up to a year after the Coronation. This meant that Bunyan's sentence could not be immediately carried out, as he had to be allowed the period in which to take legal action if he wished to do so.

In the meantime his wife had travelled to London, almost certainly for the first time in her life, and had presented a petition to the Earl of Bedford asking for her husband's release. He had, in turn, brought the matter up in the House of Lords, who had said that it was not in their power to release but recommending the judges to do so at the next assize.

Accordingly at the Midsummer Assize in August 1661, Elizabeth Bunyan attempted to present a petition. She began with Judge Hale who, according to Professor Sharrock, was lenient to Dissenters. He politely fobbed her off, so that the next day, most unwisely as it turned out, she threw a petition into the coach of Judge Twysden, who turned angrily on her saying that Bunyan would not be released until he promised not to preach. Then she again tried to approach Judge Hale, this time when he was sitting on the bench, but was intercepted by Justice Chester, who said that the case was closed.

Finally, encouraged by the High Sheriff, she made her last bid to get a hearing when Judges Hale and Twysden were sitting at the Swan Chamber (in the Swan Inn, Bedford). There were a large number of justices, including Justice Chester, present, and many of the local gentry, and with breathtaking courage the young woman, hardly more than a girl, took the stage with, as she later told Bunyan, 'a bashed face, and a trembling heart'.

'My Lord,' she said, addressing Judge Hale, 'I make bold to come once again to your Lordship to know what may be done with my husband.'

Judge Hale replied, quite kindly, that her husband had been convicted, and as he had told her before, there was nothing he could do.

Elizabeth Bunyan said that his conviction was not lawful. 'They clap'd him up before there were any proclamation against the meetings; the indictment also is false: Besides, they never asked him whether he was guilty or no; neither did he confess the indictment.'[20]

There followed a wrangle about whether or not Bunyan was convicted, either lawfully or unlawfully, and Judge Hale sent for the statute book to check. Justice Chester, having been present at the earlier judgment, took the matter very personally and began to repeat 'It is recorded, woman, it is recorded' over and over again with increasing temper.

Elizabeth Bunyan explained to the judges what had occurred on her visit to London and how she had been led to expect 'either releasement or relief' and everyone fell silent except for Justice Chester who continued to repeat 'He is convicted and it is recorded'. Indignantly she replied, 'If it be, it is false.'

Stung by this, Justice Chester described Bunyan as 'a pestilent fellow' and Judge Twysden said it was for Bunyan to give up preaching, that he seemed to feel he could do whatever he liked, and that he was a breaker of the peace.

Near to breaking-point Elizabeth Bunyan said that all her husband desired was to follow his calling, and live at peace. 'I have four small children, that cannot help themselves, of which one is blind, and have nothing to live upon, but the charity of good people.'[21] Judge Hale remarked that she was young to have four children, and she explained that she was their stepmother and then, with touching garrulity, went on to explain that she *would* have been a mother by this time, but for the miscarriage precipitated by her husband's arrest.

Hale was obviously moved by this story and said, 'Alas poor woman!' but Twysden accused her of playing on their sympathies and implied that Bunyan had made a good thing out of his preaching, much better than he had done from his calling.

'What is his calling?' asked Judge Hale, and several of the company called out that he was a tinker.

'Yes,' said Elizabeth Bunyan with spirit, knowing she must turn this quickly to advantage if she was to save her husband, 'and because he is a Tinker, and a poor man: therefore he is despised, and cannot have justice.'[22]

Judge Hale told her 'mildly' that as far as he could see she had only three options, since whatever she thought her husband had been convicted. She could apply to the king, 'sue out' a pardon, or get a writ of error.

The last suggestion with its hint of a miscarriage of justice somewhere threw Justice Chester into a rage, and he complained furiously that Bunyan would continue to preach 'and do whatever he lists'.

'He preacheth nothing but the word of God,' said Elizabeth Bunyan loyally. At this Twysden got so angry that she thought he was going to strike her.

'He preach the word of God! He runneth up and down, and doth harm.'

'No my Lord,' said Elizabeth Bunyan, 'it's not so, God hath owned him, and done much good by him.'

'God!' said Twysden, 'his doctrine is the doctrine of the Devil.'

'My Lord,' she replied, 'when the righteous judge shall appear, it will be known, that his doctrine is not the doctrine of the Devil.'[23]

This interchange, which may possibly have influenced a scene in Shaw's *St. Joan*, shows her as a loyal and a loving wife, ready to brave considerable ordeals to save her husband; the petition to the House of Lords for a working-class woman, almost certainly illiterate, who was unused to travel, was in itself a remarkable undertaking. She left the Swan chamber, Bunyan records, in tears, just as they were bringing in the statute book to look up his conviction; her heroism had been in vain.

The next assize was not until January 1662 and Bunyan managed to persuade the gaoler to allow him to leave the prison occasionally, as he had not done to begin with, a practice that seems to have been fairly common among long-standing prisoners in small local prisons. True to his convictions he continued to preach, and even took the foolish step of going to London and preaching there. Word leaked out that this had happened and both Bunyan and his gaoler were in trouble, the gaoler being threatened with dismissal and Bunyan being confined much more strictly 'so that I must not look out of the door'. His enemies clearly feared that he was trying to start an insurrection.

Meanwhile he was hoping that, as a result of suing for pardon, his whole case was about to be reopened, but the quarter sessions came and went without him being called and in an attempt to force the issue Bunyan asked the gaoler to put his name on the Kalendar, or list of felons to be tried. Also he approached the High Sheriff, who had already been kind to Elizabeth, and the Judge, and got them to promise that his name would be called. In less than two years he had advanced a long way in his understanding of legal procedures.

At this point, however, Paul Cobb, the clerk to the justices, visited the prison and told the gaoler that Bunyan must not come up before the Judge and that his name should not be included on the Kalendar. The gaoler said that it was already included, and that the Kalendar had been sent to the Judge. Cobb took the gaoler's list and scribbled out the accusation so vigorously that Bunyan, seeing it later, could not read what the gaoler had written, and wrote that Bunyan was already lawfully convicted for upholding of unlawful meetings and conventicles. He also went to the clerk of the assizes and the Justices, saying that Bunyan was not to be tried, and he threatened the gaoler that if Bunyan appeared before the Judge and was released he, the gaoler, would have to pay the fees of the case, and he also threatened to accuse him of making false kalendars.

Bunyan felt intensely bitter against Cobb, being convinced that if he had been allowed to appear in court he would have been released. With historical hindsight this seems doubtful. Bunyan had committed the 'crime' of which he was accused, and in the period of intensified persecution of Nonconformists which followed the Act of Uniformity, many were to suffer greatly for deeds no worse. The uncertainty which surrounded Bunyan's case, together with the Coronation amnesty, had had the useful result that the full rigour of the sentence of banishment had fallen into suspension; if he had drawn attention to himself by a reappearance in court the sentence might have been carried out. Is it possible that Cobb, who had seemed a kindly, if insensitive, man in his examination of Bunyan, was trying to protect him against himself?

Bunyan certainly felt that it was the action of an enemy. 'And thus was I hindred and prevented at that time from appearing before the Judge. And left in prison.'[24]

The pain and sense of abandonment in the last sentence is plain enough. Despite all the loyal efforts of his wife and friends, and his own strenuous attempts to free himself, he was still confined to the Silver Street prison, obliged to live in the company of the crazy and the criminal when his own dearly loved family were only a street away. The worst fears of transportation or the gallows had subsided, but his sentence was indeterminate; he had no means of knowing when he would again be free to pursue his trade or live a normal life.

Confinement was far less strict than in any modern prison. In the twelve years that Bunyan was to stay in Bedford gaol there were probably many occasions when he was permitted to go out, perhaps as a result of bribing the gaoler, and on a number of these he was to preach and attend meetings at Bedford Meeting. There is no record that he went home on any of these occasions; if he did so it must have been a furtive visit, attended by real fears of punishment to his family.

There is, however, a puzzle about this. He had a daughter, Sarah, by Elizabeth, and all that we know about her was that she married in 1686. The question must be — when was she conceived? We know that she was not conceived before Bunyan's imprisonment and if she was conceived afterwards she would have been too young for marriage in 1686. The middle part of Bunyan's imprisonment was the strictest, so that she might possibly have been conceived on a furtive visit home towards the beginning or the end of his imprisonment. More probable, in my view, is the tradition, started by Bunyan's first editor Charles Doe, that Bunyan was released for a few weeks or months in 1666 and then rearrested, a statement for which there is no supporting evidence and which modern scholars have therefore tended to discount. If Sarah was conceived in 1666 she would have been nineteen at the time of her marriage, a favourite age for marriage at the time.

It is noteworthy that Elizabeth did not, so far as we know, conceive at any other time during Bunyan's imprisonment, though upon his release she did so almost immediately.

The family must have been very poor. The cruellest aspect of an imprisonment like Bunyan's was that it made an entire family destitute. The 'friends' of the Bedford Meeting kept the Bunyan family out of a sense of religious duty, but the congregation was a poor one, and charity is a chancy sort of income; the hardships must have been considerable.

But with the hope of an early release removed, Bunyan seems to have settled with as good a grace as he could to his painful situation. He preached in the prison, and as the persecution of the dissenters grew he had the companionship of others convicted for similar reasons. At one point there were two other ministers imprisoned with him, and they used to take it in turn to preach. Among these were the 'Keysoe group' — dissenters from the Keysoe area of Bedfordshire, one of whom, John Donne, was sentenced to be transported to Barbados. He was, however, still in Bedford in 1672, and it seems that this, along with some other severe sentences, was delayed until official policy had changed.

Reading was important to Bunyan. As always the Bible occupied him, and he is said to have had Foxe's *Book of Martyrs* in the prison. One of the positive aspects of imprisonment was that he had more leisure to read than he can have done as a working tinker and an active member of the Bedford Meeting with all its attendant duties.

Imprisonment concentrated his mind wonderfully, not only on his reading but on writing. Deprived of so many other outlets this active and sociable man turned inward. He wrote tracts which may have brought him a small income, and in 1666 he wrote *Grace Abounding to the Chief of Sinners*, a long autobiography in the genre popular among the Puritans, very possibly worked up from an account of his spiritual struggles given to his brethren in Bedford. Above all he wrote *The Pilgrim's Progress*. There is a small table which belonged to Bunyan, given by him to John Donne, which he is believed to have used as a desk. Writing must have been a good way of using up the interminable hours and of shutting out the lamentations and cursing, the aimless chatter and the mindless rambling of his fellow-prisoners, a way of remaining sane in an intolerable situation.

Writing was not his only occupation nor his only source of income during his imprisonment; he spent hours making many gross of 'tagg'd laces' which were sold for the support of his family. Both his mind and his hands were kept busy. Tradition has it that he made a flute out of the leg of a prison stool, and played it.

Busyness must have been necessary, since these were dark days for Dissenters. The Act of Uniformity in 1662 had effectively denied them existence. They could meet only secretly in deadly fear of discovery. One such meeting-place was Wain Wood at Preston, near Hitchin, about an hour's journey by horse-back from Bedford. Here in a hollow in the wood congregations used to gather and they were addressed more than once by the prisoner John Bunyan so that the place is known to this day as Bunyan's dell.

Baptism rites could only be carried out surreptitiously after dark at a lonely place on the River Ouse.

Those who were caught breaking the law were subject to terrible penalties. John Fenne, one of Bunyan's brethren, had his goods seized. Brother Harrington was in hiding. Other Nonconformists were transported. Some like Prynne, Burton, and Bastwick had holes cut in their ears, an eventuality for which Bunyan tried to prepare himself.* Some were fined or hanged.

A black day for the Bedford Meeting was Sunday, 15th May, 1670, when, tipped off by informers, the town constables arrived at the house of John Fenne where some twenty-eight of the congregation were meeting secretly. As a result of this John Fenne and Nehemiah Cox appeared in court. There was provision in such cases for fines of £20 for a first offence, (it was doubled for subsequent offences), together with a £20 fine for holding a meeting on one's premises. If the person charged could not pay then the charge was levied upon the congregation. It was presumably because of inability to pay (and the congregation's inability to raise the balance) that John Fenne's possessions were sequestered.

Amongst the townsfolk of Bedford, however, there was a great deal of sympathy for the dissenting cause. When Thomas Battison, the church-warden of St. Paul's, was sent to collect the fines imposed on those who did not attend church 'The common sort of people covertly fixing a Calves tayl to Battison's back, and deriding him with shouts and hollows the day was seen to have been won by the dissenters.' The fines never were collected.

But this crude form of sympathy could not soften the rigour of the law. For five and a half years the Bedford Meeting no longer dared to record its meetings, and perhaps did not meet for a time.

In 1671, while Bunyan was still a prisoner, the Bedford Meeting met and chose him as pastor. It seems likely that by this time there was a feeling of 'thaw' in the political and religious atmosphere, and that they knew Bunyan would soon be free.

* I am most free that men shoulde see
  A hole cut thro' mine ear;
  If others will ascertain me,
  They'll hang a jewel there. J. Bunyan *Prison Meditations* (1665).

Bunyan came out of prison in 1672 under the 'Quaker pardon' and in the same year Elizabeth gave birth to a son, Joseph. In 1673 the Church Book records that Thomas Bunyan, by then a youth of seventeen or so, had become a member of the Meeting.

Bunyan had entered prison as a comparatively young man and came out as a middle-aged one. He had changed none of his original beliefs, nor had he bowed to persecution; there is, however, a richness of humanity in *The Pilgrim's Progress* which seems to owe much to suffering. He had entered prison as a man of unusual imagination, of natural verbal gifts and of genuine talent as a preacher. He left it as a literary genius.

First, however, he had to undergo a second term of imprisonment, for a year in 1676–7. This is thought to have been for not attending his parish church. Controversy has raged about whether this, or even his original term, was served at the cramped little gaol on Bedford bridge (destroyed in the late eighteenth century). Victorian piety liked to dwell on Bunyan's heroism by exaggerating his sufferings, and so the damp, confinement, and squalor of the old town gaol particularly appealed to them. The strength of their claim comes from the fact that this prison was supposed to have been locally known as 'the Den', and Bunyan refers to 'the Den' in which *The Pilgrim's Progress* was partly written.

Modern authorities, such as Professor Sharrock, however, are convinced that both terms of imprisonment were served in the county gaol since both were county offences. On the face of it it appears that they are right, yet in Bedford the tradition that Bunyan spent at least some time in the town gaol over the river remains strong, and since Bunyan has been a figure of continuing interest in the town since well before his death until now, it cannot quite be discounted.

Bunyan was finally released in June 1677 and found himself something of a hero. Mankind love a man who has suffered for a cause and survived, even if they do not care for the cause and would not dream of suffering for it themselves. The persecution of Dissenters under Charles had produced the usual crop of bullies, cowards, waverers, turncoats and betrayers; once the agony was past men were glad to identify with those who had behaved as well as they would have liked to have done themselves.

Bunyan was a ready-made hero, not only because he had bravely endured a harsh term of imprisonment or because his cheerful, sturdy character was much to the English taste, but because he had made himself known to a huge public by writing the first part of *The Pilgrim's Progress*. He offered it modestly, humbly, enough in 1678, not even sure that it should be published at all. It is easy to see why he doubted, and why friends advised against it, just because it is a work of such astonishing originality. However we may search for precedents among the emblem writers and others there *is* nothing written in his own time that has the same ability to discuss spiritual themes with such vitality, naturalness, and superb use of words and imagery. The dullness, the ponderous elaborations of such books as *The Plaine Man's Pathway* and *The Practice of Piety* must have made it too difficult and boring for many plain men to follow the arguments at all, whatever their religious zeal. Bunyan's book came at exactly the right moment, just as many of 'the common people' of England were struggling to come into their spiritual and cultural inheritance. It sold for 18d.

The second half of *The Pilgrim's Progress* and the *Holy War* show the delight of the successful author. Bunyan was far too natural, too childlike, to try to conceal his pleasure.

In addition to his success in authorship Bunyan was in enormous demand as a preacher. He travelled over wide areas of the countryside on horseback and was nicknamed 'Bishop Bunyan'. He gained new friends, among them a Lord Mayor, John Shorter, who presented him with a silver-mounted walking-stick.

He continued faithfully as pastor to the Bedford Meeting and the Church Book contains many entries with Bunyan's signature.

It seems unlikely that he could have found time to take up his old vocation of tinker. No doubt others had taken on his customers, and twelve years without regular exercise must have made it difficult for a man in his forties to take up such a strenuous calling again. Probably the Bedford Meeting raised money to support him.

Nothing is known about how much money he made from his writing. The usual method in the seventeenth century was for authors to be paid an outright sum for their copy which then became the property of the publisher/bookseller. Since Bunyan's reputation as a writer was not large when the first part of the *Progress* was published the payment must have been small and most of the profit must have gone to his bookseller 'Bunyan' Ponder. No doubt Bunyan knew how to value his work more highly when the second part of the *Progress* was ready for publication.*

In 1688 he rode to Reading, according to tradition, to patch up a quarrel between father and son. Travelling to London afterwards he was caught in a storm and arrived at the house of his friend John Strudwick, the grocer, at Snow Hill in the City, obviously unwell. He recovered sufficiently to preach a sermon two days later, but again fell ill and died quite suddenly, too suddenly for his wife to be sent for. The Church Book records the numb horror that fell upon those close to him.

Wednesday the 4th of September was kept in prayre and huemilyation for this heavy stroak upon us, the death of dare Brother Bunyan. Apoynted allso that Wednsday next be kept in praire and humiliation on the same account.

Apoynted that all the brethren meet to gether on the 18th of this month, September, to humble them selves for this heavy hand of God upon us. And allso to pray unto the Lord for counsell and direction what to doe in order to seek out for a fitt person to mak choyce off for an elder.

Three years before his death Bunyan had been afraid that with the accession of James II he would once again be singled out for persecution. He had therefore made out a deed of gift transferring his property to his wife in the following terms:

I . . . John Bunyan as well for, and in consideration of the natural affection and love which I have, and bear unto my wellbeloved wife, Elizabeth Bunyan, as also for divers other good causes and consider-ations, me at this present especially moveing, have given and granted, and by these presents, do give, grant, and conferm unto the said Elizabeth Bunyan, my said wife, all and singuler my goods, chattels, debts, ready mony, plate, rings, household stuffe, aparrel, utensills, brass, peuter, beding, and all other my substance . . .

The Deed was witnessed by four witnesses, John Bardolph, Nicholas

* Professor Sharrock points out that Bunyan used other publishers after Ponder, particularly Dorman Newman for *The Holy War* (though he continued to use Ponder for some of his work), possibly indicating a sense of grievance. He also drew my attention to the fact that Milton's payment for *Paradise Lost* consisted of two payments of five pounds from his printer, Samuel Symmons. It seems unlikely that Bunyan kept himself and his wife by writing.

Malin, William Hawkes, and Lewes Norman, and sealed with a silver twopenny piece. If Bunyan had again been imprisoned, or suffered transportation or hanging, his property would have been safe from the threat of distraint.

Bunyan hid this Deed so successfully that at his death it was not discovered and it was only many years later that it was found concealed in the chimney of his house.

He was buried at Bunhill fields, the burying-ground for Dissenters opened in 1666, in the tomb of his friend Mr. Strudwick. He lies near to Daniel Defoe and Isaac Watts. Victorian piety insisted on a bigger and better tomb for the evangelical hero and they placed an effigy of him on a large stone catafalque. By Victorian standards, however, it is a simple and unpretentious memorial, and if it seems a pity that it is not in the town of Bedford where he lived out the remarkable experiences of a pilgrim, he is at least surrounded in death by many who showed similar courage in the face of adversity and intolerance.

NOTES

1 John Bunyan, *A Relation of My Imprisonment* (1666).
2 Ibid.
3 Ibid.
4 Ibid.
5 Ibid.
6 Ibid.
7 35th Eliz. cap. 1.
8 *Grace Abounding*, pp. 332, 334–5.
9 Ibid.
10 Ibid., pp. 327–8.
11 Ibid.
12 Ibid.
13 Ibid., p. 325.
14 *A Relation of My Imprisonment*.
15–24 Ibid.

4

The Pilgrim's Progress, Part I

The first part of *The Pilgrim's Progress*, Bunyan's greatest masterpiece, was published in 1678, by Nathaniel Ponder (later to be generally known by the nickname of 'Bunyan Ponder') of the Poultry near Cornhill. It reveals Bunyan, for the first time, as a literary genius. His sermons had already shown that he had a fine mind, a total mastery of language and of metaphor, and a profound grasp of theology. His spiritual autobiography, *Grace Abounding to the Chief of Sinners*, published in 1666, had hinted at the poet struggling to obtain release from his mental torment. In the *Progress* the poet and the theologian move as one, imagery and belief achieving a perfect union.

It is generally agreed that Bunyan wrote parts of the book in prison (he himself suggested this in the margin of later editions of the book), but because of the date of its publication it was long thought that it was written during his second term of imprisonment. Professor Sharrock and others claim that this dates it far too late, that the book was written between 1666–1672, in the second half of the first term of imprisonment.

Bunyan's *Apology* (1678) is vague about the date and place in which he began the *Progress*, but wonderfully informative about everything else. He describes how, when he was already busy on another book his mind began to fill with an allegory about pilgrims on their way to glory. He wrote with growing speed and excitement, ideas pouring in upon him.

'In more than twenty things, which I set down; This done, I twenty more had in my Crown.' Ideas for the allegory became so fertile that he realised it had burst the bounds of the book he was originally trying to write. The allegory would have to be a book on its own.

It felt quite different from the tracts and sermons he had written in the past. He had no very conscious idea of *what* he was trying to do, nor whether he would ever show it to anyone else. He was not trying to edify or to entertain others; on the contrary, 'I did it mine own self to gratifie.' And the compulsion was wonderfully enjoyable; he 'set Pen to Paper with delight', he says, and gradually had the joy of seeing a method and a style evolve, as it seemed by itself. There was the strange effortlessness which many artists describe when at the height of creation, almost as if the book was writing itself. Bunyan used the homely metaphor of the spinner who merely controls the flow of the thread, 'Still as I pull'd, it came.'

Though he had written it only for his own gratification he felt, as soon as he had finished it, the author's usual mixture of pride and hope on the one hand, and shyness and fear of ridicule on the other. He could not resist showing the work to his friends, and with good humour he passes on the contradictory advice he received.

> Some said, John, print it; others said, Not so.
> Some said, It might do good; others said, No.

Without too much difficulty Bunyan persuaded himself that it would be better to print, but not before he attempted to anticipate (in the introductory verses of the *Apology*) the criticism he was likely to reap, criticism doubtless already voiced by the friends who said 'No'.

He felt vulnerable on the grounds that he had used 'metaphor' as a way of expressing religious truth. Of course, the sectarians made good use of metaphor in their sermons, and Bunyan was already a master of the metaphor, but such a protracted metaphor as that used in the *Progress* must have seemed dangerously close to the fiction or romance of which Calvin's followers were intensely suspicious, feeling, in their exact and literal way, that it was a sort of untruth. Here, for the first time, there is evidence of an inner conflict between Bunyan the poet to whom metaphor is as natural as breathing, and Bunyan the Calvinist.

Unconsciously Bunyan hit on the best possible answer for reconciling his two disparate personalities. The idea of the salvific journey was a commonplace of seventeenth-century theology — it appeared in innumerable sermons and books of pious instruction. What Bunyan had done was to take up this commonplace idea and transform it with imagination and deep psychological insight, born of his own terrible experience. His beliefs were so thoroughly assimilated that they did not clash with the artistic purpose of the book, in fact they gave it its passion and its energy. He managed simultaneously to outline the stages, so important to his theological system, by which a man achieved regeneration, and to write a profoundly moving story capable of touching those to whom his theology had little appeal. Calvinism, being an essentially dramatic conception of human life, lends itself to fictional interpretation; perhaps it also touches the imagination because, even in its narrowest manifestations, it reflects something true and universal about the human condition.

Bunyan's reflections on the subject of metaphor in the *Apology* (probably written just before the publication of the *Progress*) are interesting in that they suggested that his understanding of the Bible has undergone a change. The rigid literalism of many of the sectarians, and the agonised shredding of texts that Bunyan had described in *Grace Abounding* lead us to expect an excessive literalism in Bunyan, yet it is clear that he understands, or has learned, that the Bible is not to be naively interpreted. 'Was not God's Laws . . . in older times held forth by Types, Shadows and Metaphors?' he asks. This more sophisticated Bunyan employs his ingenuity to discover.

> what by pins and loops,
> By Calves, and Sheep; by Heifers, and by Rams;
> By Birds and Herbs, and by the Blood of Lambs;
> God speaketh to him: And happy is he
> That finds the Light, and grace that in them be.

Relaxed, almost humorous, in his approach to the Bible Bunyan presents a very different picture from his former self, tortured by the passage in Deuteronomy about the beasts that chewed the cud or parted the hoof. Then too, he had read a metaphorical significance into the passage, identifying with the unclean swine, yet the literal way in which the metaphor was worked out, under the stress of genuine terror about damnation, had lacked the balance and detachment with which he writes of metaphor in the *Apology*.

This latter Bunyan glows with the extraordinary personal liberation he has achieved. No longer terrified of his fate he can say 'let Truth be free, to make her Salleys upon Thee, and me'. The *Progress* has a clear purpose, namely that it 'chaulketh out before thine eyes, The man that seeks the everlasting Prize'. It is not so much improving or edifying in the usual Puritan fashion, as a kind of map, or sea-chart, of the sort drawn by sailors who have already travelled a hazardous route.

The *Progress* opens with the account of a man falling asleep and dreaming a dream. 'As I walk'd through the wilderness of this world, I lighted on a certain place, where was a Denn; And I laid me down in that place to sleep: And as I slept I dreamed a Dream.' The Den has been identified with the gaol in which Bunyan was imprisoned, ever since the seventh edition of the *Progress* which had the words 'the Gaol' as an annotation in the margin.

The dreamer dreams of a Man in a terrible state of distress. He is dressed in rags, and he carries a great burden upon his back. He has a book in his hand in which he reads, but what he reads makes him tremble and weep and he keeps calling out 'What shall I do?'

He goes home to his wife and family and tries to keep his trouble to himself but he is too distraught to do so. Finally he tells them that he has heard that the city in which they are living is about to be destroyed by fire from heaven and that they are all going to be killed. His family think him quite simply mad, the victim of a 'frenzy distemper', so they put him to bed and hope for the best. The next day, however, he is just as miserable, and they grow angry with him. They try bullying him out of his depression, and as the days go on, they alternate this with teasing, chiding, and leaving him to his own devices. Gradually he withdraws from them into loneliness, shutting himself into his room, or going for long walks in utter despair.

It is on one of these walks that, as he cries aloud 'What shall I do?' he is answered. Evangelist meets him, asks him about his despair, and tells him that he must indeed flee from the wrath that is about to come upon him. He points across the field with his finger to a wicket-gate. The Man cannot see the wicket-gate but he can see a shining light beside it, and

Evangelist advises him to go towards the light, to find the gate and to knock upon it.

The Man begins to run, and his wife and children, who are watching the whole episode from the house, cry out to him to come back. The neighbours, hearing the commotion, also come out to see the fun, and jeer at him, threaten him, and even pursue him to bring him back by force. The Man, however, having started his journey, runs on, with his fingers stuffed in his ears, shouting, 'Life, Life, Eternal Life.'

The first thing that happens to 'the Man' (whom Bunyan begins to call Christian once he has embarked upon his journey) is that he falls into the Slough of Despond, a treacherous bog. It takes him entirely by surprise — he had been walking along chatting comfortably to a neighbour called Pliable about how lovely it would be to be saved — when suddenly there they both are 'grievously bedaubed with dirt', up to their necks in the mire. Pliable struggles out of the bog on the same side as the City of Destruction. Christian fights to get out on the far side in order to continue his journey, but is terribly handicapped by the burden on his back. When he is unable to move a man called Help gives him his hand and pulls him out. Help explains how all the discouragement which attends a man when he discovers how sinful he is, settles in this area in a sewer of scum and filth. 'The King' does his best to keep the ground in good repair, and he places stepping-stones through the middle of it, but men have a way 'through the diziness of their Heads' of missing them, and they end up feeling and looking as filthy as Christian does.

Christian's next encounter is with Mr. Worldly Wiseman. Christian is terribly oppressed by the weight on his back, but Mr. Worldly Wiseman urges him to consult a gentleman called Legality in the village of Morality who will help him get rid of his burden. Christian follows his instructions and arrives at a 'high hill'. He is afraid to walk past it in case it falls upon his head, the weight on his back seems heavier than ever, and he begins to sweat and quake with terror. At this point Evangelist reappears in the story to enquire what Christian is doing so far from his original route. Bunyan explains and is rebuked by Evangelist for his credulity.

Deeply afraid that he has lost his chance of salvation Christian collapses on the ground weeping and blaming himself, but Evangelist raises him, comforts him, and redirects him to the wicket-gate.

At the wicket-gate, Christian knocks and is drawn quickly inside by

Goodwill, for fear that Captain Beelzebub should shoot him with an arrow before he is safe. Once inside Goodwill shows him a 'straight and narrow' pathway that will be his road to the Celestial City and says that he may distinguish the right paths from the wrong on his journey because the wrong ones are crooked and wide. He also tells him to be patient with his burden, and that at the right time it will fall away from him.

Soon after leaving Goodwill, Christian arrives at the House of the Interpreter, where he is shown a series of tableaux or emblems, each with a message for him. In one a man sweeps a dusty room and the dust rises in clouds until 'a damsel' sprinkles it with water and cleans it; the analogy is the soul of a man before and after sanctification. One exalts the virtue of patience, another shows Christ quenching the flames of temptation by his grace, another 'a valiant man' struggling against violent men. The most moving scene in the House of the Interpreter is in a dark room where Christian is shown a man in an iron cage. 'I am now a Man of despair,' he cries, 'and am shut up in it, as in this Iron Cage. I cannot get out; O now I cannot.' The Man is convinced that he has sinned beyond all hope of redemption, that there can never be any hope or forgiveness for him.

Alarmed by what he has seen Christian runs up a steep path with fences on both sides (called Salvation), bent double under the appalling weight of his burden. Suddenly, upon a little hill, he comes upon a cross with a sepulchre below it at the bottom of the hill. With dramatic suddenness, the great burden drops off Christian's shoulders, and tumbles down the hill until it rolls into the sepulchre out of sight. It is a cathartic moment. Filled with joy, Christian 'looked . . . and looked again, even till the springs that were in his head sent the waters down his cheeks'. As he stands at the cross weeping with happiness, three Shining Ones appear. One says, 'Thy sins be forgiven.' Another takes off his rags, and clothes him in new garments. The third sets a mark on his forehead, and gives him a parchment roll with a seal upon it, a kind of certificate that he will have to produce at the Celestial Gate. Christian goes on his way, leaping for joy and singing.

He passes, and briefly talks to, a number of other passers-by, including Formalist and Hypocrisy, but he continues on his way, sometimes reading his Roll to comfort himself, until he arrives at the Hill Difficulty. The Hill is very steep, and he has to climb it on his hands and knees, until, mid-way up it, he discovers an Arbour 'made by the Lord of the Hill, for the refreshing of weary Travailers'. He sits there, reading his Roll and enjoying his new garment until he falls into a deep sleep. When he awakes it is almost dark, and he starts up and continues hurriedly on his way up the Hill. He meets two men, Timorous and Mistrust, who tell him that they have come back because there are lions on the route, and Christian wonders what to do, daring neither to go back nor forward. It is at this moment that he realises that he has lost his precious Roll, and guessing he must have dropped it in the Arbour he goes back for it. He finds it in the Arbour, but by now the sun has gone down and he fears that he will be torn to pieces by the lions in the dark.

At this point he sees the House Beautiful in the distance and thinks he will ask there for a night's lodging. He enters the narrow pathway leading to the porter's lodge and only after he has done so perceives that there are lions on the path. He stands hesitating, until the porter calls out to him that the lions are chained. He approaches them with fear, hearing them roar, but by keeping to the middle of the path is able to get past them safely.

At the House Beautiful he is entertained by the Virgins Discretion, Prudence, Piety and Charity, who question him closely about his history and beliefs before entertaining him to supper. Christian spends several days at the House and before he departs they take him up to the roof of the House and show him the Delectable Mountains in the distance, 'a most pleasant Mountainous country, beautified with Woods, Vinyards, Fruits of all sorts; Flowers also, with Springs and Fountains, very delectable to behold'. From the mountains, when he gets there, they tell him he will be able to see the gate of the Celestial City.

The Virgins see him on his way downhill, giving him bread, wine and a cluster of raisins. He complains of the slipperiness of the route, and they say yes, it is hard going down into the Valley of Humiliation.

The Valley at once provides terrifying contrast to the courtesy and refinement he has just left. He has scarcely set foot in it before he sees a hideous fiend, Apollyon, coming across the field to meet him. He has some armour with which the Virgins have provided him but not enough to protect him from this monster, who has wings like a dragon, scales all over his body, feet like a bear, and a mouth like a lion.

Apollyon's quarrel with Christian is that he has deserted him, the Prince of this World, in order to become the subject of another King. He insists that he return. 'I am an enemy to this Prince: I hate his Person, his Laws, and People.' He then throws fiery darts at Christian, which Christian deflects with his shield; in spite of this, however, he is wounded in several parts of his body. The fight continues for hours, until Christian is utterly exhausted and weak from his wounds.

In a last life-and-death struggle Christian is thrown to the ground, and his sword is knocked out of his hand. Apollyon gloats 'I am sure of thee now' in the manner of many fictional villains, and it seems as if it is all up with Christian. But with one last effort Christian manages to snatch up his sword and to inflict a serious wound upon his oppressor. At this Apollyon speeds off and leaves him alone. It has been a stupendous battle, Christian's ears almost deafened by the yells and roars of Apollyon, and groaning himself in fear and agony. As the injured, bone-weary man gives thanks to God for his victory, something magical happens. 'There came to him an hand with some of the leaves of the Tree of Life, the which Christian took, and applyed to the wounds that he had received in the Battel, and was healed immediately.'

The Valley of Humiliation leads into the Valley of the Shadow of Death, and there is no way to the Celestial City that does not go through this solitary place. It is a desert, a drought-stricken land, and Christian is met by men who tell him of its darkness, hobgoblins and dragons, and the dreadful misery of those who dwell there. Christian advances upon it with his drawn sword in his hand. On his right hand he discovers a deep ditch into which it would be fatal to fall; on his left a quagmire with no bottom to it. Between the two runs a path so narrow that he can scarcely walk along it, and to make things worse darkness has fallen so that he can only feel his way with his feet.

Suddenly Christian finds himself looking down into the mouth of hell, hears its blood-curdling screams and cries, and sees the flames and smoke pouring from it. He knows that his sword is of no use to him here, and takes refuge in something he calls All-Prayer, a giving up of himself in all his helplessness to the care of God. He is surrounded by fiends, and some of them troop up behind him and whisper blasphemies against God in his ear. The worst thing about this was that the blasphemies seemed to be in his own voice, and Christian therefore feared they came from his own mind, and was filled with shame at himself.

In this state of mental agony and despair he hears the voice of a man going before him through the Valley singing, 'Though I walk through the valley of the shadow of death, I will fear none ill, for thou art with me.' He is given new strength by this to continue, and to his relief the sun begins to rise. Looking back, he is horrified to see what a difficult and dangerous path he has travelled, and feels gratitude for his deliverance. The rest of his journey through the Valley is no less dangerous, since it is set with snares, traps, gins, nets, deep pits and holes, but because he is now travelling by daylight, he feels safer. At the end of the Valley is a horrible mess of blood, bones, ashes and mangled bodies, the handiwork of two giants, Pope and Pagan, who live there in a cave. Pagan is dead and so past hurting anyone, but Pope is still alive. However, by reason of his age, he is too 'crazy and stiff in his joynts' to do much harm, and he contents himself with shouting after Christian the mad threat, 'You will never mend, till more of you be burned.'

Christian sings a little song, rejoicing over his deliverance from the Valley, and then ahead of him he sees Faithful on the road (the man whose voice had so comforted him) and runs until he overtakes him. They rejoice at having each other's companionship, and they describe their different experiences on the journey so far. Faithful never suffered the Slough, as Christian did, but instead was severely tempted by Wanton. The old Adam also stopped him on the way, tried to persuade him to join his service, and nearly killed him when he would not agree. He passed the lions of the House Beautiful without difficulty; it was noon when he reached them and they were asleep, and he also had arguments by the way with Discontent and Shame, Shame trying to ridicule him for being a religious man, since 'few of the Mighty, Rich, or Wise, were ever of my opinion.' Unlike Christian, Faithful enjoyed sunshine through both the terrible Valleys.

Together Christian and Faithful encounter Talkative, and Faithful in particular is impressed by his glib religious chatter. Christian knows him of old, however, and remembers him as a man who is 'best abroad, near home he is ugly enough'. 'Religion hath no place in his heart, or house, or conversation; all he hath lieth in his tongue, and his Religion is to make a noise therewith.' By questioning Talkative closely Faithful discovers that this is, in fact, the case, and hurt, Talkative flings away in a huff; 'A good riddance' as Bunyan tartly writes in the margin.

Evangelist then reappears, talks warmly of their courage hitherto, and warns them that in the Town they are approaching a new trial awaits them, in which one of them will suffer death. In the context of their journey this is to be rejoiced at, as a kind of short-cut to the goal, and a deliverance from prolonged suffering and hardship. 'He that shall die there, although his death will be unnatural, and his pain perhaps great, he will yet have the better of his fellow; not only because he will be arrived at the Celestial City soonest, but because he will escape many miseries that the other will meet with in the rest of his Journey.'

The pilgrims soon arrive at the town of Vanity where Apollyon and others have set up a perpetual Fair where everything is for sale 'as Houses, Lands, Trades, Places, Honours, Preferments, Titles, Countreys, Kingdoms, Lusts, Pleasures, and Delights of all sorts, as Whores, Bauds, Wives, Husbands, Children, Masters, Servants, Lives, Blood, Bodies, Souls, Silver, Gold, Pearls, Precious Stones, and what not'. The Fair also abounds in cheating, thieving, murders, adultery and lies.

The citizens of the town notice at once that Faithful and Christian are strangely dressed. They also talk differently from the local people since they speak 'the Language of Canaan'. The townsfolk think they must be madmen, or anyhow foreigners, and they begin to mob them until the whole place is in an uproar. The pilgrims are arrested and taken before the magistrates, to whom they explain 'that they were Pilgrims and Strangers in the world, and that they were going to their own Countrey, which was the Heavenly Jerusalem'. The magistrates have them beaten, daubed with dirt, and put them into a cage to amuse the townspeople, who at once begin to torment them. Some of the spectators, however, are so moved by their courage that they begin to defend them, and get into a quarrel with other sections of the crowd. This starts another fight, as a result of which Christian and Faithful are again brought before the magistrates, are beaten again very severely, put in irons, and led up and down the fair in chains. Their patience angers the powers-that-be, and after various misadventures they are brought to trial under Lord Hategood. Envy, Superstition and Pickthank (a flatterer) give their testimony and then, after a speech from the Judge, the Jury are asked to give their verdict. In his satirical style, always at its best when perceiving insincerity of motive, Bunyan sums up their objections to poor Faithful.

And first Mr. Blind-man, the foreman, said, I see clearly that this man is an Heretick. Then said Mr. No-good, Away with such a fellow from the Earth. Ay, said Mr. Malice, for I hate the very looks of him. Then said Mr. Love-Lust, I could never indure him. Nor I, said Mr.

Live-loose, for he would alwayes be condemning my way. Hang him, hang him, said Mr. Heady. A sorry Scrub, said Mr. High-mind. My heart riseth against him, said Mr. Enmity. He is a Rogue, said Mr. Lyar. Hanging is too good for him, said Mr. Cruelty. Lets dispatch him out of the way, said Mr. Hate-light. Then said Mr. Implacable, Might I have all the World given me, I could not be reconciled to him, therefore let us forthwith bring him in guilty of death.

The passage has the cheerful repetitive rhythm of a nursery rhyme or folk-tale, carrying the narrative along in a brisk and interesting style; the insight, however, that each of the speakers has an axe to grind introduces the note of satire. Their absurdity is not incompatible with the cruelty of their deeds, deeds which Bunyan catalogues without comment, as if only to be expected in such a place. 'First they Scourged him, then they Buffeted him, then they Lanced his flesh with Knives, then prickt him with their swords, and last of all they burned him to Ashes at the Stake. Thus came Faithful to his end.'

In the end Christian escapes from Vanity Fair, and continues his journey, this time accompanied by Hopeful, who, as a looker-on to the sufferings of Christian and Faithful has been converted by their example. 'Thus one died to make testimony to the Truth, and another rises out of his Ashes to be a Companion with Christian.' Almost at once they fall in with Mr. By-Ends of Fair-speech. Bunyan's perception of him reveals a more confident satirical touch even than that revealed by Faithful's jury. Mr. By-Ends is a man to whom family connections are very important. He is related to 'almost the whole Town' that is to say 'my Lord Turn-about, my Lord Time-server, my Lord Fair-speech (from whose Ancestors that Town first took its name:) Also Mr. Smooth-man, Mr. Facing Bothways, Mr. Any-thing, and the Parson of our Parish, Mr. Two-tongues.' He is the kind of gentleman who takes pleasure in remembering that his ancestors, a long way back, are of the common sort. 'My Great Grand-father was but a Water-man, looking one way and Rowing another.'

'Are you a Married man?' Christian enquires. By-Ends is delighted to answer this question, because he is married to 'my Lady Faining's Daughter'. He and his aristocratic wife are devoutly religious, differing only in two small respects from clumsier believers like Christian. 'First, we never strive against Wind and Tide. Secondly, we are alwayes most zealous when Religion goes in his silver Slippers; we love to walk with him in the Street, if the Sun shines, and the people applaud it.' Christian says that if By-Ends is to accompany the pilgrims, as he wishes, then he must go with Religion in rags, as well as in silver slippers, and in irons, as well as when it gains applause. By-Ends soon falls behind on the journey.

Christian and Hopeful pass on to a Hill called Lucre and a Silver-mine with a treacherous surface where many had been maimed and 'could not to their dying day be their own men again'. The mine is owned by Demas, the Demas mentioned in the Epistle to Timothy as having 'loved this present world'.[1] He begs them to come and dig for some treasure, and they resist, having heard that treasure is dangerous to pilgrims. (By-Ends, coming after them, gives way to the blandishments and disappears into the pit.)

Further on they arrive at a beautiful river surrounded by a meadow full of lilies and they drink of the water of the river and lie and rest in the meadow in safety. The rest seems to make them aware of the hardships of their life, and as they leave they notice how rough the path is and how sore their feet. It is this which tempts them to leave the stony path and to try to take a short cut over a stile and across By-path Meadow. It is a fatal detour. They are overtaken by darkness, and a terrible thunder-storm. They find themselves surrounded by floods, and see another traveller, one Vain-Confidence, fall into a pit and destroy himself before their very eyes. They almost quarrel, trying to work out who is to blame for their predicament. Finally, finding a shelter, they fall asleep.

Here Giant Despair, the owner of Doubting Castle, finds them. He accuses them of trespassing, drives them before him back to the Castle, and throws them into a stinking dungeon. 'Here then they lay, from Wednesday morning till Saturday night, without one bit of bread, or drop of drink, or any light, or any to ask how they did.'

Worse is to come. The giant's wife, Diffidence, tells him to beat them, and this he does, with 'a grievous Crab-tree Cudgel' cursing at them as he does so. 'He falls upon them, and beats them fearfully, in such sort, that they were not able to help themselves, or to turn them upon the floor.' The next day he returns, and seeing them in agonies of soreness he suggests suicide to them. He is considering whether to kill them himself on the spot but has a kind of fit to which he is subject in fine weather, and temporarily loses the use of his hand. In his absence they seriously debate killing themselves, Christian being tempted, Hopeful counselling otherwise. They continue in a state of terrible suffering, in which they are little more than alive. 'What for want of Bread and Water, and by reason of the Wounds they received when he beat them, they could do little but breathe.' The Giant threatens them about what he will do if he returns and finds them alive, and the next day, on his wife's advice, he shows them the bones and skulls of other trespassers he has torn to pieces.

But there is a turn in their fortunes. 'Well, on Saturday about midnight they began to pray, and continued in Prayer till almost break of day.' In what is the weakest dramatic moment in the book, Christian suddenly remembers that he has a key called Promise hidden in his bosom. It unlocks all the doors that lead out of the Giant's estate, even though some of the locks 'went damnable hard'. The creaking of the final Gate wakes the Giant, who leaps out of bed to pursue them, only to be taken by one of his fits. By the time he has recovered the pilgrims are safely back on the King's highway.

After the terrible sufferings of Doubting Castle the pilgrims arrive at the Delectable Mountains, where they drink from the fountains, wash themselves, and eat the fruit of the vineyards. The shepherds inform them that Immanuel owns the mountains and the sheep, and that they are within sight of the Celestial City. The pilgrims stay and solace themselves on the comforts of the place, yet even here they are not quite safe. They notice a steep drop called Errour where the bones of men lie dashed to pieces at the bottom, and what is more terrible, a by-way to Hell, especially for hypocrites, a door cut in the hillside through which comes smoke and the scent of brimstone. But the shepherds also show them the Celestial City through a perspective glass, and though their hands shake from the last terrible vision, they catch a glimpse of glory.

At this point Bunyan announces that he woke from his Dream. As in the very next sentence he says that he slept and dreamed again, this interruption seems to serve no literary purpose, and is thought to announce his release from prison in 1672.

In the second dream the pilgrims escape, with a certain amount of difficulty, the net of the flatterer (but are beaten soundly by a Shining one for falling into such a silly trap). They have a brush with Atheist, they struggle not to fall into the deadly inertia of the Enchanted Ground, and they have a long discussion with Ignorance about how a man shall be saved. Ignorance is full of sensible ideas about his faith, and a number of commentators have agreed that he is anything but Ignorant, but he falls into what was, for Bunyan, the ultimate error — that of supposing he can be saved in his own strength, and not through Christ, and Christ alone.

Talking of these things they arrive in the country of Beulah, a beautiful land where they are safe for good from the horrors of the Valley of the Shadow and out of reach of Giant Despair. For the first time they can see the Celestial City clearly and they fall sick with desire. Even in their sleep they talk of the wonders of the City. Shining ones come to them and inform them their difficulties are nearly over. They must, however, cross the River of Death, an ordeal that must be undertaken on foot since there is no bridge.

Christian is deeply afraid of this ordeal. A great darkness and horror falls upon him, he is troubled with apparitions of hobgoblins and evil spirits. He avoids drowning only because Hopeful holds him up and comforts him, but suddenly, by thinking of Christ, he finds his feet are on solid ground again. The two exhausted pilgrims are received by the heavenly host, reclothed in heavenly garments, and received into the King's city to the blowing of trumpets and the pealing of bells.

Ignorance follows them, and typically, gets across the river with the help of a renegade ferry-man. He knocks boldly on the Gate, but when they ask him for his Certificate he cannot produce it. The shining ones take Ignorance away and fling him through the doorway of the hill that leads down into hell. 'Then I saw that there was a way to Hell, even from the Gates of Heaven, as well as from the City of Destruction. So I awoke, and behold it was a Dream.'

It is possible to analyse Bunyan's allegory as a story, as a careful exposition of the stages by which a Calvinist believed man achieved regeneration or as a parallel of his own religious and social crisis as described in *Grace Abounding*.

As a story it is extremely effective. It employs nearly all the devices by which fiction beguiles (only romance is notably missing); there is a hero with whom we can identify, and there are action, suspense, violence, humour, lively characters, and a happy ending. The evil characters are genuinely frightening; Giant Despair's casual brutality and Apollyon's beastliness both chill the blood.

Part of the reason that it is all so effective is that the story is built upon the foundations of innumerable folk-tales and mythological stories. In these the hero sets out from a haven that has become constricting, travels through the world, has a series of adventures, is helped by 'allies' who frequently have supernatural powers, and finds the treasure, the goal, the prize, the princess, often killing a monster or overcoming an enemy in order to do so. Bunyan admits to having loved such adventures as a child, and to have preferred them to improving literature.* His faith and his poetic vision have now fused.

Christian has all the humanity of the peasant folk-hero. He is not well-born, nor is he particularly gifted. He makes mistakes, some of them of a rather comical nature as when he dashes past Faithful, wanting to be first on the road, smiles 'vaingloriously' to himself at his cleverness, catches his foot and trips and has to be helped to his feet by Faithful. His courage is largely born out of desperation, since the thought of returning frightens him even more than the thought of going on. He 'gives up' on several occasions and has to be comforted by his friends. He nods off to sleep at inopportune moments, is frequently scared out of his wits, and is susceptible to the wiles of Worldly Wiseman and to the Flatterer. Whatever his weaknesses, however, he is a man armed with one important piece of knowledge; life as he used to live it is no longer tolerable, and the only remedy is to persevere in his difficult journey.

Christian moves through a pastoral landscape of meadows and plains, of hills and rivers, or tracks and roads, of stiles and by-paths. There is only one town, that of Vanity, though others such as Deceit and Fair-speech are mentioned. There are stately houses, like the House Beautiful and the House of the Interpreter. On the whole it is a similar landscape to that which Bunyan saw daily on his travels around Bedfordshire. The exception is the nightmarish landscape of the Valley of the Shadow of death. Seventeenth-century Bedfordshire had its quagmires and its ditches, and its paths strewn with gins, but none of such a terrible aspect as these. These, like the Delectable Mountains, derive from Bunyan's imagination, stimulated by the romances of his youth.

Christian encounters (or hears tell of) some ninety characters. Seventeen of these are good characters, including the Shining ones who play an individual part in the drama; the rest, and by far the more interesting and

---

* 'Alas! What is the Scripture? Give me a ballad, a news-book, George on horseback, or Bevis of Southampton; give me some book that teaches curious arts, that tells of old fables; but for the holy Scriptures I cared not.' *A Few Sighs from Hell* (1658).

colourful characters, are all bad. It is possible to examine Bunyan's beliefs by tabulating the kinds of error to which his villains were subject, and all but three characters — Liar, Hate-light, and Atheist — seem to belong to one of seven categories. The seven categories are Worldliness, Pretentiousness, Conceit, Spite, Lust, Being Easily Led, and Laziness. Worldliness is by far the biggest category of sinner, sixteen of the bad characters belonging to it, two of whom are the outstanding sinners, Mr. Worldly Wiseman and By-Ends. The next biggest category is that of the easily led, with ten members, including Pliable, Simple, Timorous and Ignorance. Then come the pretentious, with Talkative and Hypocrisy as members. Lust has six characters, but these were mostly just names rattled out by Pickthank at Faithful's trial; my old Lord Lechery and my Lord Carnal Delight do not seem to trouble Christian very much on his journey. Faithful's brush with Wanton, later reported to Christian, is the only time in this book that Bunyan gives importance to lust.

The real temptations of the journeying Christian, in Bunyan's eyes, are that of conforming to 'this world', losing one's integrity by trying to please others, and soothing one's conscience by legalistic arguments. The man who conformed to this world enjoyed its honours and its rewards, but lost his soul. The next, not dissimilar temptation, was that of abdicating choice, of letting oneself be led by others into beliefs or conduct of which there was no inner understanding, and to which there was no genuine consent. Weakness of this kind, as Bunyan saw with great clarity, led to the mindless cruelty of 'the mob', a cruelty meticulously mapped out in the events of Vanity Fair.

These sins, like the sins of pretentiousness and conceit, reveal Bunyan's obsession with genuineness of belief. It is a typically Puritan emphasis to insist that belief and conduct must match to the last detail, but Bunyan seems to go beyond that in his contempt for those who say one thing and do another. No doubt the years of persecution, with the hard choices they enjoined upon the Nonconformists, had made him especially sensitive on this subject.

In addition to the characters who acted out sins, there are six characters, seven if you count my Lord Beelzebub who is merely mentioned, who themselves embody sin. These are Apollyon, the Prince of this World, Pope and Pagan, who represent their respective bodies of belief, Adam/Moses who are a kind of composite character representing unredeemed man condemned by legality, and Demas, who represents money. Christian has to navigate between his unredeemed condition, false religious beliefs, and the illusions created by money and 'this world'. These are the really catastrophic mistakes from which there may be no going back.

As an exposition of Bunyan's Calvinism the allegory works splendidly. At the core of Bunyan's belief was a rejection of the covenant of works with its death-dealing 'legality', and a turning to the 'new covenant' with its promise in Christ, and scene after scene of the *Progress* captures either the despair that attends the 'old covenant' or the liberation that attends the new. This contrast was Bunyan's intellectual preoccupation (as in his Sermons where it is meticulously worked out), and the inspiration for his artistic achievements.

He employs it naturally and without forcing or artificiality. Belief for Bunyan is closely allied to feeling, and he never falls into the mechanical approach to faith of which the Calvinists were often guilty, nor forgets that there is a feeling and suffering person caught up in the processes of salvation. The *Progress* is a fine exposition of Calvinist orthodoxy, and it is the finer for never sinking to the pettiness of a purely technical approach to the human soul. Among the adventures that attend Christian and his companions it is possible to find all the steps (except election which Bunyan regarded as having taken place before the Fall) by which a man comes to regeneration, that is to say — calling, conviction, faith, repentance, justification, forgiveness, sanctification and perseverance, but they are perfectly woven into the story, and it is through feeling, not through intellectualisation, that Bunyan asks us to become aware of them.

What matters when Christian's burden drops off his back at the sight of the Cross is not the doctrines of justification and forgiveness which it expresses but the actual experience of liberation which makes Christian cry with joy.

Inevitably, reading between the lines of the *Progress*, we remember the other story of Bunyan's own religious journey, as described by him in *Grace Abounding*. There are strong similarities and strong dissimilarities, both of which are instructive. At every stage of the *Progress* we feel Bunyan measuring Christian's experiences against his own, testing them for reality.

What is dissimilar is the two characters of Bunyan (as the hero of *Grace*

Abounding) and Christian. Bunyan, as described by himself, was, during the period of his religious crisis, an intolerably tortured man, tormented particularly by the uncertainty of whether he was going anywhere at all or was damned before he started. Christian, for all his very real bouts of suffering, is a calmer, more optimistic personality, basically confident once he had started that all was going to be well, provided each hurdle could be overcome. The whole tone of the *Progress* is more cheerful, humorous, and hopeful than that of *Grace Abounding* (and the second part of the *Progress* more so than the first). Bunyan may have seen Christian as a more typical pilgrim than he was himself — a sort of Everyman. The work of spiritual counselling which Bunyan performed before and during his term of imprisonment must have helped him to become more detached from his personal drama and to discover that not everyone lived at the spiritual intensity that he did. But what the *Progress* also suggests is a very profound change in Bunyan, a movement away from the persecuting fantasies of *Grace Abounding* towards a new confidence, balance, and joy in living.

Nothing indicates this new confidence better than the daring, almost impudent, way that he introduces colloquialisms and salty country speech. His first sermons, published in the late 1650s and early 1660s, are splendidly, irreproachably, literate; although his tinker origins were known to all, he was giving no ammunition to his university-educated adversaries. In the *Progress*, however, he at last drops the mask; he *is* the common man, is not ashamed to be so, and intends to use the knowledge this gives him to his literary advantage. This device is particularly noticeable in reported speech and conversation — as if the gossiping of his characters makes it possible for him to reveal his identity at third-hand, as it were — and it brings a wonderful vitality and humour to the book. In the following passage, where Christian is telling Hopeful about a 'mugging', nothing comes over more clearly than the peasant's enjoyment of telling a good story.

Now there happened at that time, to come down that Lane from Broadway-gate, three sturdy Rogues; and their names were Faint-heart, Mistrust and Guilt (three Brothers), and they espying Little-faith where he was, came galloping up with speed: Now the good man was just awaked from his sleep, and was getting up to go on his Journey. So they came all up to him, and with threatening Language bid him stand. At this Little-faith look'd as white as a clout, and had neither power to fight, nor flie. Then said Faint-heart, Deliver thy Purse; but he making no haste to do it (for he was loth to lose his Money), Mistrust ran up to him, and thrusting his hand into his Pocket, pull'd out thence a bag of Silver. Then he cried out, Thieves, thieves. With that Guilt with a great Club that was in his hand, strook Little-Faith on the head, and with that blow fell'd him flat to the ground, where he lay bleeding as one that would bleed to death . . .

In less dramatic passages, Bunyan reveals his unpretentious origins naturally and unselfconsciously, as when Mr. Worldly Wiseman urges Christian to settle with his wife and children in the village of Morality 'where there are houses now stand empty, one of which thou mayest have at reasonable rates'. Like all poor men Bunyan knows about the problems of credit. 'If a man runs an 100l. into the Shop-keepers debt, and after that shall pay for all that he shall fetch, yet his old debt stands still in the Book uncrossed; for which the Shop-keeper may sue him, and cast him into Prison till he shall pay the debt.'

Characters in the *Progress* 'swet', complain of being 'in dumps', find things 'damnable hard', and know a great deal about the weariness and the hazards of travelling about the countryside on foot. They use proverbs, much as Shakespeare's characters did — 'Thou talkest like one upon whose head is the Shell to this very day' — 'A Saint abroad, and a Devil at home' — 'His house is as empty of Religion, as white of an Egg is of savour' — 'I would have given my life for a penny.'

They quote the Bible continually, sometimes knowingly, sometimes apparently falling unconsciously into biblical phrases and ideas. The Bible is totally enmeshed in their speech, as it was in Bunyan's own thinking, phrases sometimes coming into his head which he could not identify; had he made them up or were they in the Bible?

Some of the vitality of the *Progress* comes from the cheerful irreverence the speakers reveal for biblical characters, mentioning them as if they were old acquaintance whose deeds had been a continual talking-point in their lives. In a conversation with Hopeful about the sufferings of the faithful Christian remembers that Haman and Hezekiah in fights with others 'got their Coats soundly brushed'. It seems to afford him amusement. St. Peter had a rough time too. 'Peter upon a time would go try what he could do; but, though, some do say of him he is the Prince of the Apostles, they handled him so, that they made him at last afraid of a sorry Girle.' Even God does not escape this familiar treatment. 'Their King,' says Christian talking of the faithful, 'is at their Whistle.' These affectionate observations seem reminiscent of the way that subjects sometimes discuss a well-liked monarch and his family.

Some of the speed and immediacy of Bunyan's style comes from a judicious use of the present tense. Giant Despair 'getteth him a grievous Crab-tree Cudgel, and goes down into the Dungeon to them; and there, first falls to rateing of them as if they were dogs, although they gave him never a word of distaste; then he falls upon them, and beats them fearfully . . . This done, he withdraws and leaves them . . .' It is again the style of peasant story-telling, vivid, and full of relish, and is sometimes helped along by short, buttonholing words typical of conversation. 'Well, on Saturday about midnight . . .'

If the *Progress* represents a new departure in style, however, it is also the literary and psychological heir of *Grace Abounding*. It is unlikely that Bunyan could have written with such detachment of the soul's misadventures if he had not already undergone the cathartic experience of writing *Grace Abounding*; it is as if the act of doing so released the painful and troublesome memories so that they could emerge transformed on to a universal stage.

The parallels between the two books are interesting. Certain events, such as the walk through the Valley of Humiliation and the Valley of the Shadow have a detailed similarity. In the Valley of the Shadow Christian teeters between the ditch and the quagmire 'for when he sought in the dark to shun the ditch on the one hand, he was ready to tip over into the mire on the other; also when he sought to escape the mire, without great carefulness he would be ready to fall into the ditch'. It is easy to match this with, 'Wherefore still my life hung in doubt before me, not knowing which way I should tip.' (*Grace Abounding*, p. 175.)

When Giant Despair encourages his prisoners to commit suicide Christian cries, 'Brother, what shall we do? the life that we now live is miserable: for my part, I know not whether is best, to live thus, or to die out of hand?' In *Grace Abounding* (p. 149) Bunyan declares 'And now I was both a burthen and a terror to myself, nor did I ever so know, as now, what it was to be weary of my life, and yet afraid to die. Oh, how gladly now would I have been anybody but myself! Anything but a man! and in any condition but mine own!'

Christian is tormented by a fiend who creeps up behind him and uses blasphemy against Christ in a voice so like his own that he thinks it proceeds from his own mind. Bunyan remembers how, in one of his darkest times, 'I should often find my mind suddenly put upon it, to curse and swear, or to speak some grievous thing of God, or Christ his Son, and of the Scriptures. Now I thought surely I am possessed of the Devil; at other times again I thought I should be bereft of my wits, for instead of lauding and magnifying of God the Lord with others, if I have but hear him spoken of, presently some horrible blasphemous thought or other would bolt out of my heart against him . . . in prayer also, I have been greatly troubled at this time; sometimes I have thought I should see the Devil, nay, thought I have felt him behind me pull my cloaths: He would be also continually at me . . . still drawing my minde away.' (*Grace Abounding*, pp. 100, 101, 107.)

These passages do not necessarily 'match' in the order in which they are experienced. Many of the experiences, and in particular the experience of blasphemous thoughts, happened to Bunyan repeatedly, but only occur once to Christian, having then fulfilled their fictional purpose.

Psychologically, the most striking of parallels is that between Mt. Sinai in the *Progress* and the steeple of St. Helena's church at Elstow in *Grace Abounding*. Christian, tempted by the claims of legality, passes beside the Hill (Mt. Sinai, representing Moses and the Ten Commandments), but 'it seemed so high, and also that side of it that was next the way side, did hang so much over, that Christian was afraid to venture further, less the Hill should fall on his head . . . here therefore he swet, and did quake for fear.' Bunyan, attempting to lead a 'good' life, and to be admired for his godliness, conceived a neurotic terror of the church steeple. 'It came into my head, how if the Steeple it self should fall? and this thought, (it may fall for ought I know) would when I stood and looked on, continually so shake my mind, that I durst not stand at the Steeple door any longer, but was forced to fly, for fear it should fall upon my head.'

The wicket-gate, leading into the 'strait and narrow' path of the Christian life, is also recognisable in *Grace Abounding*. Bunyan has 'a kind of vision' of the poor people of Bedford on the sunny side of a high mountain and himself frozen, excluded, and unable to reach them. At last he finds a little gap or door-way in the wall, and tries time after time to get through it without success until when he is quite worn out he wriggles in sideways and goes and sits with them 'and so was comforted

with the light of their Sun'. The gap in the wall, he says, is Jesus 'but for
as much as the passage was wonderful narrow, even so narrow, that I
could not but with great difficulty, enter it thereat; it showed me, that
none could enter into life but those that were in down-right earnest'.
(*Grace Abounding*, p. 55.)

Images of inclusion and exclusion are among the most dominant
Bunyan reveals in his writing, matched only by excremental images, such
as the Slough of Despond, and claustrophobic images — the iron cage,
the cage into which the prisoners are put at Vanity Fair, and the prison of
Doubting Castle.

An aspect of Bunyan's thought which scarcely appears in *Grace
Abounding* but which is of fundamental importance in the *Progress* is that
of worldliness. Perhaps it became more of a temptation to Bunyan once
he was released from the worst of his spiritual terrors, perhaps his
growing acquaintance with the spiritual problems of others, particularly
those of the Nonconformists under persecution, developed his thinking.

A possible omission from *Grace Abounding* is suggested by the bullying
and neglect of Christian by his wife and children. There is a strangely
convincing ring about this description in the *Progress*, and it seems likely
that Bunyan may have suffered similarly (his spiritual crisis must have
been extremely trying to live with) and refrained from mentioning it out
of reverence for his first, dead, wife, and consideration for his children.

Some commentators on the *Progress* have tried to give the imagery
particular geographical locations — the House Beautiful as the 'big
house' at Houghton Conquest, the House of the Interpreter as John
Gifford's rectory, the wicket-gate as a little door in St. Helena's church, a
practice which seems to misunderstand the poetic imagination, and the
way it takes disparate sources, puts them together, and produces the
'sea-change' of art. The extent to which Bunyan's mind had worked
upon and transformed the same set of experiences between writing *Grace
Abounding* and *The Pilgrim's Progress* suggests that his imagination was
both more unpredictable and more profound than this.

NOTE

1 II Timothy 4:10.

5

The Pilgrim's Progress, Part II

———

The years succeeding the publication of the first part of *The Pilgrim's Progress* in 1678 were happy ones for Bunyan. The threat of a further term of imprisonment had receded, though the Deed of Gift he made transferring all his property to his wife in 1685 indicates that the fear was never far from his mind. He had become a highly successful and admired pastor and preacher, admired as one who had suffered for the cause and survived, as well as for his great gifts of rhetoric. He was a man who enjoyed social intercourse, and his regular travels to London and other parts of the country gave him unusual opportunities for a man of his time to meet others. As pastor he had to listen to people's troubles and to counsel them as John Gifford had once counselled him in his own desperate distress; there is a tender, maternal side to Bunyan, repeatedly expressed in his writings, which suggests that this must have been particularly congenial to him. He knew from first hand the torments of the mind and soul, and his sermons in particular reveal a great longing to help others in similar straits, to bring, in the biblical phrase he uses for one of his sermon-titles, 'light to them that sit in darkness'. He had an especial sympathy for the needy and the helpless.

In addition to the happiness of success as pastor and preacher, there was the general 'easing' that often comes with middle-age. All his children except the youngest, Joseph, were grown-up and the family no longer suffered acute poverty. The Deed of Gift suggests that, though never really prosperous, John and Elizabeth Bunyan had managed to establish a comfortable home. Bunyan's daughter Elizabeth (by his first wife) married in April 1677 and Thomas probably married in the early eighties, since his wife died in 1689 leaving a two-year-old son. Mary, the blind daughter, died at an unknown date in the eighties. Sarah, the daughter by his second marriage, married William Browne in 1686.

Bunyan's mental troubles had retreated. He had passed from the agony described in *Grace Abounding*, through the fearful but steady growth of the first part of *The Pilgrim's Progress* into a warm and glad serenity that glows throughout the second part of the book.

Six years elapsed between the publication of the first and second parts, years in which Bunyan published *The Holy War* and *The Life of Mr. Badman*. Both of these books were moderately successful, commercially and as pious literature, but neither of them approaches the poetic heights of Christian's journey, and in neither of them did Bunyan manage to recapture the liberated mood of the *Progress*, the astonished freedom of the peasant who has something unique to say and knows that he is saying it superbly. He needed to return to the theme of pilgrimage to find himself again, and when he did so he was not disappointed. The second part of the *Progress* has all the liveliness and poetic vision of the first part coupled with special qualities of its own. What is gone, presumably because it was by now gone from Bunyan's life, is the underlying note of fear and suicidal despair.

Whatever the psychological reasons which made Bunyan return to the theme of the pilgrimage, there were also professional ones. As he cannot refrain from gleefully pointing out in his introduction to the second part, his pilgrim has been a stupendous success.

> My Pilgrims Book has travel'd Sea and Land,
> Yet could I never come to understand,
> That it was slighted, or turn'd out of Door
> By any Kingdom, were they Rich or Poor.
>   In France and Flanders where men kill each other
> My Pilgrim is esteem'd a Friend, a Brother.
>   In Holland too, 'tis said, as I am told,
> My Pilgrim is with some, worth more than Gold.
>   Highlanders, and Wild-Irish can agree,

My Pilgrim should familiar with them be.
 'Tis in New-England under such advance,
Receives there so much loving Countenance,
As to be Trim'd, new Cloth'd and Deckt with Gems,
That it might shew its Features, and its Limbs,
Yet more; so comely doth my Pilgrim walk,
That of him thousands daily Sing and talk.

Bunyan continues in this cock-a-hoop vein for several pages, pointing out with a good deal of delight that he is so popular that his works are pirated, and enjoying, as only the successful can afford to do, the hostility his book has aroused among the narrow-minded. Half-humorously, perhaps, he compares the annoyance caused by his book to that caused by the gipsies, the stock from which tinkers reputedly sprang.

Thinking that you like Gipsies go about,
In naughty-wise the Countrey to defile.

With a touch of snobbery Bunyan notes that the 'Galants', and young gentle-women enjoy his book. His art has leaped over class-barriers that he could not otherwise have surpassed. It is in this exuberant frame of mind that he sat down to write the second part of his masterpiece.

It is distinctly different from the first part. The fact that it describes the journey of a woman, Christiana, her friend Mercy, and four children, might not in itself have made a remarkable difference, but what alters the character of the book more than anything else is the strength of Bunyan's identification with his female characters. Once, years before, when his first wife went into premature labour, Bunyan had felt, and described, a deep identification with her suffering. This identification with the woman's point of view appears again and again in the second part of the *Progress*. He feels deeply for the women when they are set upon by a fierce dog outside the wicket-gate, and again when they are pestered by two men who 'lay hands upon them' claiming that they have a 'small request' to make of them.

It is not only their suffering with which he identifies. He writes, with a kind of fascinated enjoyment, of the affection between Christiana and Mercy, of the charm of Mercy (the younger woman), and the motherly solicitude of Christiana. There is a tenderness that creeps into the conversation of all the principal characters, and it is this loving relation-ship which the book is about, not, as in the first part of the *Progress*, the hazardous adventures that befall.

Nor is this surprising. At several stages of Bunyan's life women had been very important. His first wife seems to have initiated the interest in religion and churchgoing which precipitated his religious crisis. We have seen how 'the poor women of Bedford' (members of the Bedford Dissenting Meeting) played a crucial part in Bunyan's conversion, a part to which both *Grace Abounding* and the first part of *The Pilgrim's Progress* testify. By the time Bunyan wrote the second part he had been pastor of the Bedford Meeting for more than ten years, he had three grown-up daughters, and a wife; he had had considerable opportunities to observe women, and during the persecution had had reason to respect their loyalty and courage. No trace of patronage appears in his attitude.

He takes their pilgrimage with entire seriousness, yet there is a kind of gaiety, almost a frivolity, which creeps into the book. It is a far more cheerful book than the first part of the *Progress*, as if the introduction of women makes for a new lightheartedness. Women, for Bunyan, also seem to be associated with refinement. The entertainment Christian received at the House Beautiful is expanded in Christiana's case into a kind of house-party. 'Christian goes on a pilgrimage, Christiana on a walking tour', wrote Ronald Knox.[1] Bunyan, at the later date, was writing about the Christian life as it was lived by ordinary people going about their ordinary everyday concerns, a very different situation from the crisis of persecution which had arisen in the 1660s, or the personal and religious crisis he had endured and described in his earlier writings.

In the later book Bunyan no longer identifies only with the pilgrim, but also with the gallant, fatherly figure of Great-heart who protects the women and children and is afraid of nothing.

There are other differences, too. There are fewer bad characters than in the first part — only twenty-seven bad characters against twenty-nine good ones, an interesting change in the balance. The problem of lust becomes more important, partly perhaps as a result of Bunyan's pastoral concerns, and in Madam Bubble he at last gives sexual temptation splendid dramatic form. Among the good characters there is an appeal-ingly human element of frank apprehension and Mr. Fearing, Feeble-mind, Mr. Ready-to-halt, Much-afraid, and Mr. Despondencie seem natural members of any human group bent on a difficult exercise. The book is well-seasoned also with braver, stronger personalities, and it is not difficult to identify Old Honest, Valiant-for-Truth, Mr. Standfast, and Mr. Great-heart with the older members of Bunyan's congregation who had held out through the dark days and no longer feared any danger that life could afford.

The pilgrimage grows from the original family group to a whole party waiting to cross the final River. They join themselves one by one, rather as in the golden goose kind of fairy-tale which describes a multiple quest. The note of fairy-tale is more evident throughout than anywhere else in Bunyan's writing. The made-up names have a playful quality now, rather like the names in the game of Happy Families — Mr. Brisk, Madam Bubble, Mr. Dare-not-lie, and Mr. Fearing. Proverbs contribute to the child-language of the book — 'Nuts spoil tender teeth'.

The book begins with a dream-dialogue between the Dreamer and Mr. Sagacity (a rather tedious explanatory device Bunyan had already employed in *Mr. Badman* and which he soon abandons). Mr. Sagacity tells the Dreamer of the fame Christian acquired as the result of his pilgrimage — 'he was a Fool in every mans mouth, yet now he is gone, he is highly commended of all.' Inspired by his example, and also by a letter from the King summoning her to his presence, his wife Christiana has also set off on pilgrimage accompanied by her four sons. As in Christian's case, neighbours seek to dissuade her, and only one of them, a young woman called Mercy, offers to go part of the way with her, partly out of friendship, partly from a secret yearning for the truth.

With difficulty the party crosses the 'dirt and dung' of the Slough of Despond by way of the stepping-stones. Christiana 'had like to a been in' several times, but is supported by Mercy.

At the wicket-gate, Christiana knocks repeatedly, but no one comes at first, and they are set upon by a terrifying dog, 'the Devil' as Bunyan notes in the margin. Eventually the Keeper of the Gate lets Christiana and the boys inside, on the grounds of their relation to Christian. In terror that she has been rejected Mercy swoons, but the Keeper revives her with a bunch of myrrh and invites her inside. In the distance they can see the cross of Christ.

They set off on their journey, but not before the boys have stolen and eaten some apples from an orchard as they pass. The women are molested by two 'ill-favoured ones' and are only left alone when a man from the Gate sees what has happened and comes to their rescue.

Like Christian they arrive at the House of the Interpreter, and are shown his 'Significant Rooms'. They see the tableaux that Christian saw and also others, the most remarkable of which is the Man with a Muckrake. One stands above the Man offering to crown him with a celestial crown, but the Man looks no way but downwards, and is so intent upon raking up the muck at his feet that he does not see the sublime destiny offered to him.

On the second morning at the House of the Interpreter they are taken to the Bath of Sanctification and told to wash themselves. They emerge 'sweet and clean; . . . also much enlivened and strengthened in their Joynts'. Bunyan, always open-minded on the question of adult baptism, was trying to please the Strict Baptists who had been annoyed by his earlier book.

When they leave the House of the Interpreter Great-heart is instructed to take his Sword, Helmet and Shield and see the party safely to the House Beautiful, a curious concession to feminine frailty which takes away the element of adventure, though it replaces it with a sense of relationship.

They arrive at the Hill Difficulty and it is as good as its name. 'They set forward and began to go up the Hill, and up the Hill they went; but before they got to the top, Christiana began to Pant, and said, I dare say this is a breathing Hill, no marvel if they that love their ease more than their Souls, chuse to themselves a smoother way.' Mercy says she must sit down and rest, and one of the children begins to cry. They struggle to the top, however, and have a picnic there.

When they reach the chained Lions, the boys cringe behind Mr. Great-heart, and he teases them for suddenly wanting to walk at the back of the party instead of the front. Great-heart has a victorious fight with the Giant Grim, and the party arrives at the House Beautiful. Great-heart says he must leave them and return to his master, and they vainly beseech him to remain.

They are well entertained to a dish of 'Lamb, with the accustomed Sauce'; they are shown to a peaceful chamber and they listen to beautiful music. They stay a month with the virgins of the House, and while they are there the alluring Mercy is pestered by a worldly young suitor called Mr. Brisk. Seeing her constantly busy with her sewing he thinks she will make an efficient and profitable wife. 'What can'st thou earn a day?' he asks her pointedly. However, he is rather put off when he discovers that she is making clothes for the poor. Mercy accepts the situation philosophically, remarking that it is no good for a woman to have a husband who does not share her religious beliefs, a problem which Bunyan had no doubt encountered among the women of Bedford.

One of the boys, Mathew, falls sick, as a long term result of eating the stolen apples. 'He was much pained in his Bowels, so that he was with it, at times, pulled as twere both ends together.' The doctor diagnoses 'the Gripes' and prescribes a purge and some pills. There is a touching little scene in which the boy refuses his medicine, his mother begs him, the boy refuses, and Christiana tries one of the pills herself and assures him that it does not taste nasty. The boy is cured. Professor Sharrock suggests that this whole passage has a joke-element, as 'Mathew's Pills' were one of the favourite seventeenth century remedies for stomach-ache.[2]

Just as the party is about to set off again on its travels, Mr. Great-heart reappears with the permission of his master, bringing them each a bottle of wine, some corn and pomegranates, and figs and raisins for the children with, as it were, the Lord's compliments. He is to conduct them on the way. As they set off they hear the 'Countrey Birds' singing the hymn 'Old Hundredth' and a version of 'The Lord's my Shepherd', a comment on Bunyan's liking for hymns, since the sectarians in general disapproved of their congregational use. Here, as elsewhere, the musician influences the Puritan.

They go easily into the Valley of Humiliation which suggests that Bunyan found the women members of his congregation less arrogant than the men, and once there hear the Shepherd Boy singing the beautiful lyric that depicts Bunyan's mature faith.

> He that is down, needs fear no fall,
> He that is low, no Pride:
> He that is humble, ever shall
> Have God to be his Guide.
>
> I am content with what I have,
> Little be it, or much:
> And, Lord, Contentment still I crave,
> Because thou savest such.

Fulness to such a burden is
That go on Pilgrimage:
Here little, and hereafter Bliss,
Is best from Age to Age.

Mercy comments on how well she feels in the Valley. 'The place methinks suits with my Spirit. I love to be in such places where there is no ratling with Coaches, nor rumbling with Wheels: Methinks here one may without much molestation be thinking what he is, whence he came, what he has done, and to what the King has called him: Here one may think, and break at Heart, and melt in ones Spirit.' Great-heart agrees with her.

All of them, however, feel terror in the Valley of the Shadow of Death and James, childlike, 'began to be Sick', until his mother gave him 'spirits' and Mathew's Pills. Like Christian they are troubled by hallucinations, in their case of an 'ugly thing' and a roaring lion. Mist and darkness descend upon them, they see the fire and smoke of the pit, and Christiana understands something of what her husband suffered. The cave at the end of the Valley which used to be the home of poor crazy old Pope is now inhabited by a giant called Maul, a sort of rejuvenated Catholicism who troubles pilgrims with his sophistry — He and Great-heart have a terrifying battle which the Giant nearly wins but in which his head is finally cut off.

Further on their journey they find a pilgrim asleep under an oak-tree, who turns out to be Old Honest, a brave and loyal old man bound on the same journey. As they walk along together Honest and Mr. Great-heart recount the tale of Mr. Fearing, a hopeless ditherer, who is now safe in the Celestial City.

The party of travellers stays at the inn of a man called Gaius, the same Gaius who is mentioned in the Epistle to the Romans and who, like all his favourite characters in the Bible, is for Bunyan a contemporary figure.[3] He entertains them with the loving hospitality which the sectarians were accustomed to practise among themselves and, a little oddly, arranges for the marriage of Mathew and Mercy. Since the reader has been led to think of Mathew as a naughty boy who ate too many apples and plums, and Mercy as a personable young woman, this is careless of Bunyan. He seems to be trying to establish the passage of time since the setting out of the pilgrims. Gaius suddenly refers to Christiana as 'an aged matron', something she certainly did not appear to be earlier in the narrative, clambering up the Hill Difficulty with her four young sons. The time-sense is very different from that of the first part of the *Progress*, in which Christian seems bound on a journey of a few weeks or months, rather as a man in a terminal illness, whereas in the second part Bunyan makes it clear, partly by the presence of the children, that he is talking about the journey men make in the course of a lifetime. Here again is a movement away from his own 'crisis' experience to the experience of ordinary people.

In a long, poetic speech, Gaius bursts into a eulogy of women. They have, he says, more than made up for the sin of Eve, by their simple devotion to Christ. ' 'Twas a Woman that washed his Feet with Tears, and a Woman that anointed his Body to the Burial. They were Women that wept when he was going to the Cross; And Women that followed him from the Cross, and that sat by his Sepulcher when he was buried. They were Women that was first with him at his Resurrection morn, and Women that brought Tidings first to his Disciples that he was risen from the Dead. Women therefore are highly favoured, and shew by these things that they are sharers with us in the Grace of Life.'

It seems likely, from the intensity of this speech, that Bunyan is conscious of taking part in a continuing debate about the status of women in the church.

After Gaius has, as it were, proposed the toast to the ladies, they have a marvellous feast, full of allegorical allusions — they become merry from drinking wine, the juice of the true vine, and finish with nuts and riddles. Samuel, one of the children, whispers to his mother that he likes it in this house and wants to stay a long time. Mercy puts the tired children to bed, and the rest of the company are having such a good time that they stay up all night.

The party stays a month at Gaius's house, and the gentlemen amuse themselves by setting off on a giant-hunt. Great-heart cuts off Giant Slaygood's head, and brings it back to the inn to impress the women. He also frees a pilgrim called Feeble-mind who had fallen into Slaygood's clutches.

In addition to the marriage of Mathew and Mercy which now takes place, Gaius gives his daughter Phebe in marriage to James. They have one final stupendous feast before Gaius sends them all on their way, first refusing to take any money for their stay.

At length they arrive at the River, where Christian and Hopeful had rested before them. Christiana now has 'four daughters', her other two sons presumably having married, and she advises them how to care for their 'little ones'. Leaving the women the men set off to attack Giant Despair, and after a fierce struggle they kill him, in the process liberating Mr. Despondencie and Much-afraid, his daughter. Christiana then gives a sort of dance for the pilgrims in celebration of victory, she and Mercy providing the music on the viol and lute.

The company passes on to the Shepherds of the Delectable Mountains, where Mercy, who is pregnant, admits to craving for a looking-glass that they have hanging there. Christiana tactfully puts the request on her behalf and the shepherds obligingly give it to her, as well as other presents they have prepared for the pilgrims.

Further on they meet Mr. Valiant-for-Truth, bloody and scarred from the terrible battles he has fought, his 'right Jerusalem blade' in his hand. They wash his wounds for him, and give him food, and he too joins the party. He sings them the song 'Who would true Valour see' about the constancy of the pilgrim, the rhythm of which Professor Sharrock suggests may echo Amiens' song in *As You Like It*.

Together the party now crosses the Enchanted Ground and a mist and darkness falls upon them so that 'they walked not by Sight'. The men try to help the women and children along, but the ground is muddy, the children lose their shoes in the mire and others get caught fast in the bushes. The children weep aloud from weariness. Before they emerge from the Enchanted Ground they meet Mr. Standfast there praying on his knees. He is thanking God for his deliverance from the harlot, Madam Bubble, 'Mistriss of the World', who has offered him, tired, poor, and lonely — the freedom of her bed, her body and her purse. He too joins them.

Finally, they emerge into the sunshine and beauty of the Land of Beulah, the waiting-place for those who are to cross the river to the Celestial City. Christiana is the first to be summoned and one by one the party bid her fare-well. She passes easily across the river. She is succeeded by Mr. Ready-to-halt, and then by Mr. Despondencie and his daughter. 'His Daughter went thorow the River singing, but none could understand what she said.' Mr. Honest dies, then Mr. Valiant-for-truth, in one of the most famous passages of the whole *Progress*. He makes his will, as the others have done. 'I am going to my Fathers, and tho with great

Difficulty I am got hither, yet now I do not repent me of all the Trouble I have been at to arrive where I am. My Sword, I give to him that shall succeed me in my Pilgrimage, and my Courage and Skill, to him that can get it. My Marks and Scars I carry with me, to be a witness for me, that I have fought his Battels, who now will be my Rewarder. When the Day that he must go hence, was come, many accompanied him to the River side, into which, as he went, he said, Death, where is thy Sting? And as he went down deeper, he said, Grave where is thy Victory? So he passed over, and the Trumpets sounded for him on the other side.'

The last of the pilgrims to make the crossing is Mr. Standfast (Christiana's children remain in Beulah) who sustains the high poetic vision. 'The Waters are to the Palate bitter, and to the Stomack cold; yet the thoughts of what I am going to, and of the Conduct that waits for me on the other side, doth lie as a glowing Coal at my Heart.'

Within four years of writing these lines Bunyan himself was dead, and they are the best of epitaphs for him, as the whole book is the best portrait of Bunyan's character, and in particular of the contentment of the last ten years of his life. It is the contentment of a man who has found liberation, particularly from fear and depression, and who has made peace with his own conscience. It is a contentment too which owes much to happy human relationship, not only, as we may guess, to the pleasure of children and grandchildren, but also the pleasure of a warm and loving Christian community in which he has a secure and respected identity. He seems untouched by disillusion, although he has a realistic sense of what the problems of belief are; it is as if, having been delivered from the shattering conflicts that beset his youth, he can never again lose hope.

He seems able to relax into life, to allow himself to enjoy pleasures which earlier he would have condemned, to be glad that his pilgrims can eat and drink and dance and make jokes with such obvious enjoyment of life, a far cry from the young man who had forced himself to give up dancing.

Above all, he seems to have found, in himself and others, the tenderness for which his imagery has so often reached. He projects it upon women, who give it to others, and who evoke it from others such as Mr.

Great-heart. It was the tenderness needed (and found) by the lost child drowning in the mill-pit.

NOTES

1 *Essays in Satire* (1928).
2 Roger Sharrock, *John Bunyan*, Hutchinson (1954).
3 Romans 16:23.

6

Mr Badman and The Holy War

———

Between publishing the two parts of the *Progress* Bunyan published two other major works, *The Life and Death of Mr. Badman* in 1680 and *The Holy War* in 1682; also a sermon *A Treatise of the Fear of God* in 1679. Both the major works show signs that Bunyan had been made self-conscious by his success; in the case of *The Holy War* self-conscious as an artist, so that he tackles a theme, that of war, outside his experience, thus stifling the rich humanity that enlivens his best work; in the case of *Mr. Badman*, self-conscious as moralist and spiritual writer.

In the introduction, or Apology as he called it, for the work, he gives the reason for his writing the book, a reason which innumerable moralists have given for sounding the alarm, though not always in such stirring language. 'Wickedness, like a flood, is like to drown our English world. It begins already to be above the tops of the mountains; it has almost swallowed up all; our youth, middle age, old age, and all, are almost carried away of this flood. O debauchery, debauchery, what hast thou done in England!' *Mr. Badman* is a crisis book in which a popular author is trying to influence public morals; it deals at length with blasphemy, lying, drunkenness and promiscuity.

Parallel with this catalogue of sins is a kind of sociological element in which Bunyan, using Mr. Badman's shady business ventures as a peg, ponders upon the way commercial practice works to the disadvantage of the poor. We are witnessing the first stirrings of the social conscience, later to become so important in evangelical Christianity and in Quaker practice.

Bunyan knows that in order to make these pills palatable to the reader a gripping story will be needed and he has hit upon what, in theory, is a fascinating idea, a story of a thorough-going sinner, a rake's progress. It is, in fact, a pilgrim's progress in reverse. Mr. Badman starts as a naughty boy, continues as a bad apprentice and a wild youth, contracts a marriage with a good woman only in order to get her money, is extensively unfaithful to her with whores, is a bad father, takes to drink and to dishonest business. After the death of his first wife he marries a whore, not so much from choice, as because she blackmails him into it. Eventually he dies, certainly bound, in Bunyan's opinion, for Hell.

The story is an interesting one with a number of realistic details, most of them too strong for Victorian readers, yet it lacks the psychological credibility needed for a story. Mr. Badman has not a single redeeming feature — he moves like a tram along the rails of Calvinistic fatalism, and this makes him seem an improbable human being. Unintentionally, Bunyan illuminates the flaw in Calvinism because he forces the reader to wonder about it. If the reprobate is consigned to Hell by the will of God then how can he help his wicked behaviour? And if he cannot help it then he deserves our pity rather than our censure. Bunyan never consciously makes this connection, yet there is a curious note of caricature about the book, as if a conflict troubled him as he wrote.

The caricature is most evident in the dialogue of Wiseman and Attentive, the two characters who relate the story and moralise about it. Wiseman is the major story-teller, and since he gives illustrations from his life which we know to have been episodes in Bunyan's own life, we may identify him with Bunyan. Attentive, as his name suggests, is the patient 'feed' or stooge. What is so astonishing, after the vitality and warmth of the *Progress* is how prosy and self-righteous Bunyan (Wiseman) has become. The impression is of two very old men, mumbling over the evils of youth with a smug self-satisfaction. Or perhaps of teachers or elders talking pointedly in front of a child, determined to bring home to it indirectly the error of its ways.

The book, in fact, is propagandist, and because its aim is not so much to tell a good yarn as to edify the reader, a kind of dishonesty creeps into the book. The Book has innumerable anecdotes, some of them taken from other moral works such as Clark's *Looking-glass for Sinners*, some from local *causes célèbres*, bent on assuring us that the wicked get their deserts, and not only in the world to come but in this world too. The drunken fall off their horses on the way home from the inn, the promiscuous get the pox, those who are continually calling to the Devil to take them (as the custom was in seventeenth-century cursing) disappear or die in terrifying circumstances. There is a solid folk wisdom behind this kind of morality, but it has nothing to do with Christianity, and the stupendous drama of grace that Bunyan's hero enacted in the *Progress*.

Bunyan was too intelligent and experienced to believe that the wicked always got their deserts in this world (his own Badman died 'quiet as a lamb', and nobody living in his period, which had included the terrible onset of Plague in the 1660s, could imagine that the good could not, on occasions, suffer unspeakably). So that we must recognise the note of patronage, the patronage perhaps of a pastor having to deal with simple-minded people, and using rather crude methods for their own good.

The result has, at times, an unconscious humour. When Wiseman reports how the young Badman sometimes dropped off to sleep in church, or indulged in whispering, giggling and making eyes at the girls, Attentive replies 'Why! he was grown to a prodigious height of wickedness', a comment so out of proportion to the offence, even by Calvinistic standards, that we must suspect Bunyan of playing a role.

It also makes for some lively stories, many of them with a strikingly medieval note of credulity and awe.

Take that dreadful story of Dorothy Mately, an inhabitant of Ashover, in the county of Derby. This Dorothy Mately, saith the relater, was noted by the people of the town to be a great swearer, and curser, and liar, and thief; just like Mr. Badman. And the labour that she did usually follow was to wash the rubbish that came forth of the lead mines, and there to get sparks of lead ore; and her usual way of asserting of things was with these kind of imprecations: I would I might sink into the earth if it be not so; or, I would God would make the earth open and swallow me up. Now upon the 23rd of March, 1660, this Dorothy was washing of ore upon the top of a steep hill, about a quarter of a mile from Ashover, and was there taxed by a lad for taking of two single pence out of his pocket, for he had laid his

John Bunyan

Woodcut showing Bunyan preaching in Bedford, from Dr. John Brown's collection.

An early woodcut depicting Bunyan accosted by a woman in Bedford. It was purchased by Dr. John Brown at an auction of Bunyania in London in 1877.

From Volume I of *Prints and Drawings* in the Bunyan Museum.

Bunyan being visited in prison.
This woodcut was acquired by
Dr. John Brown.

"Poor JO.ⁿ BUNYON pursued, and hooted by the Rabble, into his House at Elton, Near Bedford. From a Drawing taken on the spot by Sam.¹ Ireland." From Volume I of *Prints and Drawings* in the Bunyan Museum. Note the reference to Elton near Bedford, instead of Elstow.

Engraving by Robert White for the frontispiece of the first edition of *The Holy War*. From the 1909 volume of *Bunyan Illustrations and Cuttings* in the Bunyan Museum.

The window, Elstow Church, designed by T. W. Camm, illustrating the subject of "The Holy War." From Volume I of *Prints and Drawings* in the Bunyan Museum.

John Bunyan
Drawn by Derby, from an authentic portrait, and engraved by W. Holl.

breeches by, and was at work in his drawers; but she violently denied
it; wishing that the ground might swallow her up if she had them: she
also used the same wicked words on several other occasions that day.

Now one George Hutchinson, of Ashover, a man of good report
there, came accidentally by where this Dorothy was, and stood still
awhile to talk with her, as she was washing her ore; there stood also a
little child by her tub-side; and another a distance from her, calling
aloud to her to come away; wherefore the said George took the girl by
the hand to lead her away to her that called her: but behold, they had
not gone above ten yards from Dorothy, but they heard her crying out
for help; so looking back, he saw the woman, and her tub, and sieve
twirling round, and sinking into the ground. Then said the man, Pray
to God to pardon thy sin, for thou art never like to be seen alive any
longer. So she and her tub twirled round and round, till they sunk
about three yards into the earth, and then for a while staid. Then she
called for help again; thinking, as she said, she should stay there . . . but
immediately a great stone . . . fell upon her head, and broke her skull,
and then the earth fell in upon her, and covered her. She was
afterwards digged up, and found about four yards within ground, with
the boy's two single pence in her pocket, but her tub and sieve could
not be found.

There is an apparent accuracy about this story which could not fail to
impress the simple faithful — Bunyan is careful to give the date and the
place, although it has all happened more than twenty years before. He
has a number of other accounts of people being torn in pieces by the
Devil, or snatched away by him, and there is also an account of an
unsuccessful contemporary attempt to deal with the Devil medically (by
smoking him out). Many of the anecdotes are borrowed from Clark, and
repeated by Bunyan without comment. Did Bunyan believe the stories
were all true? He certainly believed in the devil, and there is a note of
childlike awe in his story-telling which suggests that he could suspend
reason when yielding to these gruesome fantasies. On the other hand, we
cannot exonerate him altogether from the pastoral and parental sin of
lying in what seems a good cause. In a revealing passage he describes Mr.
Badman, during an illness, being troubled with fears of Hell, and
determining to mend his life. His physician points out to him that some
of his emotions are due to fever, sleeplessness and his toxic condition —

'the vapours disturbed the brain' — and Wiseman comments un-favourably on this piece of professional advice. Even if true, he implies, it would have been better for his physician to let him believe his problem was entirely spiritual; a not very attractive view of Bunyan's pastoral method.

Equally unattractive is the note of prurience in some of the admon-itions and stories. Like certain newspapers which have flourished since his day, Bunyan has mastered the art of discussing sexually or sadistically exciting subjects at length while expressing horror and distaste.

There often follows this foul sin the foul disease, now called by us the pox. A disease so nauseous and stinking, so infectious to the whole body, and so entailed to this sin (promiscuity) that hardly are any common with unclean women, but they have more or less a touch of it to their shame. Attentive: that is a foul disease indeed! I knew a man once that rotted away with it; and another that had his nose eaten off, and his mouth almost quite sewed up thereby.

We might justify this outburst on the grounds that in Bunyan's day venereal disease did cause the most appalling suffering, but it is harder to justify the following lip-smacking account of a suicide, which has nothing whatever to do with Mr Badman who was not suicidally inclined.

Attentive: I did once know a man, a barber, that took his own razor and cut his own throat, and then put his head out of his chamber window, to show the neighbours what he had done, and after a little while died.

Wiseman: I can tell you a more dreadful thing than this . . . there was, about twelve years since, a man that lived at Brafield, by Northampton, named John Cox, that murdered himself; the manner of his doing it was thus. He was a poor man, and had for sometime been sick, and the time of his sickness was about the beginning of hay-time, and taking too many thoughts how he should live after-wards, if he lost his present season of work, he fell into deep despair about the world, and cried out to his wife the morning before he killed himself, saying, We are undone. But quickly after, he desired his wife to depart the room, because, said he, I will see if I can get any rest; so she went out; but he, instead of sleeping, quickly took his razor, and therewith cut up a great hole in his side, out of which he pulled and cut off some of his guts, and threw them, with the blood, up and down the chamber. But this not speeding him so soon as he desired, he took the same razor and therewith cut his own throat. His wife, then hearing of him sigh and fetch his wind short, came again into the room to him, and seeing what he had done, she ran out and called in some neighbours, who came to him where he lay in a bloody manner, frightful to behold. Then said one of them to him, Ah! John, what have you done? Are you not sorry for what you have done? He answered roughly, It is too late to be sorry. Then said the same person to him again, Ah! John, pray to God to forgive thee this bloody act of thine. At the hearing of which exhortation he seemed much offended, and in an angry manner said, Pray! and with that flung himself away to the wall, and so, after a few gasps, died desperately. When he had turned him of his back to the wall, the blood ran out of his belly as out of a bowl, and soaked quite through the bed to the boards, and through the chinks of the boards it ran pouring down to the ground. Some said that when the neighbours came to see him, he lay groping with his hand in his bowels, reaching upwards, as it was thought, that he might have pulled or cut out his heart. It was said, also, that some of his liver had been by him torn out and cast upon the boards, and that many of his guts hung out of the bed on the side thereof . . .

Bunyan goes on to protest rather thinly that he relates this horrible tale 'as a warning'; against what, it is hard to imagine. Not many of his flock can have felt a temptation to follow poor John Cox's example. Its real significance is that it recalls Bunyan's own suicidal tendencies; in its psychotic destructiveness he lives again his temptations to self-injury.

Here, as throughout *Mr. Badman*, we see a very different Bunyan from the artist and the Nonconformist hero — self-righteous, holier-than-thou, unscrupulous for the cause, prurient, sadistic — almost as if Bunyan is trying to live out the Puritan caricature. Since Bunyan never appears like this in his other literary masterpieces (though he does occasionally in his sermons) we must ask ourselves what it is about the theme of *Badman* which has this effect. It is worth noting that a number of Badman's vices — lying, stealing, swearing and blaspheming and going with wild companions — were vices of Bunyan's own youth, vices of which he was later bitterly ashamed. What he seems to be attempting in this book is to detach himself from Badman, to convince himself that this man and his horrible deeds have nothing in common with the converted Bunyan. But it involves a sort of radical surgery — an amputation of parts of his personality — and the ferocity he brings to the task is more unattractive, at least to the modern reader, than the sins of Mr. Badman himself.

Mr. Badman is a good example of what Jungian psychology calls 'the shadow'. The Jungian 'shadow' is the side of oneself that one would rather not see or be aware of. It is the side which all one's life one has repressed in order to be the 'good' person one would prefer to be. The 'better' one is, the larger and more threatening one's shadow will be. Jung claims that people with large shadows have a particular need for the Devil. 'The figure of the devil . . . is a most valuable and acceptable psychic possession, for as long as he goes about outside in the form of a roaring lion, we know where evil lurks.'

In order to know himself a man has to confront his shadow, to discover that it is not 'outside' him, in the person of an abstract Devil, but inside him, and very much part of himself. This is a painful and difficult step on the road to self-integration, so painful that many people never manage it. That Bunyan is so strenuously denying his 'shadow' in this book does not mean that he never managed to confront it; indeed the relaxed happiness of the second part of the *Progress* written four years later, with its gentle acceptance of weakness and of sensual need, suggests that he moved fast and far. Like many writers he writes in order to know how to live.

Mr. Badman is interesting in the main, therefore, because of the light it throws on Bunyan's personality. The 'good' Bunyan of all his other works suddenly crumbles to a man who enjoys a bit of salacious gossip, and with a taste for revenge. (Understandably enough, God knows, but Bunyan on his 'best behaviour' officially loved his enemies.) Among the other unconscious indiscretions of the book is the story of Mr. W. S. a man who must have caused unutterable misery to the little flock at Bedford.

In our town there was one W.S. a man of a very wicked life; and he, when there seemed to be countenance given to it, would needs turn informer. Well, so he did, and was as diligent in his business as most of them could be; he would watch of nights, climb trees, and range the woods of days, if possible, to find out the meeters, for then they were forced to meet in the fields.

Mr. W. S. duly informed, but then, Bunyan reports with glee, he was stricken of God. He could not speak properly, he dribbled, he had difficulty in controlling his limbs (symptoms that seem consonant with a stroke) and eventually died. Bunyan's satisfaction is evident.

Yet beside the smugness and unctuousness of parts of the book (Wiseman often sounds rather like 'Worldly Wiseman', one of the most deadly interlocutors Christian encountered) there peeps out a genuine love for people, especially for the poor and for their muddled attempts to lead a god-fearing life. There is one particularly moving vignette of a poor man, struggling, as Bunyan had once struggled, to bring up a family at a time of inflated food prices.

There is a poor body that dwells, we suppose, so many miles from the market; and this man wants a bushel of grist (unground corn), a pound of butter, or a cheese for himself, his wife, and poor children; but dwelling so far from the market, if he goes thither, he shall lose his day's work, which will be eightpence or tenpence damage to him, and that is something to a poor man. So he goeth to one of his masters or dames for what he wanteth, and asks them to help him with such a thing; yes, say they, you may have it; but withal they will give him a gripe, perhaps make him pay as much or more for it at home, as they can get when they have carried it five miles to a market . . . Now this is a kind of extortion, it is making a prey of the necessity of the poor, it is a grinding of their faces, a buying and selling of them.

Bunyan's compassion is deeply rooted in his own experience.

The Holy War, on the other hand, has a setting which is outside Bunyan's personal experience, that of a town under siege. No doubt, as a boy conscript he had found the ritual of Army life impressive, and had thrilled to stories of the siege of Leicester. The trumpets, the banners, the marching men, the crises of leadership, the agonising fears and uncertainties of military action are all carefully drawn.

The book was published in 1682, two years after Mr. Badman, and Bunyan appears to have devoted these two years of his life to it. There is a curious air of ambition about it; the homeliness of the first part of the *Progress* is abandoned in favour of an heroic theme and style as if Bunyan is trying to show that he can write a high-flown literary work with the best of them. There are passages — the meetings between the Lords of Darkness — that have a Miltonic note, and it is very possible that Bunyan had read *Paradise Lost*.

There is one very remarkable thing about the book; it has not a single female character. This cannot be explained away on the grounds of its military theme, since the siege is set in a town of normal townsfolk and women might have been allowed an interesting part in the drama, which they certainly played in any real life siege. The mood of the book, however, is one of almost aggressive masculinity. No tender feelings or indeed feelings of any kind, are described or aroused; the emphasis of the book is upon action, and this gives it at times the atmosphere of a modern 'thriller', though it is not especially exciting. What is missing is any sense of relationship between the characters. It is interesting that this book should have preceded by two years the publication of the second part of *Pilgrim's Progress* with its feminine cast and its profound sense of feeling. *The Holy War* implies that Bunyan was fighting a last ditch stand to keep feeling at bay, a battle he clearly lost.

The siege in *The Holy War* is the siege of Mansoul — Bunyan has returned once again to full allegory — and is a description of the fight between Emmanuel (Christ) and Diabolus (Satan) to take possession. Emmanuel is working for his father Shaddai (God), and he has a good deal of difficulty in securing and holding the goodwill of the citizens of Mansoul. They have an unaccountable way of preferring Diabolus.

Mansoul, at least as it was originally (i.e. before the Fall) had every advantage, and was Shaddai's special pride. He had built a castle in the middle of it, especially for his own use, and walls surrounding the town which could never be broken, so that it was only at the townsmen's invitation that an enemy could enter. There were five gates to the town — Ear-gate, Eye-gate, Nose-gate, etc.

Diabolus, 'king of the blacks or negroes' an ex-servant of Shaddai, attempts, with other devils, to take the town by force. Captain Resistance is in charge of the defences of Mansoul, supported by other leaders such as Lord Will-be-will and my Lord Innocent. There is a parley at the gates and one of the devils suddenly shoots Captain Resistance so that he falls down dead.

The townspeople let Diabolus into the town and he takes possession of the castle. Mr. Conscience, the Recorder, is put out of office, and My Lord Will-be-will takes over as governor under Diabolus. Shaddai hears the news of the rebellion and he determines to come to the rescue of his town.

He sends an Army under the Captains Boanerges, Conviction, Judgment and Execution and they camp outside the gates. There are several 'brisk encounters' between town and Army, the King's Army inflicting damage but little more. In any case, winter has come down so they entrench without attempting further attacks. Their presence reduces Mansoul to a jumpy, uneasy state, and the citizens become quarrelsome with each other. On several occasions the town is invited to surrender itself, but without success, mainly because of Lord Will-be-will and another character called Old Incredulity.

Word goes back to Shaddai from his Army that they seem to be making little progress and Shaddai sends Prince Emmanuel, with a splendid Army, who surrounds the town. This has an effect.

When the men of the town saw the multitude of the soldiers that were come up against the place, and the rams and slings, and the mounts on which they were planted, together with the glittering of the armour and the waving of their colours, they were forced to shift and shift, and again to shift their thoughts, but they hardly changed for thoughts more stout, but rather for thoughts more faint.

Emmanuel perceives that Diabolus has reduced the townsfolk to slavery, and he resolved to try to take the town by force. He charges Ear-gate by battering-ram, breaks it open, and sets up his headquarters in Conscience's house. He breaks open the castle, brings out Diabolus in chains and has him stripped of his armour before the people. He then rides in triumph through the town with his prisoner bound to his chariot wheels. Afterwards he retires in triumph to his pavilion in the camp, and orders his men to put Understanding, Conscience and Will-be-will under arrest. The three prisoners, conferring with the townsfolk through 'the gates' of the prison are terrified they are going to be executed. 'Fear possessed them in a marvelllous manner; and death seemed to sit upon some of their eyebrows.' They resolve to go down to the Prince, clad in mourning, wearing ropes round their necks, and sue for mercy. When they stand trembling before him he forgives them and the whole town of Mansoul. He dresses them in new garments, anoints them with oil, and gives them chains of gold and earrings, in place of the ropes. They swoon with joy, and are overwhelmed with gratitude to him.

Back in Mansoul the inhabitants are astonished to see the three prisoners returning. When they grasp what has happened they go wild with joy. 'No man . . . could sleep that night for joy; in every house there was joy and music, singing and making merry, telling and hearing of Mansoul's happiness . . . Who thought yesterday,' would one say, 'that this day would have been such a day to us?' Emmanuel assumes control of the town.

Once the Diabolonian officials have been removed from office, and received punishment, the town embarks on a period of peace and happiness. Unluckily however, Carnal Security becomes influential in the town, bringing about 'a coolness' between Emmanuel and the inhabitants.

Emmanuel is hurt (perhaps 'piqued' is a better word), and finally withdraws (it is tempting to say 'flounces off') to his Father's court. He wants the citizens to come and plead with him to return. Under the influence of Mr. Godly-fear and Mr. Conscience the townsfolk begin to regret the absence of Emmanuel, and they send a petition to the court of King Shaddai and his son. They become very frightened at what they have done, and they call a day of fasting and universal woe.

Meanwhile Diabolus and others are once again plotting in Hell, wondering how they can persuade the Diabolians who are still concealed in Mansoul to collaborate with them in re-capturing the town. Covetousness, Lasciviousness and Anger enter the town in the guise of good and holy men, ('Take heed, Mansoul!' Bunyan inserts in brackets), and lead many of the citizens into trouble. No answer had come from Emmanuel to the many petitions the townsmen had sent him. The Diabolonians become strong again in the town.

A plot is uncovered to massacre all the citizens by Mr. Prywell, a man with a habit of eavesdropping in a good cause, and the Mansoulians at once realise the folly of their ways and decide to appeal yet again to King Shaddai and to fight to the death if Diabolus appears. They strengthen the gates, expel Diabolonians hiding in the town and keep yet another day of fasting and 'humiliation'. Covetousness is found (disguised as Prudent-thrifty), and lasciviousness (disguised as Harmless-mirth). Their imprisonment is so severe that they die almost at once of consumption, unregretted.

Meanwhile the Army of Diabolus, reorganised, is marching on Mansoul. Diabolus commands a drummer to approach the town asking for parley. He commands them to surrender, or else he will take the town by force and it will be the worse for its inhabitants. Night after night he repeats the message without success. The town, surrounded, is 'languishing' in a state of great fear and suffering. 'There is nothing,' says Bunyan, 'to the town of Mansoul so terrible as the roaring of Diabolus's drum.' They wonder whether to send yet again to Shaddai for relief, but fear it will be useless.

Diabolus arranges his men for the final attack; Captain Cruel and Captain Torment are placed outside Feel-gate with their men with Captain No-ease as replacement. Captain Brimstone and Captain Sepulchre are at Nose-gate and Captain Pasthope at Eye-gate. Mouth-gate is too strongly manned for Diabolus, and from it the townsfolk send a last, desperate plea to Emmanuel. Diabolus tries 'if possible, to land up Mouth-gate with dirt?' (blasphemy)

Finally, he sounds the charge and attacks the town. The inhabitants fight with good words, prayer and singing of psalms, the enemy with rage, blasphemy, 'horrible objections', and 'the terribleness of their drum'. A number of citizens are badly wounded, among them my Lord Reason and Mr. Mind. After dark, a party of the Mansoulians make a sally againt the enemy camp and cause the enemy Army to retreat somewhat. However, in a few days the war turns against them. Their captains are driven back to the castle and Mansoul is overrun by the Army of Diabolus. They loot and slaughter, and rape the women, and in the havoc left behind by this disaster the town continues for two and a half years.

The Captains secretly petition Emmanuel yet again, and for this the whole town is cruelly punished by Diabolus.

Messages are received from Emmanuel praising the courage and perseverance of the town's leaders and promising help. Encouraged by this the townsfolk join battle with the Diabolonians, when, like the U.S. Cavalry arriving in an old Hollywood film, Emmanuel appears again with a great Army. 'He came with colour flying, trumpets sounding; and the feet of His men scarce touched the ground.' The Diabolonians are decisively defeated. The Prince rides into a town bedecked with lilies and branches and filled with cheering people. There is general rejoicing.

Stray bodies of Doubters continue to attack the town from time to time but without success. Diabolus remusters his scattered Army but news of this gets back to the town by Prywell, the spy. The criminal collaborators are tried and sentenced to execution (crucifixion). Emmanuel rebuilds the town.

In a postscript to *The Holy War*, Bunyan mentions a slander to the effect that he was not really the author of *Pilgrim's Progress*; *The Holy War* is intended to give that slander the lie. He is contemptuous of the slander and of those who insinuate:

> so fond I am of being sire
> I'll father bastards; or if need require,
> I'll tell a lie in print to get applause.
>   I scorn it: John such dirt-heap never was,
> Since God converted him . . .
> It came from mine own heart, so to my head,
> Then to my pen, from whence immediately
> On paper I did dribble it daintily.

'It came from mine own heart'. Like all Bunyan's major works, *The Holy War* is a repetition of the terrible experience of his religious crisis. The original emotion has now largely exhausted itself, and Bunyan can take pleasure in the extraordinary ingenuity of his allegory, getting a kind of mechanical enjoyment out of fitting the pieces together. It is done very cleverly, with real mastery of the theological material, but the lack of character, of humanity, is curiously chilling, and some of the woodenness of the military mind seems to obtrude on the story. The siege is an inflexible image, and though it represents some aspects of Bunyan's crisis quite well (he felt himself beset by the Devil, and at times invaded by him), it is a poor image to express the sense of love which was crucial in his conversion.

Also it raises, at least in the twentieth-century mind, difficult questions about Prince Emmanuel and King Shaddai. Prince Emmanuel seems extraordinarily touchy for a ruler, and strangely careless of his duty. Why did he not arrive with relief *before* the town had been seized by Diabolus at such appalling cost to the inhabitants? His feelings are scarcely an adequate explanation for the harm done; even his undoubted wish to teach the inhabitants a lesson seems pursued beyond reasonable bounds. These are twentieth-century speculations; we cannot know whether any of them occurred to seventeenth-century readers, only that by the standards of any century Emmanuel is a rather unsatisfactory prince.

Bunyan's return, in the second part of *Pilgrim's Progress*, to the image of the journey and his beloved pilgrims, suggests that he was not entirely at ease in the cold exchanges of *The Holy War*. He retreats from the grand literary scheme and returns to the common life of men. He has come back to himself.

7

The Belief of Bunyan

By the time, in the 1650s, when Bunyan first tried to work out a system of belief for himself, the clear vision of the Reformers had already splintered, like a pane of glass, into innumerable slivers. The liberation from priestly domination had affected men in a variety of ways, some accepting a far more severe discipline than anyone had endured under Catholicism, others practising the most extreme forms of licence. For some a belief in an approaching millennium was the major influence in their lives, for others it was mystical experience.

The sectarian groups, of which the Bedford Meeting was one, embraced a variety of creeds; extreme Antinomianism, mysticism, Quakerism, Arminianism, Calvinism and many more. Bunyan, though loyally committed to an Open Baptist sect makes it clear that his ultimate loyalty is a different one.

Here is one runs a-quaking, another a-ranting; one again runs after the Baptism, and another after the Independency. Here is one for free-will, and another for Presbytery; and yet possibly most of all these sects run quite the wrong way, and yet everyone is for his life, his soul, either for heaven or hell. If thou now say, Which is the way? I tell thee it is Christ, the Son of Mary, the Son of God . . .[1]

When Bunyan tells us that Christ is the way (i.e. the way to salvation) he is talking on two levels. One is the experiential and personal level — he felt himself actually accused, forgiven and loved by Christ as by a person. The other is the technical and mechanical level; according to his system of belief it was necessary to 'apprehend' Christ in order to escape the penalty of one's sins.

The experiential level is what gives so much of Bunyan's work a warmth and vitality that makes it readable today. He describes in *Grace Abounding* going to church in a state of despair at his own sinfulness, convinced he is bound for Hell. The preacher speaks of the love of Christ for man and moved by his words Bunyan hears a voice within him say, 'Thou art my Love, thou art my Love; and nothing shall separate thee from my love.'[2] Though he had many more depressions and temptations ahead of him, throughout his life he never 'got over' the sense of wonder at the forgiveness and healing he had received, a moment given perfect dramatic expression in the *Progress* where the burden drops from Christian's back.

This experiential quality of Bunyan's belief is reminiscent of Luther, who suffered a similar crisis of despair and forgiveness, and it is not surprising that reading Luther in translation was one of the formative theological influences in Bunyan's life. Erik Erikson has described Luther as a man with 'an intense need for cure', words which might equally apply to Bunyan; for both of them the cure was 'Christ', a fact which they felt bound to celebrate for the rest of their lives. 'When I have apprehended Christ by faith, and through him am dead to the law, justified from sinne, delivered from death, the Devil and Hell; then doe I good works, I love God, I give thankes to him, I exercise charity towards my neighbour.'[3]

Both Luther and Bunyan had a desperately vivid apprehension of Hell, the fear of which, in the early stages of religious crisis, filled their minds to the exclusion of the possible delights of salvation, no doubt because they could not begin to imagine they would share the latter. R. L. Greaves says that 'the emphasis of both Luther and Bunyan was on salvation *from* something, whereas most Calvinists, while acknowledging that the elect were saved from sin and divine wrath, nevertheless stressed salvation *to* something, namely, the holy life of a regenerated man'.[4]

Luther's God was a god of terrifying wrath from whom, as it seemed at first sight, no mercy could possibly be expected. Bunyan saw God as an absolutely holy and pure being, and, above all, as a Judge. It was, he believed, the function of a judge to show justice, not kindness and sympathy, and since, in his own case, the prisoner was guilty of the offences of which he was charged, then there seemed no possible grounds for mercy, in fact an all-righteous Judge *could not* be merciful in such circumstances. 'Justice once offended, knoweth not how to shew any pitty or compassion to the offender . . . '5

The prisoner (and this really meant all men) was tried and condemned to execution, but then a substitution took place. Christ, who had committed no crime (sin) took the place of the condemned man, rather as, in heroic incidents at concentration camps, one prisoner occasionally saved another by taking his place in the gas chamber. Rather oddly, to twentieth-century understanding, the Judge all along knew about this substitution and was apparently indifferent to it; what mattered was that the literal penalty was exacted, that Satisfaction (as Bunyan called it) was given. Who suffered the penalty was not, in one sense, important.

In another sense, however, it was very important, since the saved prisoner took on, to some degree, the character of the one who had stepped in to save him. It was as if they had changed clothes to effect the substitution, and by this change of raiment the guilty man had taken on, at least in part, the goodness of the one who had saved him. Luther's interpretation of this miracle was entirely triumphant. 'There is no damnation to them that are in Christ Jesus . . . O law! thou hast no power over me . . . I plunge my conscience in the wounds, blood, death and resurrection and victory of my Saviour Christ . . . '6

Bunyan is more cautious. Calvinistically, he thinks of salvation not so much as achieved fact, in the light of which a man lives, as of a process to which he must give himself up without reserve. 'To save,' he said, 'is a work of many steps.' He did not feel that either he himself, nor anyone else, could expect such a miracle on easy terms.

All the same his sense of wonder and joy was no less than Luther's. He is like a prisoner who has actually been led out to the execution and then saved at the last moment when he had given up all hope of his life, and he can never get over the sense of gratitude and joy in living with which this unexpected liberation has filled him. The best thing of all is the sense of having been loved so much by Another that such a saving sacrifice was gladly made. It is this love which makes him want to shout to the crows in the fields.

It is part of what he calls 'the Promise', and includes forgiveness, salvation from Hell and the hope of Heaven. Describing the night when he truly began to feel that 'the Promise' was for him, he says 'I could scarce lie in my Bed for joy, and peace, and triumph.' The Promise, for Bunyan, also seems to include the gaining of a new identity, a moment marked in the *Progress* when three Shining ones appear, tell Christian his sins are forgiven, place a mark on his forehead, and give him a new garment. He has changed clothes with the divine prisoner and can begin to hope.

The divine prisoner is, for Bunyan, of a collective or representative importance; he is 'the common or publick person', so that his death and resurrection achieve the same result not just for one person but for 'the whole Body of his Elect'. The concern of Bunyan, as of so many followers of Calvin, was whether he was or was not numbered in that body and so able to benefit from the sacrifice of 'the publick person'.

What leads him to believe that he is is his experience of the grace of God. Before examining grace, however, it is necessary to consider the way in which Bunyan sees God. As already mentioned, he sees him as a perfectly pure and holy being before whom sinning man knows himself as a monster of depravity, and as the Judge who knows nothing of sympathy but only of punishment. Such is Bunyan's ambivalence, however, that he also believes God loves man and wants to help him. For all his paranoid conception of God in the dark moments of his crisis he can also talk of God as having compassion and pity, 'a feeling of the Condition of those in misery' and a 'running over of infinite Bowels to objects in a miserable and helpless condition'. It is almost as if God is kept at a distance from man by his holiness and purity, or alternatively, as if there is another side of God in conflict with the righteous Judge.

Christ provides the 'Satisfaction' that the righteous judge demands, but a man's way of directly experiencing the love of God is through grace. Bunyan uses a movingly feminine metaphor to tell us of this experience. 'The Child by nature nuzles in its Mother's Bosom for the Breast; the Child by Grace, does by Grace seek to live by the Grace of God.'[7] Bunyan knows God as tender, loving and nourishing, as well as an unforgiving judge.

It is because of the grace of God that the Promise of Christ is held out to sinning man, but it is also because of grace that a man discovers what it is that Christ offers him. Under grace, fear is gradually replaced by love.

'Not the overheavy Load of Sin, but the Discovery of Mercy; not the Roaring of the Devil, but the Drawing of the Father, that makes a Man come to Jesus Christ.'[8]

What was peculiarly Calvinist in Bunyan's thought was the belief that God had decided from the outset whether or not his grace was to be extended to any individual soul. This decision, Election, as it was called, was not made because of any sin committed by the man, or even at the beginning of his life on earth, but before the Foundation of the world. Given this grace a man could not help moving through the steps towards sanctification in spite of himself. Without it, nothing could save him from reprobation.

But here again Bunyan is ambivalent. Officially, he aligned himself with the strict Calvinist position, stoutly denying that he was a 'free-willer'. But in practice, he cannot help talking as if men have a choice. The whole drama of *The Pilgrim's Progress* hangs upon the fact that Christian might fail, that he might give up or be defeated by one of his many enemies. Again in his sermons, moved by the suffering of them 'that sit in darkness' he continually urges his hearers to seek God's grace. During his own crisis he seems to have held a semi-conscious belief (perhaps influenced by millenarianism) that God might have made up his mind at a particular point in the recent past about whom he would call. Remembering what a bad life he had led he was sure that he would not be numbered among the happy band, and he cursed himself for not reforming in time. Again in *The Heavenly Footman* (written probably in the mid-sixties) he says, 'They that will go to heaven they must run for it; because perchance the gates of heaven may be shut shortly.'

Strict Calvinism, though attractive intellectually to a certain kind of personality (one, perhaps, which needed security, whether the security of Heaven or of Hell) seems to have been extraordinarily difficult to assimilate. For naturally warm and ebullient people like Bunyan, who felt a love for their fellow-men as well as concern for their own souls, hope kept breaking in. Bunyan's strict Calvinist doctrine of reprobation, one which he loyally defended in argument, is perhaps the gloomiest belief anyone ever held. Yet he manages to write with great cheerfulness, and as if it is important for his readers to make the right decisions.

The man elected (before the foundation of the world) had the experience in his lifetime of being 'called', the first step on the journey of salvation. Having been called he experienced conviction (the despairing knowledge of his own sinfulness that Christian experienced at the Slough of Despond), then faith, repentance, justification, forgiveness, and sanctification. Perseverance (also seen as the inability to give up once one had been called) ran through the whole mighty endeavour. And the root, or ground of this journey of salvation, as it was the root or ground of the fact of Predestination itself, was the divine love and grace. For Bunyan the fact of the divine love and grace, and the forgiveness, justification and hope of salvation that it brought in its train (i.e. the Promise) was the most holy, the most numinous thing in his entire experience. 'There is nothing in Heaven or Earth that can so Awe the heart, as the Grace of God. 'Tis that which makes a Man fear, 'tis that which makes a Man tremble, 'tis that which makes a Man bow and bend, and break to pieces.'⁹ And 'tis that which keeps a man like Bunyan grateful and unable to forget till the end of his days.

Bunyan reveals the strength of Calvinist influence upon him in his attitude to Predestination and again in his emphasis on the Covenants. Bunyan, in his Map Showing the Causes of Salvation and Damnation, shows the reprobates as living under the Covenant of Works and the elect as living under the Covenant of Grace. The Covenant of Works was the agreement God made with Moses that man must live under the Law. Since in practice man continually transgressed against the Law because of the influence of the Fall, then the Law doomed him to perpetual guilt, shame and failure. No amount of trying could guarantee success (this was one of the most deeply-felt of all Bunyan's beliefs; like Augustine before him, he could never forget the agony of his hopeless striving to be 'good'). The Law for Bunyan was a hated enemy which had inflicted unforgettable injuries upon him. He was not, like the Ranters, in favour of abrogating it altogether. He could see that what it proposed was in itself commendable even though man failed to live up to it; the solution for Bunyan was to lift the whole problem of conduct on to another level altogether, that of the Covenant of Grace.

Whereas the Covenant of Works fathered reprobates (since it was their failure to keep the Law that condemned them), the Covenant of Grace fathered the elect and carried them safely to their journey's end, preserving them by its power. This covenant, in Bunyan's view, was made not between God and man but between God and Christ; to put it crudely, a 'deal' by which man might be saved.

Nothing is more central to Bunyan's theology than the certainty he has about the Covenant of Grace, and the sense of security he gains from it. His greatest sermon *The Doctrine of the Law and Grace Unfolded* (1659) is entirely taken up with an exposition of the two Covenants. Drawing heavily on St. Paul, the originator of covenant theology, he sets out to show what the uses of the covenants are, and what kind of people live under one and under the other.

No man can escape the Law. A man needs to know the Law, in order to know sin, and he needs to know sin in order to appreciate the deed wrought by his Saviour.

If thou wouldst . . . wash thy face clean, first take a glass and see where it is dirty; that is, if thou wouldst indeed have thy sins washed away by the blood of Christ, labour first to see thy besmeared condition, but look on every spot thou hast; for he that looks on the foulness of his face by the halves, will wash by the halves; even so, he that looks on his sins by the halves, he will seek for Christ by the halves.[10]

It is a homely metaphor, but an impressive plea for self-knowledge.

The Covenant of Works is, for Bunyan, an expression of the terror and pain in religion, the awe and shame and fear which are, for him, inseparable from the holiness of God; the underside of that sublime holiness, Bunyan knows well, is Hell. It is what a man suffers when he cannot find a way to live in the light of holiness.

The Covenant of Grace, on the other hand, expresses the tenderness, forgiveness and love which Bunyan's maturing faith had brought him. It is another face of God altogether, and the face is called Christ.

He saw the Covenant of Works as imposing an obsessional necessity upon a man to be perfect. 'Though thou shouldest fulfil this covenant, or law, even all of it, for a long time, ten, twenty, forty, fifty, or threescore years, yet if thou do chance to slip and break one of them but once before thou die, thou art also gone and lost by that covenant.'[11] What it is clear he is renouncing is the conviction, known as Pelagianism, that a man can achieve salvation by his own efforts. If there was one lesson that Bunyan's religious crisis had taught him it was that this was not so. He not only thought that man's only hope was surrender to Christ, but deeply influenced by Calvinist thought, and by his own self-hatred, he thought that man was utterly sinful and polluted. It was this which made it necessary for him to surrender his identity and take on, however partially, the identity of Christ. The sanctified man achieves 'sonship'.

Bunyan sets out 'the deal'. Because Christ died 'to give the justice of his Father satisfaction, and so to take away the curse that was due to us, wretched sinners' and because 'God, his Father, being every ways fully and completely satisfied' the way was cleared. Christ had been 'made a curse' and 'through him sinners should be inheritors of the blessing.' Bunyan puts it firmly into legal terms.

> His first office, after the covenant was made and concluded upon, was that Jesus should become bound as a surety, and stand engaged upon oath to see that all the conditions of the covenant that were concluded on between him and his Father should, according to the agreement, be accomplished by him; and that after that, he should be the messenger from God to the world to declare the mind of God touching the tenor and nature of both the covenants, especially of the new one.[12]

How literally did Bunyan take this elaborate structure of belief? Did he see God and Christ sitting down together with documents like a pair of lawyers or business associates or was he consciously using a metaphor to express a deep insight he had about different aspects of godhead? Bunyan's first excursions into religion and his description of them suggest that his understanding of religious truths was then almost wholly literal, an interpretation he shared with many of his fellow sectarians. The more relaxed way he talks of God and of scripture later in his life, together with what little we know of the religious development of individuals, suggests a move away from literalism into a deeper understanding of the deeper truth of metaphor.

Bunyan's authority for all his ideas was Scripture. His friend Charles Doe gives an interesting example of the supreme position the Scriptures held in his thinking. 'I once asked him his opinion in a common religious point, and offered some arguments to prove my opinion for the general of it; but he answered, that where the Scripture is silent we ought to forbear our opinions; and so he forbore to affirm either for or against, the Scripture being altogether silent in this point.'[13] Thought outside Scripture (Bunyan's whole education, library and cultural environment) comes to a stop.

Like many of his contemporaries Bunyan gloried in the idea that the Spirit worked by revelation through Scripture using ignorant men such as himself. Ignorance was thought to give the Spirit room to manoeuvre unhindered by intellectual conceits and Bunyan has not much time for the intellect and the reason. 'I am not ashamed to Confess, that I neither know the Mode nor Figure of a Sylogism, nor scarce which is Major or Minor . . .' Though he was not trained in formal logic, and felt an ideological need to justify this, he used his mind carefully and well when arguing doctrinally. Perhaps part of the sectarian belief about the importance of allowing 'the Spirit' room was a plea for feeling to have some place in the religious scheme. For Bunyan, even more than for many of his contemporaries religion was inseparable from feeling; this was the distinctly Lutheran strain in his thought. Remembering the time when he swung helplessly between the two Covenants, he cannot talk of what he believes without passionate feeling resonating in his words. It undoubtedly was what made him so successful a preacher.

Bunyan has described how deeply he was influenced through reading a book of Luther's. We know less about how he acquired his deep Calvinist dye, in some ways one antipathetic to Bunyan's character with his spontaneity, warmth, and intense sympathy for the suffering of others. Almost certainly it is due, in the main, to 'the poor women of Bedford' and the general influence of the Bedford Meeting upon him, coming as it did at a time in his life when he was desperately in need of friendship and help.

For Bunyan, as for many of his class, it provided a welcoming and accepting *milieu* in which religious ideas could be tried and worked out, and if the ideas seem to us narrow and sometimes naive, it is clear that the sense of fellowship and love between the members was a very rich experience. They were caught up in a fervour and excitement that was partly religious, partly political (in the broader sense that it had to do with class and social struggle). 'Barred by society from high political, economic, intellectual, and social attainment,' writes R. L. Greaves, 'tinkers and farmers, mechanics and day labourers could find in the sectarian churches a distinct spiritual superiority. That superiority, based on the free working of the Spirit in whom it will, psychologically compensated for all the more materialistic frustrations of life.'[14]

The separatist churches, says Greaves, saw the Church rather like a garden where souls were watered and tended by God. Their members were 'separated' from the world, their fellowship depended upon shared belief, they came together (were 'gathered' as they preferred to say) in freedom and from choice, unlike the 'conforming' Anglicans, and they aimed at nothing less than leading holy, 'sanctified' lives.

Before a new member was accepted he had to furnish verbal or written proof of the working of God within him (*Grace Abounding* is thought to have had its origins in such a statement of belief), and his life was expected to continue to provide signs that he was 'on his journey', the journey of salvation. Bunyan supremely demonstrates how deeply the concept of 'the journey', with its stylised stages, bit into the Calvinist imagination.

The Church Book of Bedford Meeting suggests the very powerful hold that the separatist system had on its members. On the one hand, there was a deep and moving concern for the sick, the dying, the impoverished and those in any kind of trouble. The keener members of the congregation were continually visiting other members in their homes, as well as paying charitable visits to selected non-members, such as those in prison. Side by side with this loving concern, however (or as the members would have thought an extension of it) was a determination to see that fellow-members did not fall from grace. A member who did not appear at church would be asked questions about not coming. The Church Book contains a long correspondence with William Whitbread who developed so many spiritual doubts that he gave up attending meetings for a while, and even took the offensive step of attending Anglican worship. He returned to the fold later. Some, like the drunkard John Rush, were expelled from the congregation. The meetings tended to be more understanding about spiritual difficulties, which they expected to be part of religious development, than sudden bursts of irresponsible behaviour, especially if these exposed the Meeting to ridicule and censure.

Bunyan, first as elder, then as pastor, took an important part in many of these decisions and was clearly a key figure, partly because of his superior intelligence, in all that happened. Together with his fellow-members he joined in prayer, the hearing, reading and expounding of the Scripture, baptism rites and 'the Supper of the Lord'. Baptism, like other 'ordinances' as he called the sacraments, was not very important to Bunyan and his sect. Unlike the Strict Baptists they did not make it a condition of Church membership. What mattered to them was the 'baptism of the Holy Spirit'. This indifference to outward form, while insisting on a deep sincerity of intent, is characteristic of Bunyan. It may have been what drove him to such an agony of searching and questioning in the first place at the time of his youthful crisis. In the *Progress* his richest scorn is reserved for those who, like By-Ends, are insincere.

The Calvinist sects did not, in general, use hymns, but Bunyan's quotation from two hymns in the second part of the *Progress* suggests that he, at least, enjoyed them. It is possible that he was trying to persuade his congregation to use music, or more probably, natural musician that he was, he played and sang them at home with his own family.

One of the difficulties in assessing Bunyan's religious thinking is that he is often most explicit when taking part in an argument, as for instance, in his first tract *Some Gospel Truths Opened* (1650) when he was opposing the Quakers, or in his other books and sermons where he is clearly continuing a topical and ongoing debate. This leads to a certain over-emphasis which is not entirely typical of Bunyan's character, and means that we see him negatively, through what he opposed rather than through what he believed. We know that what he opposed was what he considered the excessive spiritualising of the life of Jesus by the Quakers, who talked in a rather modern way of 'the Christ within' and thought that crucifixion, resurrection and much else was experienced in this way. Bunyan's method of dealing with the 'historicity' of Jesus and other biblical characters was to treat them as if they were contemporaries of his own, as if history was parallel to the life of his own day. It is puzzling to know how he justified this; it is reminiscent of the way some people, even in our own time, believe that characters in a radio serial are genuinely alive, not in fiction, but in reality. No more than reminiscent, since the biblical characters do have historical basis, but what is similar is the mental confusion between different orders of reality, a confusion which is more likely where knowledge of literature, and literary device, is not very extensive. The mind lacks facility in moving in and out of different orders of reality, and so takes what it reads or hears at its face value. Like the mind of a child it cannot detach imaginative reality from factual reality.

Another of Bunyan's targets was the extreme Antinomianism of the Ranters. He has described in *Grace Abounding* how tempted he was to try to escape his unendurable sense of guilt by becoming a Ranter (to whom all things were permitted since he believed), and since Bunyan's thought had a strong Antinomian cast throughout his life he probably always felt an unconscious attraction to them which had to be stoutly denied. Bunyan's commonsense, and probably his obsessionalism, convinced him that the Ranter solution was too easy, there must be a catch in it; he could feel no confidence in what Bonhoeffer later called 'cheap grace'.

He also opposed at length the extreme randiness of some sections of seventeenth-century society, and the cold worldliness of others, particularly when this coincided, as it did with Mr. Worldly-Wiseman and Mr. By-Ends, with an outward show of religion. His deepest hatred is reserved for those who, like the Pharisees in the New Testament, observe the legal niceties of religion.

With the dreadful exception of *Mr. Badman*, Bunyan, the writer, is not often a prig; his beliefs are too deeply and honestly felt for this. He is never proper or prim — his metaphors are pungent — and what is disquieting in his work to a modern reader is not his moral attitudes which are basically sensible and traditional. Much harder to accept is the profound and detailed interest he takes in Hell, and the dreadful agonies of those who go there. Early in his writing career (1658) he wrote his most thorough-going 'hellfire' sermon *A Few Sighs from Hell*, one which explores in considerable detail the mental and physical agony of the damned. He chooses as his text the story of Dives and Lazarus, but gives it a strange emphasis. In the original, Dives, the rich man who let the sick beggar die at his gates from hunger, is sent to Hell, and asks, in vain, that Lazarus may come to him from Abraham's bosom bringing him a drop of water to cool his tongue. This request is refused because of 'the great gulf fixed' between Heaven and Hell and Dives asks that a messenger may be sent to warn his relatives of the fate that is in store for them. This is again refused on the grounds that they would not believe it, not even 'if one rose from the dead'. There is, as in many of Christ's stories, a hint of irony.

Bunyan interprets the story with considerable license and total solemnity, adding to it many details of his own — lengthy descriptions of pain, the sneers of God overheard by the tormented sinner, above all the endless broken pleas of the sufferer which are peremptorily refused.

This sermon perhaps says more of Bunyan's psychological make-up (to be discussed in the next chapter) than of his doctrinal belief, but because Hell was so real to him a certain morbid twist is given to much of his theological thinking, a twist that often strikes a note of discord in a loving and compassionate man. It is a morbidity not unusual in the history of Puritanism and probably in a far wider circle, but it cannot be entirely dismissed as a peculiarity of the times. Even in the seventeenth century it filled some people with a sense of disquiet.

As Mr. Bunyan was preaching in a barn, and showing the fewness of those that should be saved, there stood one of the learned to take advantage of his words; and having done preaching, the schoolman said to him, You are a deceiver, a person of no charity, and therefore not fit to preach; for he that in effect condemneth the greatest part of his hearers hath no charity, and therefore not fit to preach.

Then Mr. Bunyan answered — The Lord Jesus Christ preached in a ship to his hearers on the shore, and showed that they were as four sorts of ground — The High-way, The Stony, The Thorny, and The good ground; wherof the good ground was the only persons to be saved.

And your position is — That he that in effect condemneth the greatest part of his hearers hath no charity, and therefore not fit to preach the gospel.

But here the Lord Jesus Christ did so; then your conclusion is — The Lord Jesus Christ wanted charity, and therefore not fit to preach the gospel.

Horrid blasphemy; away with your hellish logic, and speak Scripture.

Then replied the learned: 'Tis blasphemy to call logic hellish, which is our reason — the gift of God; for that which distinguisheth a man from a beast is the gift of God.

But Mr. Bunyan replied: Sin doth distinguish a man from a beast; is sin therefore the gift of God? Etc.

They parted.[15]

Despite Doe's scorn of 'the learned' we can perceive a fair and genuine question behind this debate, one to which Bunyan can only reply with the sort of quick, cheap answer used to crush a heckler. It illustrates very well the deterministic twist of Calvinism. What in Christ's story had been perhaps no more than a statement of fact and observation — that many men lose any sense of spiritual things in the course of their lifetime — becomes in Calvinist hands something harsh, guilt-laden, and punishable. Man is wicked. God sits in judgment upon him. Yet even this judgment is, in a sense, rigged, since God has decided, before the Fall, which of his victims he is going to let off punishment because of the action of Christ. Nothing can save the unlucky ones; Bunyan quite certainly believed in unspeakable and eternal suffering.

We are fairest to Bunyan when we note what a huge and insoluble contradiction lay at the heart of his theological thinking; no wonder he spoke sharply and quickly when, as in the incident described above, this contradiction was challenged. He loved his fellow-men, longed to help them, to 'mend' them, as Henry Denne said, as he had once mended kettles and pans. His life's work, as pastor and writer, was to talk of the love and mercy of Christ, to encourage men to lead better lives, and to travel, with Christian, to the Celestial City. And yet he could brood with total callousness, indeed with a good deal of satisfaction, on the agonies of Hell, on the many who would go there, and the sadistic satisfaction of the same 'loving' God. Such splits in men are not unusual, though they may take a different form in our own time. We learn to grow accustomed to contradiction. Bunyan was, however, reaching for something that lay on the far side of it.

What he is reaching for is freedom, a kind of unchallengeable buoyancy in a world full of destructiveness. His word for freedom is 'to be saved' and the way to achieve it is through 'faith'. The man of faith moves into a new and original pattern of behaviour, freed from the terrible, death-dealing compulsions of his past, cleared of his guilt and his shame. 'The Holy Ghost is sent into our Hearts, not to Excite us to a Compliance with our Old and Wind-shaken excellencies, that came into the World with us, but to Write new Laws in our Hearts: even the Law of Faith, the Word of Faith, and of Grace, and the Doctrine of Remission of Sins . . . that Holiness might flow from thence.'[16] It is a subversive statement, but one filled with a profound and hopeful wisdom.

Bunyan's faith took him far beyond the conventional waters of his belief, out into the deep ocean where all contradictions are reconciled. He could experience — the second part of the *Progress* in particular is about this experience — but he could no longer accommodate what he experienced within the framework of his doctrine, or any doctrine.

NOTES

1 *The Heavenly Footman* (1968).
2 *Grace Abounding*, pp. 91–2.
3 Luther, *An Abstract Commentarie on the Epistle to the Galathians.*
4 R. L. Greaves, *John Bunyan*, Sutton Courtenay Press.
5 *The Doctrine of the Law and Grace Unfolded* (1659).
6 *Commentarie on the Galathians.*
7 *The Saints Privilege and Profit* (1692).
8 *The Water of Life* (1688).
9 Ibid.
10 *Doctrine of the Law.*
11 Ibid.
12 Ibid.
13 Charles Doe, *The Struggler* (1691).
14 R. L. Greaves, *John Bunyan.*
15 Charles Doe, *The Struggler.*
16 *A Defence of the Doctrine of Justification by Faith in Jesus Christ* (1672).

8

The Mind of Bunyan

─────

It is impossible to read Bunyan without acquiring a strong curiosity about the mind of the man who wrote such works. The man who was so ashamed of his parentage, yet who came into his own as an artist when he wrote in their vernacular: the man who devoted his life to spiritual search, yet who struggled for years with the longing to pour out streams of blasphemy: the man who preached, from deep experience, of God's love, yet who also imagined God secretly sneering at him behind his back, as well as gleefully rejecting the desperate pleas of those writhing in Hell with a triumphant 'You had your chance!': finally the man who, as the second part of *The Pilgrim's Progress* bears witness, seemed to win through, in his late fifties, to a new serenity, a new tenderness, a new forgiveness of himself and others.

Bunyan's psychology has attracted a good deal of interest from those professionally qualified to write about it, but regrettably none of those who have done so seem fully acquainted with all his works, as well as with all the relevant details of his life, and their conclusions seem often to stand on too narrow a base. In particular there is an attempt to make him fit certain pre-conceptions about Puritanism whether he does so or not. Thus William James, in a brief but famous study of Bunyan in *Varieties of Religious Experience* (1902) quotes the following passage as an example of Bunyan's Puritan rejection of the world.

I must first pass a sentence of death upon everything that can properly be called a thing of this life, even to reckon myself, my wife, my children, my health, my enjoyments, and all, as dead to me, and myself as dead to them; to trust in God through Christ, as touching the world to come; and as touching this world, to count the grave my house, to make my bed in darkness, and to say to corruption, Thou art my father, and to the worm, Thou art my mother and sister . . . (*Grace Abounding*, pp. 325, 326.)

While it is true that some strands of Puritan thought gave this world over to the devil, this is not a striking feature of Bunyan's thought, and in fact, he took the greatest pleasure and pride in his wife and children. What James does not say, and it is an extraordinary omission, is that at the time Bunyan made this harsh resolution he was under sentence of transportation, which could under certain circumstances be commuted to hanging (and Bunyan feared this darker fate at one stage), with the knowledge that were such a sentence to be carried out, as he had every reason to suppose it would be, his family would be evicted and their possessions sequestered. It is scarcely surprising that, torn by an intolerable conflict, Bunyan felt a need to pass 'a sentence of death' on all that was precious to him. James continues 'the full flood of ecstatic liberation seems never to have poured over poor John Bunyan's soul', an astonishing statement in view of the final ecstasies of Bunyan's pilgrims, or even the rapturous passages in *Grace Abounding* (p. 263): 'Then with joy I told my Wife, O now I know, I know! but that night was a good night to me, I never had but few better . . . I could scarce lie in my Bed for joy, and peace, and triumph thorow Christ.' Again and again Bunyan, or his characters, feel themselves overwhelmed by ecstatic experiences, and though these may only have been partial liberations — the true and complete flowering of the man occurring much later in his life — James's remark is an odd one, and makes one wonder how thoroughly he knew his subject's work.

Perhaps the adjective 'poor' is significant. (Elsewhere James refers to him again as 'poor, patient Bunyan'.) There is a tendency in writers to label Bunyan as neurotic or psychotic, as 'obsessive' or 'paranoid'. 'He was,' says James, 'a typical case of the psychopathic temperament, sensitive of conscience to a diseased degree, beset by doubts, fears and insistent ideas, and a victim of verbal automatisms, both motor and sensory.' R. H. Thouless saw Bunyan as a 'melancholiac' and noted that some of his symptoms, in particular the preoccupation, fairly brief in Bunyan, with the 'unpardonable sin', was one he had often noted among acutely depressed patients in mental hospitals.[1] W. N. Evans, in a very interesting Freudian study of Bunyan's conversion, written in 1943, sees Bunyan very much as a victim of the Puritan ideology, 'the most repressive movement in history' as he calls it. He also seems totally unaware of the way that Bunyan continued to develop once his religious crisis was past.[2]

The tendency of some writers to make Bunyan 'nothing but' a neurotic, or worse, has the unfortunate effect not only that he is thereby belittled, but that those who do admire his life or his artistry, or both, feel obliged to fall over backwards to make him seem normal, or to deny the weight, interest, or importance of Bunyan's psychological conflicts. R. L. Greaves dismisses the tortured period of Bunyan's twenties, with its mental and physical collapse, as 'a psychologically-trying period of despair', and 'a disquieting psychological state'.[3] Professor Sharrock warns against translating Bunyan's beliefs 'into purely psychological terms which neglects their devotional content . . . The saints and mystics are not psychopathological cases . . . '[4]

If we are to look more closely at Bunyan and understand him better then it is necessary to avoid both these extremes. It is possible to look without patronage, or any hint of 'poor Bunyan' at the remarkable range of traits and complaints Bunyan displayed, and to try to see how these helped to establish his beliefs and create his art. Bunyan *was* neurotic, if the word has meaning, and a doctor presented with his symptoms nowadays might well feel disposed to seek expert psychiatric opinion. Whether it would help Bunyan more than, or as much as, the therapy he found for himself by way of Mr. Gifford, Bedford Meeting, preaching, writing, and sharing in family life, it is impossible to say. But, *pace* Professor Sharrock, the saints and mystics *may*, like many great men in history, be 'psychopathological cases', that is to say that they may, by the normal standard of Joe Bloggs, behave in a peculiar way.* A Michelangelo, a Shakespeare, a Beethoven are not 'normal', nor could they contribute so uniquely to mankind if they were. The saints, or those with special religious insights are similarly not 'normal', but this does not

---

* 'We have come to take it for granted that any greatness . . . harbours massive conflict.' Erik Erikson, *Young Man Luther*, Faber (1959).

make them contemptible or unworthy of attention; on the contrary, it deepens their experience and insight.

They are also, like the rest of us, to some degree affected and formed by their physical make-up. All that we know of Bunyan — his strong physique, his pleasure in active pursuits like games and dancing and bellringing, his strenuous calling — suggests that he fits Sheldon's category of the 'mesomorph', the physical type of the strong, sturdy and firmly muscular. Sheldon linked this physical type with a tendency to be energetic, assertive and to take action. He went on to build up a picture of the temperament which accompanied mesomorphy (somatotonia) — a picture which included 'love of physical adventure', 'need of exercise', 'love of dominating', 'bold directness of manner', 'physical courage for combat', 'claustrophobia', 'unrestrained voice', 'general noisiness' and 'competitive aggressiveness'. They form a striking parallel to the portrait of Bunyan as he appears in his life and works, and it is particularly useful to be reminded that traits like 'aggressiveness' may be 'built-in' to the personality and are not necessarily the result either of faulty development in infancy, nor, as the too-glib Christian view sometimes has it, of sinfulness. Bunyan *is* aggressive by nature, just as he has reddish hair and a powerful body.

In his case it must be admitted that there are real difficulties in reaching the roots of his psychological suffering, the chief of which is that we know so little of his early life. He does not mention his mother, apart from mentioning the 'meanness' and 'inconsiderableness' of his parents, and his father is allowed very little space in his work, a query about whether the Bunyans are descended from the Israelites, and an implied rebuke for permitting his little boy to grow up with the habit of swearing. Bunyan claimed that he sprang 'out of the dunghill', implying that the dung had given birth to him (it is almost as if he thought of himself in later years as a man who had had no parents).

His earliest recollections are of himself as 'a bad child', continually swearing and lying and going with bad companions. He also remembers himself as a frightened child, suffering dreadful nightmares, and deeply troubled by fears of Hell and of devils.

There is no word in his autobiography of the death of his mother and sister, nor of his father's remarriage. In fact the narrative only really comes alive at the point of his marriage and the 'romantic' attachment to the Church, religious rituals, and to the Vicar, which occurred at about the same time. The sermon he heard preached about Sunday observance was the immediate cause of the beginning of his spiritual crisis, the moment during the game of 'cat' when he felt that Jesus was 'hotly displeased' with him. What followed was a desperate attempt to 'be good', in particular to overcome his uncontrollable cursing and blaspheming. He began to be troubled by neurotic fears of approaching the church building in case the bells or the steeple itself should fall on him and kill him. He became agonisingly scrupulous, renouncing all his pleasures one after another but still unable to feel 'good'.

This part is really only the introduction to his account of his spiritual adventures. He wants to feel religious faith deeply and sincerely, he wants to feel that God has touched *him*, that he has been personally chosen, and hence becomes desperate for assurance that he has faith, that he is called. He even tries to test God, as it were to lay a trap for him, to decide the issue one way or another, but his fear of discovering himself rejected is too great. At about this time he overhears the conversation of 'the poor women of Bedford' and at once recognises that they have the sort of inner assurance he longs for.

He has a dream, a 'birth-dream' as Evans calls it, in which he is trying desperately to wriggle through a tiny space but cannot do so. He is in cold and darkness, but he can see 'the poor women' sitting on a hillside in the sunshine. Rather like Kafka determined to get into the Castle, he struggles and struggles. Unlike Kafka, he succeeds, and joins the fortunate group in the sun. He felt painfully split by the dream, however, which he interpreted as meaning that there would only be room for him to get through 'the narrow gap' (the wicket-gate of the *Progress*) if he left sin outside, that is became wholly good, and he could not find a way to do it, however hard he tried.

He was, he says, 'driven to my wits end', tormented by contradictory texts in the Bible which he shredded for minute shades of meaning; even the animals that 'parted the hoof' and the ones that 'chewed the cud' were treated as deeply relevant to his own case, as if everything that happened in his life, and every word that he read, was 'meant' in a peculiarly threatening way. No 'call' came from God, that is he could not manage to 'feel' anything, and his disappointment turned to an extreme of self-hatred. 'I was more loathsom in mine own eyes than was a toad, and I thought I was so in Gods eyes too: Sin and corruption, I said, would as naturally bubble out of my heart, as water would bubble out of a fountain.' (*Grace Abounding*, p. 84.)

He felt a tremendous envy of animals, with their ignorance of the conflict of good and evil, an envy which Luther shared (and, according to William James, many others of a Puritan cast of mind).

At this desperate moment of crisis two good things happened to him, however. One was his friendship with the older man and minister, John Gifford, who shared his belief that one should not 'take truth upon trust'. Gifford led him 'from truth to truth' and was 'much for my stability'. The other good thing was a sudden glimpse, no more than a glimpse, eclipsed by despair, of the loving face of God. 'Thou art my Love, thou art my Love, and nothing shall separate thee from my Love.'

This tiny, but precious, interlude soon gave way to the most hellish phase of his crisis. He heard voices, his mind was filled with blasphemy, with curses against God and Christ. He was plagued with doubt, he would have committed the 'unpardonable sin' if only he had been sure what it was. He imagined himself as a terrified child kicking and screaming in the arms of a gipsy who was attempting to steal him away from his family and home. The image suggests a sense of possession by an alien force, and in this state he was troubled by hallucinations of the Devil. Yet he could only imagine God jeering at him and his suffering (as a few years later he was to picture God jeering at the pain of the damned in Hell).

He was troubled by a voice commanding him, over and over again, to sell Christ. 'Sell him, sell him!' He suffered extreme physical agitation so that he could not sit still or concentrate upon anything, so great was his agony of mind. On an impulse he rejects Christ — 'Let him go then, if he will' and reaches his lowest point of mental and physical collapse. He is in total despair, his body shakes continually, he feels as if his breast bone is splitting. His sense of envy of happier people, of exclusion from all love and joy, is intolerable.

He is saved by a text to which he clings like a drowning man to a spar. 'My grace is sufficient...' As the image of terror was that of being snatched away by unloving arms, the image of love was of being held lovingly. 'Now it was as if it had arms of grace so wide, that it could not onely inclose me, but many more besides.' (*Grace Abounding*, p. 204.) He felt as if his mind was a scales, seesawing between two alternatives — peace and joy at one moment, and fear and guilt the next. Gradually, the scales came down upon the side of peace and joy. Identifying with his wife in her premature labour, he felt that the cessation of her pangs was a sign from God. At about this time he discovered his preaching gift and his symptoms began gradually to decline, though for a number of years he was troubled by the longing to pour out blasphemy when he was in the pulpit.

He was arrested at Samsell in circumstances which might easily have been avoided without dishonour, and removed, at least in part, from the responsibilities of husband, father and breadwinner for more than twelve years.

The predominant images in his writing are images of mothers and children, children either loved or in distress; the child who 'nuzels' in its mother's bosom for milk, the child whose mother both hugs and scolds it at once, calling it 'slut' and 'naughty girl', the child kidnapped by the gipsy, the child struggling in the mill-pit and others. Another frequent image is of prison, or of a cage — the man in the iron cage, the cage at Vanity Fair, the dungeon in Doubting Castle, and these are accompanied by other claustrophobic images — the 'narrow gap', the narrow pathway between the Walls of Salvation, etc. Excremental images are also frequent — the dunghill from which Bunyan claimed to have come, the filth of the Slough of Despond, the dirt from which a man not in a state of grace had to be cleansed. *The Awakened Child's Lament* (1686) describes his state of mind perhaps as concisely as anything Bunyan ever wrote:

> As I was born naked
> I was with sin bespaked,
> At which when I awaked
> My Soul and Spirit shaked . . .
>
> A sin has me infected
> I am thereof detected
> Mercy I have neglected
> I fear I am rejected.
>
> The Word I have misused
> Good Council too refused
> Thus I my Self abused
> How can I be excused? . . .

> Mercies Gate is locked,
> Yea, up that way is blocked,
> Yea some that there have knocked,
> God at their cryes hath mocked.
>
> Thus I have sin committed
> And so my self out-witted
> Yea, and my Soul unfitted
> To be to Heaven admitted ...
>
> O Lord! do not disdain me,
> But kindly entertain me;
> Yea in thy Faith maintain me,
> And let thy Love contain me.

Bunyan, in depression, saw himself as dirty, wantonly wicked, and worthless, deserving of rejection and half-expecting it, a fit object for the mockery of God; his vision of God as sadistic implies a curious kind of self-importance. God, the sadist, clings to his victim, and his victim is therefore, of great significance to him. The victim is not, at least, forsaken. Bunyan refuses to regard himself as of no account to God, or as simply insignificant to him, and, despite the pain, finds a kind of reassurance in this.

The other side of this frightened, self-accusing submission to God, was the longing to attack God by pouring out streams of blasphemy. Love for God, fear of God, fought with hatred of God and of Christ, a hatred very evident in Bunyan's identification with Judas during his crisis, and his subconscious longing to 'sell him'. 'God does not hate you. You hate him', the young Luther was told by his monastic superiors, and the same might have been said with equal truth to Bunyan at the period of his religious crisis. The image of the scales perfectly expressed the ambivalence of his feelings, an ambivalence which nearly destroyed him.

According to Evans such ambivalence is associated with an ambivalent attitude to one's father; if the father is simultaneously loved and hated then the child will alternate between feelings of rage and fear on the one hand and submission and a longing for acceptance on the other. These feelings may, in the grown man, be projected on to God, and there will be a cleavage of the parental image, into 'good' and 'bad', that is to say on to God and the Devil, or on to 'good' and 'bad' people.

We do not know enough about Bunyan's father to guess the predominant feelings he aroused in the child — we can only work backwards from the feelings Bunyan had as a man. It may be profitable, however, to compare the young Bunyan with the young Luther. Luther revealed an extraordinary number of the characteristics we see in Bunyan — the terror of hellfire, the constant awareness of the Devil, the longing for God's love and the fear of being rejected by him, the persistent sense of guilt and unworthiness, the agonised scrupulosity, and the compulsion to blaspheme. Luther, however, unlike Bunyan, was very frank about his relations with his father.

As a child he was deeply afraid of him, constantly beaten by him, and on one occasion ran away from home in order to escape from him. Yet at times he also felt close to him, longed for affection and approval, and suffered greatly when, as in the case of his monastic vocation, he opposed his father's wishes. His younger son, Hans, was called after his father (as Bunyan's younger son, Thomas, was called after *his* father). Erik Erikson, writing about the relationship between the Luthers, *père et fils*, says:

Martin, even when mortally afraid, could not really hate his father, he could only be sad; and Hans, while he could not let the boy come close, and was murderously angry at times, could not let him go for long. They had a mutual and deep investment in each other which neither of them could or would abandon, although neither of them was able to bring it to any kind of fruition.[5]

Erikson considers that though the boy could not, dare not, hate his father openly, he did hate him 'underneath'. The resentment he felt against him, resentment he was forced to hide, made him deeply guilty, causing him to develop 'an obsessive mixture of obedience and rebelliousness', one which was more than illustrated in his later relations to the Pope and the Roman Catholic church. He never felt 'good enough' — Erikson says that Luther felt himself a criminal all his life, and in a futile attempt to counter the inner sense of guilt fell prey to scrupulosity and the rituals of obsession. 'In the obsessive fulfilment of detailed rituals ... the negative conscience takes over, dividing every minute of the day into a miniature last judgment.'

Bunyan too felt like a 'criminal', showed signs of being tormented by alternate feelings of obedience and rebellion, and was a victim of his own compulsions and obsessions. It is not perhaps fanciful, therefore, to form a hypothesis that his childhood experiences followed a similar pattern to those of Luther, that his basic conflict was his ambivalent attitude to his father, and that, as with Luther 'a transference had taken place from a parent figure to universal personages', i.e. God, the Devil, the Pope, etc.

Evans saw Bunyan's ambivalence not so much in terms of his individual childhood experiences as part of the whole Puritan system, which he felt played upon childhood conflicts.

The whole technique of Evangelical Protestantism rests upon the early parent-child situation where the child is alternately scolded and cajoled. By thus exploiting the ambivalent feelings of the child this mixture of threats and coaxing usually results in the submission of the child into "good behaviour".

The Puritan tradition has revived and exploited that parent-child relationship. The voice conveying the super-ego threat is again heard, in circumstances calculated to heighten dramatically the authority of the voice and so evoke the repressed feelings of guilt. The reasonable arguments of the ego are explained away as pride and self-will. Thus the sinner is reduced to abject dependence on God in the knowledge of his complete worthlessness and guilt.[6]

Evans does not explain why, just at that point in history, there should be such an outbreak of ambivalence; parents had, presumably 'alternately scolded and cajoled' their children for centuries without thereby making them Puritans. What he seems to be implying, with some reason, is that in the sixteenth and seventeenth centuries men discovered, consciously, or much more probably unconsciously, a technique which touched powerfully upon repressed guilt, so mobilising guilt feelings. Those most affected by it were those in whom the childhood feelings of ambivalence had been particularly strong, of whom Bunyan was very probably one.

As a Freudian, Evans is particularly interested in the Oedipal conflict. Here again, he argues from the general to the particular, necessarily in Bunyan's case since we can only guess at the form his Oedipal conflict must have taken. Evans' generalisation is to note that there is no presiding female figure in Protestant Christianity as there is in Catholicism in the person of the Virgin Mary. In Protestant religion the only important personages were Father and Son. The Catholic boy, in his view, suffered fully the conflicts of the Oedipal situation, that is to say he felt rage, jealousy, envy and fear towards his father, but was then able to sublimate these feelings by way of the religious personages who were important to him.

Protestants, on the other hand, behaved rather more like Luther's father (admittedly a Catholic) who, according to Erikson, harshly and abruptly removed the boy from his mother's sphere of influence when he was far too young, trying to make him 'precociously independent of women'. Innumerable attacks Luther was later to make upon the Mother of God make Erikson, he says, feel like exclaiming 'Didn't the man have a mother?' Evans feels that Protestants by their severity tried to prevent the Oedipal situation from ever arising. The situation was anticipated, the libido pruned and checked, long before the genital stage was reached.

The intense suspicion felt by Puritanism of the senses caused their vigilance to begin in earliest infancy, denying little children the sensual and instinctive satisfactions which, according to Erikson, give a 'basic trust' in life and in other people. Neither Luther nor Bunyan show this basic trust — on the contrary, they show the greatest doubt and suspicion, together with a desperate need to establish a trust.

This prepared the way for a later crisis. In adult life they found themselves presented with a terrible ultimatum. 'Wilt thou leave thy sins and go to Heaven? or have thy sins and go to Hell?' was the form in which it came to Bunyan. In other words was he prepared to renounce all instinctual desires — thus submitting himself utterly, and masochistically to God, or would he live in terror of Hell (which Evans translates as fear of annihilation and castration)? No wonder the mental agony was so acute. 'Few,' says Evans, 'are able to retort, like Shelley, that they would prefer to burn with Plato, rather than go to heaven with Archdeacon Paley; those brought up in the severity of the Puritan tradition elect only too often to pay the terrible price that is exacted.'

Many, like Luther and Bunyan, tried to pay the price but encountered unexpected difficulties. The suppression of the instincts proved to be neither totally effective nor final. Their return, in the form of renewed temptation, re-aroused guilt which was already there repressed and dormant. Their attempt to reduce the guilt feelings by an ever-increasing scrupulosity gave only temporary relief; fear, anxiety, depression continued to gain on them. The ego tried to reassert itself against the tyranny of the superego, a conflict that expressed itself in feelings of anger against God, feelings which both Bunyan and Luther blamed on the Devil. The Devil, too, filled their minds with blasphemy and obscenities. 'The typical Puritan,' says Evans, 'is like a ship's captain with a mutinous crew beneath the hatches: he dare not relax his attention lest they batter down the hatches, overwhelm the captain and take charge of the ship.'

This image catches the mood of ceaseless nervous activity, of being unable to rest in being. Yet for all his busyness, his expiatory rituals, the Puritan seems to have difficulty at arriving at a point of lasting contentment and peace. Always he must try harder, harder. 'He is constant in training, his moral athleticism knows no bounds, yet in the eyes of his dread task-master, he is never fit.' It never seems possible to prove to the harsh father that they can live up to his expectations. God himself was the dreaded and untrustworthy father.

Feelings otherwise felt by a young child in relation to his father became mixed with the grown man's feelings about God. 'Beneath the virtues of humility, the acceptance of one's lot and the spirit of submissiveness which were extolled in the sermonic literature of the time, was concealed the jealousy and envy which are associated with the father-son relationship.'

In much Puritan writing and thinking we can note an incipient paranoia. This is particularly marked in both Bunyan and Luther. According to Erikson 'suspiciousness, obsessive scrupulosity, moral sadism, and a preoccupation with dirtying and infectious thoughts and substances go together. Luther had them all.' So did Bunyan.

We have noted Bunyan's fears that God was jeering at him behind his back as well as his tortured scrupulosity, what he called his 'tenderness of conscience'. He is more inhibited than Luther about using excremental imagery, but dirt, dung, filth and similar euphemisms abound in his work. And 'moral sadism' appears in his fascination with the torments of Hell, and in particular with his fantasies of the damned pleading for relief and being rebuffed. (The Marquis de Sade in *Justine* recommends, as a source of pleasure, a situation in which a mistress refuses the pleas of a servant — an orphan girl without friends to help her — for adequate food and clothing.)

Given such problems and preoccupations Bunyan might have suffered a full and lasting paranoid breakdown, and it is likely that, at the worst point of his spiritual crisis, this was not far off. The 'voices' were beginning to interfere more and more with his everyday living, and his mind seems to have become filled with blasphemy, thoughts of threatening devils, and the conviction of certain damnation.

A series of events, however, led him towards a sort of therapy, a therapy so effective that within a few years his agony largely abated, joy took the place of perpetual suffering, and he was able to produce two major works of art. The first of these events seems to have been his friendship with the older man, Mr. Gifford who, on his own admission 'stabilised' him. It is interesting to compare Mr. Gifford's role in Bunyan's life with that of Dr. Staupitz, the monastic superior, in Luther's. Dr. Staupitz (who became important to Luther at the height of *his* youthful crisis) listened to the young man, understood, at least in part, the conflicts which troubled him, and set him to work as preacher and lecturer. Erikson feels that part of Staupitz' value for Luther was that he encouraged him to laugh 'and humour marks the moment when our ego regains some territory from oppressive conscience'. Dr. Staupitz became a kind of fatherly sponsor for Luther, and though some of Luther's ambivalence was transferred to him, and so he experienced him at times as punishing and revenging, he trusted him as much as he would ever be able to trust a 'father', and interestingly described him as the 'father' of the two most important ideas of Lutheran theology; that faith, not works, is of supreme importance, and that Christ was a man like himself with whom he could identify. It was not that Staupitz was an original theologian, or even a particularly discerning one; it was rather that his fatherhood brought these ideas to birth in Luther, who allowed himself to be fertilised.

Bunyan's fatherly sponsor also listened to him and welcomed him into the small community of the Bedford Meeting to which Bunyan was later to have so much to give. It was here, though probably not until after Gifford's death, that he discovered his *métier* as a preacher. Gifford led Bunyan 'from truth to truth', and understood something of his desperate need not to take truth on trust, at a time when others were urging him to stop worrying. If, as is often claimed, Bunyan gave dramatic expression to Gifford's personality in the person of Evangelist in the *Progress*, then we have an interesting picture of a firm, but loving personality, able to

comprehend fully the depths of Christian's despair, and give him clear
instructions as to how to proceed. A revealing moment comes where
Christian is caught by Evangelist on the wrong road, since he has
followed the advice of Worldly Wiseman. At a hint of rebuke from
Evangelist Christian is beside himself with terror, prostrate on the ground
and conviced that he is due for annihilation. Evangelist refuses this
savage, punishing role, however. He raises Christian up gently, and tells
him that he is forgiven. He advises him where to go next, kisses him,
smiles upon him and wishes him Godspeed. Mr. Gifford, it seems, has
refused to be made over into the role of the punishing father, and by his
love makes a new start possible.

With this new start comes a new role for Bunyan, almost a new
identity. He discovers that he is a gifted preacher, and that he is valued
and admired by others for his unique talent. His delight in this turn of
events comes to us with a moving clarity down all the years:

> I at first could not believe that God should speak by me to the heart of
> any man, still counting my self unworthy; yet those who were thus
> touched would love me, and have a peculiar respect for me; and though
> I did put it from me that they should be awakened by me, still they
> would confess it and affirm it before the Saints of God, they would also
> bless God for me . . . and count me Gods Instrument that shewed to
> them the Way of Salvation . . . then I began to conclude it might be
> so, that God had owned his Work in such a foolish one as I; and then
> came that Word of God to my heart with much sweet refreshment . . .
> At this therefore I rejoyced. (*Grace Abounding*, pp. 273-5.)

The greatest difficulty in understanding the thought of a man like
Bunyan is in grasping the role that Christ played in his mind. That he is of
supreme and therapeutic importance to him we have his own words over
and over again, yet quite how the therapy worked, or 'who' as you
might say, he is to him, is a puzzling and not entirely soluble problem.

Bunyan first mentions Christ at the time of the game of tipcat when he
experiences him as an accuser, one who is 'hotly displeased' with him.
Yet as time went on he gradually relinquished this idea, and began to
perceive him as what one might call 'the loving face of God' in contrast
to the wrathful face which found expression in the divine Judge. The
writing of Luther had, he admits, something to do with this change in his

thinking, but it seems likely that he also needed the experience of human love to know what he was talking about, and it was perhaps the fatherly love of Mr. Gifford that made this new step possible. The change of heart is complete when Bunyan imagines the Lord Jesus looking down at him through the tiles of his house, not with the guilt-producing anger of the first encounter, but benevolently and with love.

In the *Progress* it is the apprehension of Christ's love as discovered by Christian when he sees the Cross that suddenly, magically, relieves him of the burden of sin and clothes him with a new identity. Up to that point all is tears, pain, desperate anxiety and fear; beyond it Christian is transformed into a man who, although he has much difficult travelling ahead of him, knows what life is about and where he is going.

Luther came to feel that the accusing Christ was somehow a 'false Christ' to which he must not listen. 'When Christ comes and talks to you as if to a sinner and tortures you like Moses: "What have you done?" — slay him to death. But when he talks to you as God does, and as a saviour, prick up both ears.' The 'real' Christ is the consoler and forgiver. 'Christ . . . is no Tyrant or Judge, which will condemne us for our sinnes, hee is no caster down of the afflicted, but a raiser up of those that are fallen, a mercifull releiver and comforter, of the heavy and broken-hearted.'

Luther discovered this 'loving face of God' because, with Staupitz's help, he learned to look on Christ as a man like himself, that is to say, to separate him from the terror with which he thought of God. Christ became the 'good' God. Bunyan, influenced by Luther and his own contemporaries, made a similar separation. The thought of 'the Blood' of Christ, or the wounds of Christ, with their reminder of sacrificial love, were one of the few comforts he could find to cling to in his darkest hours.

What is noticeable in Bunyan's Christ is how feminine he is. He is all tenderness, gentleness, understanding, quite separate from the aggressive sides of Bunyan's character; Bunyan thinks of love, and the loss of it, almost entirely in terms of maternal imagery. Emmanuel, in *The Holy War*, the princely Christ, exhibits another aspect of femininity — its capricious, teasing, almost flirtatious side, a kind of 'playing hard to get'. More generally, however, the tender qualities predominate, qualities so reminiscent of a Madonna, that one must wonder whether Protestantism, having despatched the Virgin Mary from the Oedipal trinity of God,

Christ, and the Mother of Christ, has not had to bring her back in disguised form.

Evans thinks that the Protestants identified with a Christ who had succeeded (as they longed to do) in renouncing all instinctual desires, that is to say a Christ who was not so much a woman as a kind of psychological eunuch. It was, he thinks, Bunyan's unconscious refusal to make such a sacrifice of his instincts that made him long to destroy Christ, e.g. to 'sell him' as Judas had done, and it was this inner rage which accounted in part for Puritan compulsions to curse God and Christ.

Those who went through the conversion process, however, with its unspeakable agony of renunciation, found compensation for themselves in identifying with another aspect of Christ, the role of saviour. Strongly marked in almost everyone who was converted, and outstandingly so in the cases of Bunyan and Luther, was a sense of mission, a compulsion to 'save' others, and a tendency to behave in a 'Christlike' way, not so much through the 'imitation' of Christ, in any conscious sense, as because there was a strong identification, both conscious and unconscious, as by someone in love. Erikson says of Luther that he

abandoned the concept of Christ as an ideal figure to be initiated, or abjectly venerated, or ceremonially remembered as an event in the past. Christ now becomes the core of the Christian's identity: *quotidianus Christi adventus*, Christ is today here, in me. The affirmed passivity of suffering becomes the daily Passion and the Passion is the substitution of the primitive sacrifice of others with a most active, most masterly, affirmation of man's nothingness — which, by his own masterly choice, becomes his existential identity.

In this sense the converted man takes up his cross daily.

The saved man turned saviour himself becomes a giver, using his suffering to speak with authority of what suffering means. 'You must preach,' said Luther, using a simile that anticipates Bunyan, 'as a mother suckles her child'. In this passion of giving, a man could forget for long periods his own hunger, his own unhealed wounds, and unresolved conflicts. It is not the perfect solution for those who suffer what James called a sense of 'radical bad being', but it has dignity, and perhaps useful social consequences.

If Christ becomes the 'good' face of God, and a man identifies as wholly as he can with this 'goodness', then what becomes of the badness, either of God — the wrathful, punishing aspects of which Bunyan and Luther were so heartbrokenly aware — or of man? Men like Bunyan all too easily saw badness only in themselves, as in the period of 'conviction' common to all conversion processes, in which they saw themselves as 'the worst of sinners'. The badness in themselves seemed to 'match' with the badness of the persecuting God, sneering at their helpless struggles and their pain.

In the relative health of the post-conversion period, however, the badness was withdrawn from themselves, and to some extent from God, and became projected either on to individuals or to causes, or to the Devil, or to all three at once.

Luther's projection was principally on to the Pope. Bunyan too thought badness resided in Catholicism, as his spiteful, though amusing, portrait of 'Pope' in the *Progress* makes clear. He has, like all paranoid people, his *bêtes noires* — Paul Cobb, the clerk who struck his name off the Kalender, the Quakers, the whole apparatus of 'the World'. One can imagine that such subjects had only to crop up in conversation for Bunyan to 'sound off' about them.

But alongside these human vessels of badness there was the major vessel, or as Bunyan and Luther believed the source, of badness, the Devil. The Devil was curiously close to God — in Bunyan's view of Hell, for example, the Devil is, as it were, performing a useful function for God in his superintendence of Hell, rather as the governor of a prison performs a function for a monarch. The Devil was 'the prince of this World', as for example, personified in Apollyon, and the converted man had to detach himself from the illusions of 'this World' and prepare himself, mentally and spiritually, for one which he could not see. In the everyday conduct of his life the pilgrim was continually influenced, cajoled, tempted and harassed by the Devil or by his demons, and he needed to keep his wits, and his suspicions, about him, not to be deceived.

The Devil was the crystallisation, or personification, of all evil, either the 'bad' things a man felt in himself such as sexual temptation or the bad things he saw in the world about him. There was no real distinction between the two — both were joined in the Devil — yet for men as constitutionally guilty as Bunyan and Luther there may have been some relief from the sense of personal responsibility in the sense of being worked upon by an enemy, possessed, as the town of Mansoul in *The Holy War* was invaded by Diabolus. The Devil was, in psychological terms, an externalisation of evil. 'The belief in demons permitted a persistent externalisation of one's own unconscious thoughts and preconscious impulses of avarice and malice, as well as thoughts which one suspected one's neighbour of having.' Fear of the hostility of others, together with deep and dangerous wishes of one's own, both get pushed on to the Devil. 'In all magic thinking, the unknown and the unconscious meet at a common frontier: murderous, adulterous or avaricious wishes, or sudden moods of melancholy . . . are all forced upon me by evil-wishing neighbours. Sexual fantasies, too, can thus be treated as extra-territorial.'

In modern times we no longer find it easy to place blame on the Devil, since he is too magical a figure for 'scientific man'. This does not necessarily mean that we are better able to recognise our unconscious impulses, but rather that we externalise them solely upon human beings, upon unpopular racial groups, or religious groups (as in Northern Ireland).

At times Bunyan half knows that the Devil is also himself, as when he puzzles over *who* was actually speaking, or more important, feeling, the blasphemy against God and Christ that filled his mind. What he cannot permit himself at this stage of his life is the discovery that he is murderously angry with God; the fear of punishment, and of his own badness, is still too great for that.

Erikson makes the point that swearing, of the kind of which Bunyan had been so free as a young man, is a kind of verbal defecation. It would seem, from the persistent use of excretory imagery, that anality played a very important part in Bunyan's make-up, as it undoubtedly did in Luther's. Freudian psychology regards the infant as encountering two major crises. The first, depending on the way a mother feeds and cares for the helpless infant, decides the child's later ability to trust. This period determines what Freud calls 'orality'. The second crisis has to do with the development of the child's will, with the ability to, as Erikson puts it 'combine an unimpaired will with ready self-discipline, rebellion with responsibility'. This period determines anality.

Where this second crisis is handled harshly or unsympathetically by those caring for the child then it grows up with a sense of shame and self-doubt. It may be both frightened of authority, yet intolerably rebellious, as Luther was eventually to become. It may be excessively obstinate, or obsessed with cleanliness, punctuality and 'carefulness' over money.

Many writers have suggested that the whole Puritan movement was marked by this kind of 'anality', the excessive retentiveness of which Luther complained so bitterly in the form of constipation, finding expression in a joyless thrift, and a remarkable capacity to amass money and wealth. The discovery that 'time was money' was made in the seventeenth century, and to drive the point home, watches were invented and clocks for the first time recorded the minutes as they passed.

We have no evidence that Bunyan shared this excessive thrift; such evidence as there is, and there is little of it, suggests the opposite, that he was careless of financial considerations when his work or his duty conflicted with the chance to earn money.

Yet a sense of inner shame troubled him, as in the extraordinary statement that he came 'out of the dunghill'. In medieval thought the Devil had been associated with faeces (something Luther makes abundantly clear), and perhaps Bunyan never felt himself wholly free of the dunghill's taint. The first ordeal Christian has to undergo on his journey is to cross a kind of sewer into which he is in imminent danger of falling in and drowning, and Bunyan's metaphor for the grace of Christ in a famous sermon is that of having dirt washed away.

It is upon this kind of unconscious fear of a primal taint that the guilt of men like Bunyan rested, and this is why when they give their conscious reasons for regarding themselves as 'the worst of sinners' — swearing, lying, etc. — they seem so unconvincing. We feel them casting around for some sin big enough to impress us, and failing completely. They *are* their wickedness, because of their inner association with the devil, or the dunghill, and no rational argument is going to help. What does help, according to them, is to make a new identification, not with the dunghill this time, but with the opposite of the Devil, Christ. They pass from the extreme of degradation to the extreme of purity.

Christ was the man who had succeeded in renouncing instinctual desires, in freeing himself from the shame that was fundamental to the self-awareness of men like Bunyan. What began perhaps, as envy of him, as of a hero, continued as identification, whether with entire success we may doubt. Bunyan's emphasis on the recurring nature of temptation, together with Freud's insistence that such suppression was never truly effective, suggest otherwise.

Christ also represented, however, a 'letting be' or a 'letting go'. Erikson makes much of the fact (one of great embarrassment to nineteenth-century Protestants) that Luther's revelation that it was faith and not works that justified a man came to him on the lavatory, a fact which Luther himself reported with evident satisfaction. The tortured need for expiation in the case of men like Bunyan and Luther, with every form of works, scruples, confessions, compulsions and obsessions suggest a desperate, a supreme need to 'let go' and 'let be'. This was matched in Luther's case — we have no evidence for Bunyan — with a chronic inability to 'let go' in the bodily sense, a severe form of constipation and urine retention about which he is extremely frank. Body and mind together lead him to a marvellous revelation — one that was to seem equally revelatory to Bunyan when he came upon it in Luther's writing — that there is no need to 'prove' oneself, to a father or to anyone else. One is; and one is satisfactory.

The astounding sense of liberation brought about by identification with the passivity of Christ is particularly evident in Bunyan's account of what happens to Christian when, on his journey, he reaches the Cross. The burden that has made life insupportable rolls from his back, he is told that he is forgiven, he has a mark placed upon his forehead, he is given a certificate which will take him into the Celestial City, he is stripped of his old 'filthy' garment and given a new coat. He has acquired his new identity. The sense of miraculous liberation reduces him to tears.

Though Bunyan the artist describes this drama of conversion better than it has ever been described, except possibly in the Biblical description of St. Paul's conversion, what he put into words was a commonplace of Puritan and later, of Evangelical, experience. What one needs to know is what happened later when the first wonder of this experience had worn off. Did the convert find, as Freud suggests, that the suppressed desires continually returned?*

From the frequent references to 'the Devil' in the writing of Bunyan and others, we must suppose they did. It could not, after all, be 'in

---

* 'Possibly on account of the sexual elements which are also involved, possibly on account of some characteristics of instincts in general, the suppressive action in religion proves to be neither completely effective nor final.' Freud, *Obsessive Acts and Religious Practices*, Coll. Papers II, 33 (1907).

Christ' that they experienced them, since in identifying with Christ they were identifying with someone they regarded as a kind of psychological eunuch who was not troubled by such desires.

What desires did trouble Bunyan? We know nothing directly of Bunyan's sexual feelings. He denies specifically that he was ever an adulterer or a fornicator, or that he is even attracted to any woman beyond his own wife. We may feel that he overdoes his protestations somewhat, and wonder what it is he is defending himself against when he will not even give his fellow-worshippers the 'holy kiss' or allow himself to 'so much as touch a Womans Hand' but he makes it clear that he does not consciously suffer sexual desire.* The absence of any very effective sexual temptress in his writing, until the magnificent Madam Bubble, 'Mistriss of the World', towards the end of the second part of the *Progress* suggests that it was only late in his life, in his middle fifties, that he could permit himself to recognise the force of his sexual feeling.

The dating of his being 'shie' to the time of his conversion does suggest that a repression of his sexual feeling had taken place, probably reinforcing an earlier attitude; only much later in his life could he bear to look at 'a Woman' again.

So far as marriage is concerned he seems to have been particularly fortunate in his second marriage to Elizabeth. He writes with obvious love of the pain of being separated from her, of the joy of sharing his religious ideas with her, and she in her turn obviously recognised what was important to him in his life and work, and supported him, even when, as during his imprisonment, it involved her in considerable suffering and hardship. We cannot ignore, however, the almost suicidal way, fairly soon after his marriage to her, he allowed himself to be arrested at Samsell, when this could easily have been avoided, an arrest virtually bound to lead to imprisonment. Unconsciously, by opting out of his heavy responsibilities as breadwinner, he provided himself with the leisure — twelve years of leisure — to become a major writer and minor theologian.

It may be worth bearing in mind that his first marriage had also

* 'If all the Fornicators and Adulterers in England were hang'd by the Neck till they be dead, John Bunyan . . . would still be alive and well. I know not whether there be such a thing as a woman breathing under the Copes of the whole Heaven but by their apparel, their Children, or by common fame except my Wife . . . [God] . . . made me shie of women from my first Convertion until now. Those know, and can also bear me witness, with whom I have been most intimately concerned, that it is a rare thing to see me carry it pleasant towards a Woman.' *Grace Abounding* (1666).

coincided with a crisis, though of a different kind; by encouraging in him an interest in religion, and in church-going, his first wife precipitated the landslide of guilt and scruples which brought about his mental break-down. The bitterness with which the treatment of Christian by his wife and family is described, as the time of *his* breakdown, implies that this marriage may have been less idyllic than that with Elizabeth.

For all the liberation achieved by Bunyan through his conversion — and we cannot doubt that it changed his life profoundly, giving him a new kind of confidence, joy and sense of direction — there are hints throughout his writing of the Bunyan who was *not* liberated, and who continued to suffer. The most persistent of these hints occurs in the recurrence of images of imprisonment and of claustrophobia. These might be explained away by the fact that Bunyan, after all, *did* suffer the most wearisome physical confinement for a protracted period, though alternatively Bunyan's imprisonment might be viewed as an unconscious attempt to reproduce in his outer life the conditions of his inner life. Whatever the source of the imagery, Bunyan, even after the liberation of his conversion, still felt 'unfree'. As he showed in the *Progress*, in the extremely menacing description of the prison of Giant Despair, even when far advanced on his spiritual journey, or perhaps particularly when far advanced (that is, a long way from the simplicities of conversion), a man could find himself intolerably constricted, and like Christian and Hopeful, barely alive. In fact, this is the worst suffering of the entire journey, the only point at which Christian contemplates suicide.

Erikson suggests that the claustrophobic image is linked with anxiety. 'Anxiety comes from *angustus*, meaning to feel hemmed in and choked up; Martin's use of *circumvallatus* — all walled in — to describe his exper-ience in the thunderstorm indicates he felt a sudden constriction of his whole life space.'

We may wonder what constriction Bunyan felt, beyond the confines of Bedford gaol, in the years in which he was writing the first part of the *Progress* and thereafter. If, as Erikson suggests, anxiety is the problem to which his imagery gives a key, then in what did this anxiety consist? Possibly a return of the instinctual desires of which Freud speaks, of the rage against God which still occasionally troubled him in the desire to blaspheme. Given too powerful a return of such passions, the precious sense of identification with the 'pure' Christ could no longer be successfully maintained, yet the passions themselves continue to simmer within him unacknowledged as part of his present character.

Bunyan found a temporary, and not very satisfactory way of solving this problem by writing *The Life and Death of Mr. Badman*. Mr. Badman is a counter-hero, the opposite of brave, good Christian, though not the exact opposite, since whereas Christian, for all his struggling, sometimes does 'bad' things, Mr. Badman never, ever, does anything good. He is entirely black, the repository of every kind of sin; he cheats, lies, swindles, bullies, whores and blasphemes on an extraordinary scale, and in fact outside pornographic literature it would be difficult to find a book so occupied with perverse behaviour. Bunyan does not, of course, own to a pornographic purpose — quite the contrary, he writes in rejection of what he describes. It would be impossible, however, for any writer to produce a lengthy book on such a subject without discovering, and finally admitting to himself, a strange affinity with his subject. *Mr. Badman* effected an introduction for Bunyan to what can scarcely have been very welcome — a whole range of repressed desires.

That the writing of *Mr. Badman* produced strange emotions in Bunyan we can feel from studying his style. The extraordinary note of caricature — as if Bunyan is parodying his own sermons and making fun of them — suggests a note of acute dissatisfaction with himself and his adjustment to life. His middle-age experience of life makes nonsense of the old simplistic view of good and evil. He does not know how to change something so fundamental to his whole theological position, but unconsciously he attacks his own position by making it ludicrous.

The Holy War, his next book, touched upon another repression, by simply eliminating women from its pages altogether. If 'the Mistriss of the World' had begun to trouble Bunyan at this stage of his life he is determined to look in the opposite direction, not to notice that there are any women besides his wife, in an attempt to shut out unwelcome thoughts. His choice of a military theme, of a brisk, no-nonsense style (no maternal imagery in *this* book, nor any other imagery that is particularly memorable), and the absence of any feeling relationship between the characters, apart from the coquettishness of Emmanuel, suggest what the feminine stood for in Bunyan's life and work, and how impoverished he was when he rejected it.

It is a pity that we know nothing of the two years between the publication of *The Holy War* and the second part of *The Pilgrim's*

Progress. Bunyan was fifty-six when that last great work was published, and only four years from his death. It represents a change so astonishing that we cannot fail to be curious about what had occurred in Bunyan's life to produce a feeling of such serenity, such tenderness, and such joy, a peace of heart and mind which for all the wonder of his original conversion was like nothing which he had known before; *this* joy was less dramatic, the sense of contentment and calm we would like to associate with old age.

If in *The Holy War*, women had been excluded, in the second part of the *Progress* they not only return but are the principal characters. If in *Mr. Badman* there is ludicrous exaggeration of the wickedness of the sinner, in the second part of the *Progress* there is forgiveness, even a humorous understanding of those who err, as in the case of the boy Mathew who eats fruit from the Devil's orchard and gets the tummy ache. There is an extraordinary sense of pleasure in the body and its delights — the characters dance, eat, drink to the point of being 'merry' and stay up all night talking for the sheer fun of it. The warm, motherly figure of Christiana presides over the whole enterprise (somehow it is impossible to imagine anything very dreadful happening to anyone while Christiana is around), together with the pretty Mercy, a kind of grown-up sister-figure. Most moving of all is Bunyan's new compassion and respect for those who are not cast in the heroic mould — Mr. Dispondencie and his daughter Much-afraid, Mr. Fearing, Mr. Ready-to-halt, and the children who grumble, get tired, fall ill, lose their shoes, make loud and embarrassing remarks about the hospitality, ask riddles, and generally behave not as Puritan models, but as real children.

We can only guess what had happened to Bunyan in the last decade of his life; that with the writing of *Mr. Badman* he made the discovery that the wickedness he had so roundly condemned was not something he could leave behind like an unwanted garment but was still very much part of him. What he needed to do was forgive himself, know his frailty and so become less scornful of the weakness of others.

With the writing of *The Holy War* came the discovery of how much he needed his feminine side, how dull, mechanical and unimaginative he was without it. He could now take it up again without shame or a sense of weakness. And with this discovery came, on the evidence of the *Progress*, a new and unashamed pleasure in the body.

When we think of the young Bunyan, tortured by scruples, sick with guilt, mercilessly denying himself the pleasure of dancing, troubled with compulsions to blasphemy and sadistic fantasies, it is hard to believe that this happy and relaxed grandfather is in fact the same person. *His* progress, his individual progress, not the progress of the universal Christian, shows marked signs of the psychological and spiritual process Jung called 'individuation', the inner development by which a man moves towards wholeness. Individuation, which Jung said took place in the second half of a man's life, involves the rediscovery of repressed parts of the personality and the reintegration of them in the whole personality. At the same time the personality learns something of its relative unimportance; it recognises and accepts a truth beyond itself around which it revolves and in the light of which it has meaning and purpose.

There are many stages in the individuation process, but an early and important one is confronting and integrating the 'shadow' or negative personality, a stage which I would like to suggest coincided for Bunyan with the writing of *Mr. Badman*. Another, very important, stage, is discovering within oneself the traits and the character of the opposite sex, known, in the case of a man as 'the anima'. It is this joining of the opposites within one which makes creativity possible. Perhaps we may also see in Bunyan a final detachment from the inadequacies of his parents; the warm, capable motherliness of Christiana, and the strong benevolence of Mr. Greatheart seem to reach beyond the ignorant and poor tinker couple who happened to breed a genius to a grateful new awareness of what true motherliness and fatherliness consist of.

The crippled Mr. Ready-to-Halt dies with the words 'Welcome Life!' on his lips. It seems to have been 'Life' that for all his neurotic wounds Bunyan succeeded in finding.

NOTES

1 R. H. Thouless, *The Psychology of Religion*, Cambridge (1923).
2 W. N. Evans, 'Notes on the Conversion of John Bunyan', *International Journal of Psycho-Analysis*, XXIV (1943).
3 R. L. Greaves, *John Bunyan*.
4 Roger Sharrock, *John Bunyan*.
5 Erik Erikson, *Young Man Luther*.
6 W. N. Evans, 'Notes on the Conversion of John Bunyan'.

9

The Influence of Bunyan

The remarkable sales of the first part of *The Pilgrim's Progress* — eleven editions in the first ten years — took Bunyan's ideas into many homes in which, as in Bunyan's youthful home, there were few books apart from the Bible, Foxe's *Book of Martyrs*, and a chap-book or two. Upon such virgin soil it must have made the same forceful impact that Bayly and Dent had made upon Bunyan, though his readers were luckier than he had been. They had an exciting story, laced with the heroism and adventure of the chap-books, through which to learn Bunyan's interpretation of the human condition. Later Macaulay was to observe that *The Pilgrim's Progress* was 'loved by those who are too simple to admire it'.[1] 'In the wildest parts of Scotland *The Pilgrim's Progress* is the delight of the peasantry. In every nursery *The Pilgrim's Progress* is a greater favourite than Jack the Giant-killer.' Part of Bunyan's remarkable success in his own time was due to the fact that a whole new class, one barely educated, was passionately interested in theological thinking in a way that seems scarcely imaginable today. He gave them theology in a digestible form.

He was so perfectly suited to the needs and tastes of the second half of the seventeenth century that he became the kind of household name that is not rooted out of men's memory for several generations. The eighteenth century, with its classical taste, and its dislike of raw natural feeling, was a long way from Bunyan's rough pilgrims and folksy asides, and few writers championed him openly, yet there was a warm underground stream of sympathy for Bunyan noticeable among distinguished men.

Richardson, writing in 1742, made a guess that most people probably preferred Bunyan to the fashionable Pope. 'A Quarles or a Bunyan may be of greater Use to the Multitude who cannot taste, or edify by, the Superlative than Mr. Pope's writing . . . Are all Men born to Taste? No. If they were, what an infamous Death would hardly be too severe a Punishment for those petty Writers who were to mishandle it . . . But neither are the Works of all even fine Writers, to be compared to the Works of the two I have named, in their Morality and Piety.'[2]

Dr. Johnson had a deep and unashamed love of Bunyan. Impatient with long books to the point where he scarcely ever read any of them right through, *The Pilgrim's Progress* was one of the three books — the others were *Don Quixote* and *Robinson Crusoe* — which he wished longer.

Boswell has a story of Johnson taking Dr. Thomas Percy's little daughter on his knee and asking her what she thought of the *Progress*. She said she had not read it.

'No!' replied the Doctor, 'then I would not give one farthing for you,'[3] and he set the child down and pretended to ignore her.

He thought the best evidence of the merit of the book was its 'general and continued approbation' among mankind. 'It is remarkable that it begins very much like the poem of Dante; yet there was no translation of Dante when Bunyan wrote. There is reason to think he had read Spenser.'

Boswell, borrowing the idea from Mrs. Piozzi, suggests that Johnson, with his pathological terror of death, bears a strong resemblance to Bunyan's Mr. Fearing. His fear is not about petty everyday things — he is full of courage — but about 'Acceptance at last'. 'It was only sin, death and hell that were to him a terror.'

Swift, about to publish *Gulliver's Travels*, hoped that it might have as good 'a run' as 'Bunyan', and Pope talked of having his works handed out free in the streets as he claimed Bunyan's had been.

Nevertheless, in the eighteenth century, Bunyan was not in fashion. Richardson is slightly apologetic for his championship, Johnson can only afford it because his stance is that of an oldfashioned Tory, Cowper observed that he dare not mention Bunyan in his verse, 'for fear of moving a sneer'. It is the fate usually suffered by supremely successful authors a generation after their death.

Bunyan might have dwindled into oblivion but for the shift of taste towards the lone hero which came with the Romantic movement in the early part of the nineteenth century. What did more to rehabilitate him than anything was the edition of *The Pilgrim's Progress* published by John Murray in 1830 introduced by Robert Southey with a life of the author. Southey was a warm and generous man, with real gifts of insight and appreciation, and his fair but enthusiastic assessment of Bunyan's importance is immediately appealing. He comments on the way Bunyan's fame had recently begun to increase, and the way the common people had understood and appreciated him long before the intellectuals — 'the opinion of the multitude had been ratified by the judicious' is how he puts it. He makes a rather startling comparison between Bunyan and Rousseau; Rousseau also set the question of his salvation upon a cast, (as Bunyan was tempted to do on the road between Elstow and Bedford); he suffered similar agonies of unbelief and deadly fear, and he was troubled by a constant awareness of 'The Enemy'.

What is most interesting about Southey, however, particularly in view of the naïveté of so much that was written about Bunyan in the Victorian period, is his clear-sightedness about Bunyan's psychological make-up. He notes the 'prurient scrupulosity of the man' and warns his readers (would that later writers like Offor had remembered!) that 'the wickedness of the Tinker has been greatly over-charged'. He says bluntly that Bunyan was unreasonable and intolerant at his trial (so far as I know this makes him the only critic of Bunyan to make this observation), and he is psychologically offended by some of Bunyan's early sermons, no doubt *A Few Sighs from Hell* among them. 'Some passages occur in them which may make us shudder; these are very few.'

He sees Bunyan with admirable clarity, criticising with justice some of his feebler verses, yet he loves and admires and commends him. Such cool detachment is rare among those who write about Bunyan, since those who admire him seem to have a tendency to want him to be perfect, and those who dislike him notice only his mental conflicts and his bleak Calvinism. With a zest that the Victorians would not have appreciated, Southey remarks that Bunyan was 'no mealy-mouthed writer'; he would not have appealed to the Romantics if he had been.

Southey was trying to assess Bunyan's literary significance as distinct from his religious insights, an attempt which reaped considerable scorn from Coleridge. A copy of the Southey *Pilgrim's Progress* was sent by John Murray to Henry Coleridge, Samuel Taylor Coleridge's son, and in this copy, now in the British Museum, the father made notes of his opinions of both Bunyan and Southey. Coleridge wrote on the fly-leaf:

I know of no Book the Bible excepted as above all comparison — which I according to my judgment and experience could so safely recommend as teaching and enforcing the whole saving Truth according to the mind that was in Christ Jesus, as The Pilgrim's Progress. It is in *my* conviction, incomparably the best *Summa Theologia Evangelicae* ever produced by a Writer not miraculously inspired.
Grove, Highgate.   S. T. Coleridge.

14 June 1830

P.S. It disappointed, nay, surprised me, to find R.S. express himself so coldly respecting the Style and Diction of the Pilgrim's Progress. I can find nothing *homely* in it but a few phrases and single words. The Conversation between Faithful and Talkative is a model of unaffected correctness, dignity and rythmical Flow.

Coleridge goes on, in notes throughout the book, to be fairly critical himself of Bunyan, in particular for his inconsistent and sometimes illogical way of using allegory. 'The allegory is clearly defective' he writes in one place, and in another, the account of Passion and Patience in the House of the Interpreter, 'One of the not many instances of a faulty allegory'. This particular bit of allegory he thinks is 'not legitimately imaginable'. Of the image of the Fire at the House of the Interpreter he says, 'This is beautiful; yet I cannot but think, it would have been more appropriate, if the Waterpourer had been a Mr. Legality, a prudentialist offering his calculations of *Consequence* as the moral antidote to Guilt and Crime.'

Coleridge was an attentive reader. He noted each of the misprints — 'Ward' for 'Word', 'Sun' for 'Son', 'heart' for 'harp' — and when Bunyan makes Great-heart ask Old Honest his name, having just called him by it a few minutes earlier, he notes, 'There seems some forgetfulness here as to the name.' One of his most interesting comments is a gloss on the passage in the Valley of the Shadow where blasphemy floats through

Christian's mind, whether originating there or put there by devils he is not quite sure. Coleridge writes:

> There is a very beautiful Letter of Archbishop Leighton's to a Lady under a similar distemperature of the Imagination. In fact, it can scarcely not happen under any weakness and consequent irritability of the nerves to persons constantly occupied with spiritual self-examination: No part of the pastoral duties require more discretion, a greater practical psychological science. In this, as in what not? Luther is the great Model — ever reminding the individual that *not* he but Christ is to redeem him — and that the way to be redeemed is to think with will, mind and affection on Christ, not on *himself*.

At Bunyan's reference to the Cave of Pope, Coleridge reveals the anti-Catholic prejudice that was so typical of nineteenth century England. 'O that Blanco White would write, in Spanish, the Progress of a Pilgrim from the Pope's Cave to the Evangelical Wicket-Gate and the Interpreter's House!'

Coleridge's warmest acclamation of Bunyan is reserved for the passage where Christian and Faithful are discussing the need for both 'Saying' and 'Doing' for a Christian, since 'the Soul of Religion is the practick part'. Coleridge marked the passage, 'It will not be said then, Did you believe? but, Were you Doers, or Talkers only? and accordingly shall they be judged.' Beside the whole passage he wrote, 'All the Doctors of the Sorbonne could not have better stated the Gospel Median between Pelagianism and Anti-nomian Solifidianism (more properly named, Sterilifidianism). It is indeed Faith alone that saves us; but such a Faith as cannot be alone. Purity and Beneficence are the Epidermis, Faith = Love the Cutis vera of Christianity. Morality is the outside Cloth, Faith the Lining. Both together form the Wedding garment given to the true Believer by Christ.'

Coleridge was highly critical of Southey, partly because of his detachment from Bunyan's conflicts, both mental and political; it seemed to annoy him that Southey observed Bunyan coolly, not with passionate partisanship, and did not play upon his readers' feelings of moral indignation. He clearly felt that, theologically-speaking, he himself was more knowledgeable than Southey. At one point where Southey describes Bunyan as a 'Calvinist', Coleridge notes 'Bunyan *may* have been one; but

I have met with nothing in his writing that is not much more characteristically *Lutheran*'. Again where Southey wonders whether the way Bunyan and his sectarian brethren read the Bible was not actually harmful to them, Coleridge takes up the Protestant cudgels. 'Promiscuous Bible-reading' as he rather charmingly calls it could, he admits, have its dangers, yet the advantages far outweigh them.

In Southey and Coleridge we observe two very different men approaching Bunyan's work from different points of view. Southey is much more the 'modern' literary critic, using literary criteria. Coleridge, though so well able to apply literary criteria, as in the case of the defective allegory, prefers to consider Bunyan principally within a framework of Christian orthodoxy. Southey attempts to lift Bunyan out of his narrowly Christian influence and make him universally available; Coleridge insists on examining his art solely in Christian terms.

Not everyone felt as angry with Southey as Coleridge. Macaulay on the whole approved of 'the Life', though like Coleridge he felt Southey was not sufficiently upset by the political persecution of Bunyan. While noting the imperfections in Bunyan's use of allegory, Macaulay claimed that the *Progress* was the only English allegory with 'strong human interest'. Bunyan far outdid Johnson, Addison and Spenser in his mastery of his material.

> Other allegories only amuse the fancy. The allegory of Bunyan has been read by many thousands with tears . . . This is the highest miracle of genius, that things which are not should be as though they were . . . Cowper said, forty or fifty years ago, that he dared not name John Bunyan in his verse, for fear of moving a sneer . . . We live in better times, and we are not afraid to say, that, though there were many clever men in England during the latter half of the seventeenth century, there were only two minds which possessed the imaginative faculty in a very eminent degree. One of these minds produced *Paradise Lost*, the other *The Pilgrim's Progress*.[4]

Two years before the famous Murray edition of the *Progress* appeared, Charles Lamb's friend, the publisher Bernard Barton, wrote to him to tell him about it. Lamb replied in mocking tones that incidentally revealed how much the *Progress* had meant to him in his childhood, unfashionable as it had been.

A splendid edition of Bunyan's Pilgrim — why, the thought is enough to turn one's moral stomach. His cockle hat and staff transformed to a smart cock'd beaver and a jemmy cane, his amice gray to the last Regent Street cut, and his painful Palmer's pace to the modern swagger. Stop thy friend's sacrilegious hand. Nothing can be done for B. but to reprint the old cuts in as honest a style as possible. The Vanity Fair, and the pilgrims there — the silly soothness in his setting-out countenance — the Christian idiocy (in the good sense) of his admiration of the Shepherds on the Delectable Mountains, the Lions so truly Allegorical and remote from any similitude to Pidcock's. The great head (the author's) capacious of dreaming and similarly dreaming in the dungeon. Perhaps you don't know *my* edition, what I had when a child; if you do, can you learn new designs from Martin, enameld into copper and silver plate by Heath, accompanied with verses from Mrs. Heman's pen.[5]

As it happened, when the new edition emerged the introductory verses were not by Mrs. Hemans but by Barton himself, and Lamb approved sufficiently to write and tell Southey that the book was 'beautiful', though a somewhat critical review (said to have been written by Lamb) appeared in *The Times*.

In 1829 Lamb reported in a letter to Barton that he had found an old version of the *Progress* on the stalls in the Barbican and had bought it for 4/-, along with a sheepskin' edition of Thomas Aquinas.

As the nineteenth century wore on the aesthetic pleasure that a man like Southey could take in Bunyan became less important than the evangelical attraction of his work. Innumerable editions of the *Progress* were published, many of them edited by clergymen who gave copious notes of an 'improving' kind and illustrated the text with dramatic and sentimental steel-engravings. A collected edition of the works of Bunyan was first made by George Offor in 1853, published by Blackie and Son of Glasgow in three volumes. This went into other editions. It included a memoir of Bunyan, and pages of evangelical commentary of the most cloying kind, notable for a paranoia that far outdid Bunyan, anti-Catholic prejudice, and crushing propriety. This was how Offor described Elizabeth Bunyan's miscarriage following Bunyan's arrest: 'When her partner was sent to jail, she was in that peculiar state that called for all his sympathy and his tenderest care. The shock was too severe for her delicate situation; she became dangerously ill, and, although her life was spared, all hopes had fled, of her maternal feelings being called into exercise.' (*Memoir of John Bunyan*). It is instructive to compare this with Elizabeth Bunyan's own plain words on the subject: 'I being smayed at the news, fell into labour, and so continued for eight days, and then was delivered, but my child died.'[6]

The first, and the best, of the Bunyan biographies was published by the Reverend John Brown in 1885. This was to run into many editions and to be revised by others and republished again after Brown's death. Brown was also a devoted editor of Bunyan's works, bringing out editions of *The Holy War*, *Grace Abounding*, *The Pilgrim's Progress*, and *The Life and Death of Mr. Badman*.

Those who did not share evangelical enthusiasms inevitably felt a lessening of sympathy towards Bunyan. Matthew Arnold (perhaps also reacting to his father Dr. Arnold of Rugby's, warm enthusiasm for Bunyan) called him a 'Philistine of genius'. He placed him among 'the fanatics of the *what*, the neglectors of the *why*', a group of human beings which, he claimed, not infrequently produced men of genius. 'They have the temperament which influences, which prevails, which acts magnetically upon men. So we have the Philistine of genius in religion — Luther; the Philistine of genius in politics — Cromwell; the Philistine of genius in literature — Bunyan.'[7]

In America interest in Bunyan had taken a rather different path. There was a sense in which the lone pilgrim of the *Progress* setting off into unknown country mirrored the personal experience of many Americans in the eighteenth and early nineteenth century. 'The wilderness of this world . . .' which Bunyan mentions at the beginning of the *Progress* assumed, as David Smith points out, a significance beyond Bunyan's imagination.[8] The vast untamed wilderness of the uninhabited country, with its dangers of hostile Indians, wild animals, trackless wastes and ravines was threatening in very much the same way as the unknown country which lay before Christian was threatening. Somewhere on the far side of it — westwards in American terms — lay the goal, the reward, the Celestial City.

Charles Sanford in *The Quest for Paradise* suggests that the millenial strain in Puritan thought with its emphasis on the imminence of perfection was a matrix of American culture. Closely linked with this expectation of perfection (as in Bunyan who is not, in my view, truly a millenialist) is a sense of mission or pilgrimage, of hardships to be endured in the present on the way to, or as a condition of, perfection. The early colonists had this sense of pilgrimage to a marked degree, and the hardships of their lives in a new country served to reinforce it.

One of the first writers consciously to link Bunyan's pilgrim to the American experience was Joseph Morgan. In *The Kingdom of Basaruah* (1715) he borrowed and adapted from Bunyan to form a pilgrimage account that accorded with the American experience. D. E. Smith states:

> The basic metaphor of Morgan's tale is that of a vast tract of wilderness through which some few paths lead, and on the borders of which flows a broad body of water forming an impassable barrier. The task of the disinherited inhabitants of this virtually impenetrable wilderness consists mainly of weeding out its poisonous plants and subduing its wild beasts.

As we saw earlier the New England Puritan Thomas Hooker thought of human conduct in terms of pruning and training what was wild and uncivilised in man — 'we would have garden love and garden joy, of God's owne planting'. Similarly the colonists dreaded the wilderness before it could be domesticated.

> For Puritans, the term wilderness invariably signifies chaos. What one does *with* a wilderness when one is confronted with it and cannot escape it is amply illustrated in the case of the early generations of Puritan settlers, who 'fenced it out'. Wilderness implied wildness, beasts, poison, savages. If one must venture into the wilderness it should be to change it into a garden: that is to weed out and destroy its 'poisonous fruits' and to destroy or domesticate its savage beasts

Bunyan had thus begun to acquire a symbolic meaning in America which went far beyond his literary intentions, though he would have sympathised with it. As Smith points out, the American hobo eventually became the heir of Bunyan's wandering hero; the lone traveller who suffers the hardships and adventures of living without roots, recurs constantly in American literature and appears in Westerns to this day.

The Pilgrim's Progress was a best-seller in America in the first half of the nineteenth century and reached its peak of success in the 1840s. Many adaptations were made, often to rouse sympathy for one cause or another, or to attack a point of view the author disapproved of. William R. Weeks' *The Pilgrim's Progress in the Nineteenth Century*, originally published in the *Utica Christian Repository* during the years 1824-6, was a Calvinistic attack on liberal doctrine and all that he believed went with it — mesmerism, witchcraft, fairs, light reading, intemperance, slavery, theatres and Sabbath-breaking among other targets. Above all he attacked heresy — the dangerous '-isms' — Deism, Unitarianism, Transcendentalism and others which were then flourishing in America.

Another adaptation of the *Progress* was *Pilgrim's Progress in the Last Days* published by an unknown author in 1843. It was a millennialist book but, as with many tracts being issued at about this time, its principal target was slavery, and it foresaw the tragic conflict that was to come. Bunyan was being more and more used by the abolitionists as an ally, and the phraseology he used in the *Holy War* was eventually to be applied by them to the Civil war.

There was a passionate idealism abroad in the America of the 1840s which found expression in an attempt to build little Utopias or Edens upon earth like that of Fruitlands, what we should call a 'community' founded by Bronson Alcott, Louisa Alcott's father and Charles Lane at Harvard, Massachusetts, or Nathaniel Hawthorne's equally abortive attempt to 'return to the land' at Brook Farm.

One of the most famous of Bunyan's champions in America was The Reverend George Barrell Cheever, a rather livelier version of the clergymen who pored so assiduously over Bunyan in nineteenth-century England. Cheever gave a set of lectures on Bunyan in the 1840s which were a huge success and Bunyan recurs constantly in his writing. Cheever was an evangelical millenialist who believed in temperance, and a strict observance of the Sabbath (he was against railroads operating on Sunday), and who passionately opposed slavery and the removal of the Indians. He was the enemy of liberalism in all its forms, and of 'progress', and to these ends he pressed Bunyan into his service, both by direct quotation and by imitation of his allegorical style.

Amongst these pre-war writers who were influenced by Bunyan was one who was an artist, and who saw beyond the simplicities of evangelical solutions to some of the deeper complexities of the human condition; Nathaniel Hawthorne.

Hawthorne was born, and lived as a child, in Salem, steeped in the beliefs and traditions of New England. He had read Bunyan, Spenser and Milton as a child, and he knew in his bones the solemn introspection of Puritanism, but unlike most others who were using Bunyan to promote their point of view he no longer identified completely with the religious beliefs that had inspired Bunyan. He was a Puritan by temperament and habit rather than by conviction.

The new note of ambivalence which a writer like Hawthorne expressed (no doubt on behalf of many of his generation) appears in his short story *The Canterbury Pilgrims*. A young man and woman, very simply dressed, pause to drink from a spring on the side of a hill. They have left the nearby Shaker village; they are in love, and wish to get married, thus offending against the strict celibacy of the Shaker community from which they come. So they have decided to leave and seek their fortune in the world. While they are drinking and resting, three men and a woman, and two children approach from the other direction, and ask the way to the Shaker village. Each of them, it turns out, has tried what the world has to offer, in terms of material success and human love, and found that it does not satisfy them or bring them joy, so they have decided, like Bunyan's pilgrim, to renounce the world. Somewhat depressed by their example, the young Shaker couple are still not deterred, however; they continue on *their* pilgrimage towards 'the World'.

Hawthorne's ambivalence is perfectly conveyed. He fully understands the disillusion and disappointment with the world that gives a Puritan 'yon-side' religion its attraction, yet he sees that 'the World' also demands its due, that it is part of a necessary balance, and that those denied its satisfactions develop an ineradicable yearning for them.

Hawthorne derived much from his childhood reading of Bunyan. Not just the suspicion of the world — which he imbibed in any case from his whole New England inheritance — but a kind of natural allegorical sense and an emblematic use of nature. Rocks, precipices, pine trees, forests, narrow pathways and dangerous by-ways, represent not only the New England forests of his childhood, or the country of Maine which he explored as a youth, but also the peculiar dangers and frustrations of the human spirit.

Yet he saw that the problem of human existence was more complex than Bunyan had believed. 'The World' did not 'work', it was true; a life given over to worldly objectives did not bring happiness and contentment. Yet renouncing 'the World' did not seem to work either. Hawthorne lived in a period of heroic experiments, in which unworldly men were prepared to sacrifice themselves to high ideals, just as Bunyan had recommended. Yet in Hawthorne's own case and in that of others, like Bronson Alcott, this path did not lead to Utopia but to failure and hurt. He has become disillusioned with reform, whether of the individual or of society, and it is out of his bewilderment that he writes. There is, perhaps, some envy of the original simplicity and integrity of Puritan thought.

All these strains appear in his short story 'The Celestial Railroad',[9] yet another adaptation of The Pilgrim's Progress, but one with a satirical purpose. The satire is not at Bunyan's expense, but at the expense of the many in American society of his day who thought they had found some short cut to spiritual fulfilment. Because Hawthorne himself had fallen under the influence of William Miller and the millenialist George Ripley, and come to regret it, he is particularly suspicious of lofty idealism, reform and 'progress'.

At the beginning of 'The Celestial Railroad' he explains that a railroad has now been built between the City of Destruction and the Celestial City, so that pilgrims no longer have to make that painful and difficult journey on foot. Mr. Smooth-it-away, the director and chief stockholder of the railroad corporation has seen to all that. There is a fine bridge over the Slough of Despond, and a station-house instead of the old wicket-gate, where Evangelist obligingly sells tickets. Nobody carries a burden any more; the travellers' luggage is snugly deposited in the baggage-car for the duration of the journey. Nowadays, too, there is a better class of traveller.

Instead of a lonely and ragged man with a huge burden on his back, plodding along sorrowfully on foot while the whole city hooted after him here were parties of the first gentry and most respectable people in the neighbourhood setting forth towards the Celestial City as cheerfully as if the pilgrimage were merely a summer tour. Among the gentlemen were characters of deserved eminence — magistrates, politicians, and men of wealth, by whose example religion could not but be recommended to their meaner brethren. In the ladies' appartment, too, I rejoiced to distinguish some of the flowers of fashionable society, who are so well fitted to adorn the most elevated circles of the Celestial City. There was much pleasant conversation about the news of the day, topics of business and politics, or the lighter matters of amusement; while religion, though indubitably the main thing at heart, was thrown tactfully into the background. Even an infidel would have found nothing to shock his sensibility.

It turns out that the porters, stokers, etc. who maintain the railroad are all in the pay of Prince Beelzebub, while Apollyon is Chief Engineer. A tunnel has been skilfully constructed through the Hill Difficulty, the Valley of Humiliation has been filled in, and 'inflammable gas' now illuminates the darkness of the Valley of the Shadow. The narrator of the story, an ingenuous fellow who has eagerly looked forward to meeting all the people in *The Pilgrim's Progress*, is disappointed to find that many of the old characters are gone — Greatheart has been made redundant, and the pretty young virgins of the House Beautiful are all dried up old maids.

The cave where old Pope used to sit mouthing curses at the travellers is now inhabited by Giant Transcendentalism who 'makes it his business to seize upon honest travellers and fatten them for his table with plentiful meals of smoke, mist, moonshine, raw potatoes and sawdust'.

At Vanity Fair, a place supervised by the Rev. Mr. This-to-day and the Rev. Mr. That-to-morrow the travellers feel entirely at home. Conscience, 'a sort of stock or scrip', is now the chief commodity on sale. 'A man's business was seldom very lucrative unless he knew precisely when and how to throw his hoard of conscience into the market.' The Fair offers instant satisfactions. If a man wants 'Youth', for instance, this is quickly supplied by a 'set of false teeth and an auburn wig'. If he prefers peace of mind then that too can be laid on with opium or a brandy bottle. A peculiarity of the Fair is that people 'vanish like a soap bubble'. Nobody seems to notice this, or remark upon it, however.

The nice final stroke is that no one is any longer forced to wade across the terrifying River of Death. A steam ferry boat takes the passengers across and there are coaches waiting to meet it on the far side. Just as the narrator is about to arrive he is splashed by the water of the river, he shudders, and awakes. It was a dream!

Hawthorne's wry humour is at the expense of himself and his contemporaries. Bunyan was still deeply admired. David Smith suggests that the Civil War brought about a change in American feeling about Bunyan. Before the War admiration and emulation of him knew no bounds. After the War, partly perhaps because of the self-righteous zeal of the Abolitionists, he began to be travestied and parodied on the one hand, or, by some of his greatest admirers, to be trivialised on the other. In *The Innocents Abroad* (1869) Mark Twain assumes a certain disillusion and amusement at the whole idea of pilgrimage. The New Jerusalem is now the goal only of the naive.

Or it is an ideal for children. In *Little Women* (1868) the March girls play at being pilgrims. Their mother gives each of them a copy of *The Pilgrim's Progress* as a Christmas present, and each girl tries to bear whatever her 'burden' is, in their case the burden of temperamental difficulties and impoverished circumstances. David Smith points out that, unlike Christian, who gave up all that was familiar to him, and set off into the unknown, the children in *Little Women* never leave home. Home is the setting of the journey, and in a strange way, it is also the Celestial City; the happy ending consists in the fact that all the girls, except Beth who dies, achieve homes of their own with husbands whom they love. Smith sees Miss Alcott's book as a cheapening of Bunyan's vision. The daring, the imaginative leap was gone, and in its place was a concern for the social proprieties, and a covert admiration of fashion and wealth.

> The paradox of *Little Women* is that, although Vanity Fair is repre-
> sented superficially by the elegance, conspicuous consumption, and
> vicarious leisure of the Moffats, whom Meg visits on holiday,
> ultimately the dreams of such elegance control the hopes and destinies
> of the Little Women themselves. Vanity Fair dominates *Little Women*,
> in spite of Miss Alcott's intentions to the contrary, and ultimately each
> girl becomes rich, not poor, fashionable, not unfashionable, and happy,
> not miserable. To put it another way, Bunyan's Christian were he to
> have returned to Concord in 1870, would have regarded the circum-
> stances of all the March girls as smacking of the Cities of Destruction
> and Carnality. The kind of pilgrimage undertaken by the March
> girls . . . led ultimately only as far as the City of Vanity.

Is this fair to Miss Alcott, I wonder? She was writing for children and young people who expected a happy ending, yet there is a genuine note of Puritan resolution in her work that Mr. Smith seems to ignore altogether. By nursing the sick baby of a poor immigrant German family Beth contracts scarlet fever, an illness that so undermines her health that she eventually dies, seemingly of tuberculosis. Mr. March, though past the age for active service, insists on serving in the Army during the Civil War because he believes in the ideals for which the War is being fought. The book reveals a good deal of psychological insight about just how hard it is to love others genuinely, particularly those with whom you live. The note of introspection and self-examination is sounded in the characters' struggles with anger, envy, greed, selfishness and pride, struggles skilfully dramatised in a plausible story.

Carnality does not seem to be, as Mr. Smith suggests, the underlying design of Miss Alcott, but he is on stronger ground, perhaps, when he notes the near-deification of the home and the family. It would be impossible to suggest to any of these pilgrims, as Evangelist did to Christian, that spiritual growth might lie in leaving home and family. Nor was Miss Alcott alone in her attitude. Mr. Smith quotes a 'devout church lady' of the 1880s who, watching a dramatic production of *The Pilgrim's Progress* was heard to whisper, 'Are we expected to admire Christian for running away and leaving his family in the City of destruction?' America had moved a very long way from the harsh Puritanism of Jonathan Edwards and other uncompromising forebears. Bunyan, who had once been used to uphold that same lack of compromise, had become part of the comfortable pious furniture that obstructed change.

In England, only a decade later, Bunyan was to gain the public championship of a very different kind of writer from Miss Alcott — Bernard Shaw. Shaw had loved Bunyan as a child; one of his early memories was of reading *The Pilgrim's Progress* aloud to his father at the age of about five, and of his father correcting his pronunciation from 'grievious' to 'grievous'.[10] He remembers how he thrilled to the battle between Christian and Apollyon, and again to Great-heart's struggles with giants.[11] In his old age he said that every child ought to be given the *Progress*, *Aesop's Fables* and the Book of Genesis.

Nostalgia for his childhood no doubt accounted in part for Shaw's admiration of Bunyan, yet his enthusiasm went far beyond sentimental affection. In the *Saturday Review* of 2nd January, 1897, Shaw eulogised

Bunyan at the expense of one of his favourite targets, Shakespeare. None of Shakespeare's characters, he complains 'believes in life, enjoys life, thinks life worth living'. Shakespeare 'understood nothing and believed nothing', and so the creatures of his imagination reveal no 'faith, hope, courage, conviction, or any of the true heroic qualities'. The unity for which he looks in vain in the works of Shakespeare, he claims to find in Bunyan,

to whom the true heroic came quite obviously and naturally. The world was to him a more terrible place than it was to Shakespeare, but he saw through it a path at the end of which a man might look not only forward to the Celestial City, but back on his life and say 'Though with great difficulty I am got hither, yet now I do not repent me of all the trouble I have been at to arrive where I am. My Sword, I give to him that shall succeed me in my Pilgrimage, and my Courage and Skill, to him that can get it.' The heart vibrates like a bell to such a passage as this.

Even in the matter of poetry, Shaw tries to prove Bunyan superior to Shakespeare. He compares:

Yet I will try the last: before my body
I throw my warlike shield. Lay on, Macduff,
And damned be him that first cries Hold, enough.

from *Macbeth* with Apollyon's speech uttered under similar stress: 'I am void of fear in this matter. Prepare thyself to die; For I swear by my infernal den that thou shalt go no further: here will I spill thy soul.'

He compares other fighting words of Shakespeare's with Mr. Valiant-for-Truth's account of mortal battle. 'I fought till my Sword did cleave to my Hand, and when they were joyned together, as if a Sword grew out of my Arm, and when the Blood run thorow my Fingers, then I fought with most courage.'

'Nowhere in all Shakespeare,' says Shaw 'is there a touch like that of the blood running down through the man's fingers, and his courage rising to passion at it.'

Bunyan's English, he feels, is not cluttered like Shakespeare's, with classical affectations. 'Here there is no raving and swearing and rhyming and classical allusions. The sentences go straight to their marks; and their concluding phrases soar like the sunrise, or swing and drop like a hammer, just as the actor wants them.'

The most passionate admirer of Bunyan must feel that Shaw is overdoing his partisanship. Selecting the weakest passage of Shakespeare, and the strongest passage of Bunyan and comparing them is a strange, and unfair, method of literary criticism; it ignores the astounding variety and depth of Shakespeare's perceptions, and the poetry that illuminated so many human landscapes. Bunyan's perception and his poetry is almost entirely confined to one mode of human experience — that of spiritual journey — though in that mode he is a master. The question must be why Shaw, who did not even subscribe to the belief upon which Bunyan's concept of the spiritual journey was based, valued Bunyan so highly.

An American critic, Norbert F. O'Donnell, has argued plausibly that Shaw was using Bunyan for a polemic purpose.[12] Shaw's critical intention was to establish a certain sort of play in the London theatre of his day, a play of serious social intention aimed at persuading an audience to ask fundamental questions about the world in which they lived. The questions were, following Ibsen, about the social, moral, political and financial organisation of their world, and they had a reformist intention. Shakespeare, who had no such reformist intention in his plays, and who was more interested in the workings of the individual mind and the heart than of societies, thus became representative of all that Shaw opposed. Bunyan, who was clearly a reformist writer, was similarly used by Shaw as representative of a whole class of writers, even though the reforms he had in mind were quite different from those that Shaw envisaged.

What obviously moved Shaw in artists he admired was a propagandist intention. He seemed to draw a special pleasure and inspiration from artists who had a passionately held belief for which they were prepared to sacrifice themselves — 'artist-philosophers' as he called them. They demonstrated the vitalism which was his religion, what he called 'the struggle of Life to become divinely conscious of itself instead of blindly stumbling hither and thither in the line of least resistance'.[13] It was not just that they were brave, or that they talked of life in stirring terms, but that they exhibited a sense of purpose, they seemed to know where they were going and so managed to convince others that there was somewhere to go. 'This is the true joy in life, the being used for a purpose recognised by yourself as a mighty one; the being thoroughly worn out before you are thrown on the scrap heap; the being a force of Nature instead of a feverish selfish little clod of ailments and grievances complaining that the world will not devote itself to making you happy.'

It was this sense of purpose that Shaw looked for in art, and this is the main reason that he loved Bunyan. Like Mr. Valiant-for-Truth, so fired by the excitement of battle that he does not worry about the blood dripping through his fingers, he sees man at his happiest and best when he is living beside himself or beyond himself, lost in what he believes is a good cause. What he cannot forgive Shakespeare is that he is prepared to look at, as it were, the opposite end of the spectrum to Valiant-for-Truth's exaltation, at the mood of total disillusion, the fear that man's life may be meaningless. His greatest contempt for Shakespeare is reserved for his expression of disillusion. '[Shakespeare] never struck the great vein — the vein in which Bunyan told of that 'man of a very stout countenance' who went up to the keeper of the book of life and said, not "Out, out brief candle" but "Set down my name, sir".'[14]

Shaw is determinedly optimistic, reformist and progressive, a rogue-Marxist, who seems convinced that Bunyan is, did he but know it, marching under the same banner. This becomes most ludicrously apparent when he tries to pretend, on the strength of a very few pages in *The Life and Death of Mr. Badman* on the subject of commercial sharp practice, that Bunyan is a social reformer. There have been one or two attempts, since Shaw's day, to enlist Bunyan as a Marxist born before his time,* but any careful reading of Bunyan's works makes this view impossible to sustain.

Bunyan was not 'optimistic'. He did not believe that any lasting good was likely to come in 'this world' and when he paid the sacrificial price of a long imprisonment for his beliefs, it was more from loyalty to a 'yon-side' state of joy and happiness, than from any hope or ambition of making a world safe for Nonconformists to live in. We may guess that Bunyan knew more of the feeling of disillusion than Shaw permitted himself; he had languished in Doubting Castle as well as enjoying blood-stirring fights with Apollyon.

At times Shaw can admit that Bunyan disappoints or repels him. Shaw

* See Alick West, *The Mountain in the Sunlight* (London, 1958) and Jack Lindsay, *John Bunyan, Maker of Myths* (Methuen, 1937).

disliked St. Paul, feeling that it was he who had ruined Christianity before it had properly started, and he could only deplore the Pauline flavour of Bunyan's Christianity. He failed entirely to grasp the significance of the crucified Christ for Bunyan. 'If Jesus could have been consulted on Bunyan's allegory as to that business of the burden of sin dropping from the pilgrim's back when he caught sight of the cross, we must infer from his teaching that he would have told Bunyan in forcible terms that he had never made a greater mistake in his life, and that the business of a Christ was to make self-satisfied sinners feel the burden of their sins and stop committing them instead of assuring them that they could not help it, that it was all Adam's fault, but that it did not matter as long as they were credulous and friendly about himself.'[15]

Shaw has totally and wilfully misunderstood the very essence of Bunyan's thinking which, as we have seen, was that however hard man tried he *could not* be good. The importance of Christ and his cross for Bunyan, as for Luther, was that a man was released from the torment of hopeless trying. This was scarcely a point of view which was likely to recommend itself to the reformist and progressive Shaw — all reformists have a touch of Pelagianism about them — but it is interesting to notice that Shaw, like many nineteenth-century Americans, appeared to admire Bunyan on a totally mistaken premiss; they believed that he represented moral effort, the victory of the will over hostile circumstances. Whereas Bunyan clearly believed that excessive moral effort was a dangerous and doomed course of conduct (see Lord Will-be-will in *The Holy War*) and that hope lay in giving up the sovereignty of the will.

For all Shaw's misunderstanding of Bunyan, however, we cannot doubt that he did exercise an influence upon him and his work, particularly perhaps in his tendency to recognise courage in the person of the lone hero, a Romantic concept which owes much to Puritan thought. The trial scene of *St. Joan* is reminiscent of Elizabeth Bunyan's real life appearance before the justices of Bedford on behalf of her husband, and it is possible that there was a link in Shaw's mind, conscious or unconscious, between these two lonely and uneducated women, each exposed to the sophistication, the sarcasm, and the disbelief, of a male court. They are the epitome of weakness that takes on powerful forces yet wins a moral victory. Shaw, whose principal concern was how to bring about change in society, could not fail to be fascinated by their comparative success. Bunyan too, and his literary creation, Christian, had similarly challenged 'respectable society', and, instead of being overcome, had brought about change.

There may also be another link between Bunyan and Shaw. Chesterton suggested that Shaw was himself a Puritan, citing his contempt for social tradition, his refusal to drink alcohol, his 'desire to see truth face to face even if it slay us, the high impatience with irrelevant sentiment or obstructive symbol; the constant effort to keep the soul at its highest pressure and speed'.[16] O'Donnell points out, in addition, Shaw's attacks on the prurience of the London theatre, but he absolves Shaw from Puritanism, on the naive grounds that Shaw himself rejected the idea. Shaw claimed that the Puritan regarded the sex instinct, together with any form of beauty which might arouse it, as his great enemy, and on these grounds did not think he was a Puritan. O'Donnell adds that 'the sense of sin' and a 'belief in Christ' are at the heart of a Puritan's character. Obviously much depends upon how the word 'Puritan' is to be defined, a matter that is the concern of the next chapter. What Shaw quite clearly had in common with Bunyan and the whole Puritan movement was a dramatisation of the human condition, and in particular the conflict between good and evil; the battle lines were drawn in different places, but both saw life in soldierly terms.

A very different admirer of Bunyan was the poet e. e. cummings. When little more than a boy, cummings served as a driver with the American Red Cross in France during the First World War. On what appears to have been a mistake of identity, or anyhow guilt by association with a friend who had annoyed the French authorities, cummings was arrested and detained for several months in filthy and brutal prison conditions, and he later wrote a book about the experience, *The Enormous Room* (1922). Accustomed as we now are to books about prisons, labour-camps and worse, it does not fill us with a sense of shock or outrage, but in 1922 when it was published it did shock readers. It seemed to rip off the skin of conventional decencies and moralities, and suggest that the human animal underneath was cruel and ruthless. Part of the shock came from the fact that cummings used *The Pilgrim's Progress* — by now a classic completely domesticated to middle-class prejudices — to indicate the various discoveries that came to him in his personal hell.

At first sight the parallel appears vague — he does not attempt to follow the original with any precision — yet his deep, if disillusioned, understanding of Bunyan's meaning is moving. On the interminable journey to his place of confinement, the exhausted prisoner finds himself climbing a little hill. 'Every muscle thoroughly aching, head spinning, I half-straightened my no longer obedient body; and jumped: face to face with a little wooden man hanging all by itself in a grove of trees.

The wooden body clumsy with pain burst into fragile legs with absurdly large feet and funny writhing toes; its little stiff arms made abrupt, cruel, equal angles with the road. About its stunted loins clung a ponderous and jocular fragment of drapery. On one terribly brittle shoulder the droll lump of its neckless head ridiculously lived. There was in this complete silent doll a gruesome truth of instinct, a success of uncanny poignancy, an unearthly ferocity of rectangular emotion.

For perhaps a minute the almost obliterated face and mine eyed one another in the silent of intolerable autumn.

Who was this wooden man? Like a sharp, black, mechanical cry in the spongy organism of gloom stood the coarse and sudden sculpture of his torment; the big mouth of night carefully spurted the angular actual language of his martyred body. I had seen him in the dream of some medieval saint with a thief sagging at either side, surrounded by crisp angels. Tonight he was alone; save for myself, and the moon's minute flower pushing between slabs of fractured cloud.'

The prisoner had nearly arrived at his destination where he was to lay down the burden of his bed roll and duffel bag and begin in earnest the spiritual journey of captivity, the desperate struggle by way of starvation, brutality and despair to achieve an inner liberation.

The most striking feature of this terrible prison is its filth. Open buckets of urine, women and children staggering about carrying brimming pails, the perpetual stench of excrement, prisoners handcuffed together forced to urinate and defecate in unhappy unison, are, as it were, the canvas upon which cummings paints his infernal vision. Only the captors are clean and immaculate; the prisoners can never forget for a moment the filth which belongs to the human body; it becomes for them a sign of their brotherhood. David Smith sees in this cummings' rage, in the post-war years, against those who refused to face the stinking horror of the war, and, by extension, of human civilization — those who refused 'the actual smell' of life.

The Enormous Room was addressed to (the) unscented majority in the hope that it would be not merely shocked but that it would sense, somehow, beyond its Wrigley's Spearmint, Nujolneeding, Odorono values, that Christian brotherhood existed among human odors, not beyond them . . . In choosing for his prototype fool the overcivilised American with a supersensitive nose, cummings discovered an essential symbol. Inevitably, therefore, his own pilgrim would need to be able to smell his fellow human beings in order to progress with them towards the Delectable Mountains.

The Delectable Mountains of *The Enormous Room* are people, four prisoners, who, amid all the horror, remain as beacons of hope for the demoralised and degraded prisoners who live alongside them. They embody, says Smith, 'all possible human values — notwithstanding a totally corrupt civilisation which has unjustly attempted to destroy them'. The Delectable Mountains were not men of words — words were inadequate in such an extreme situation — but men who could simply 'be' and could communicate being. The greatest of these, was a sort of Christ-figure called Surplice, whose name, in the mouths of Dutch and Belgian prisoners emerged as 'Syph'lis', the symbol of human disgust and contempt. In him being is so complete that he feels no need to push his own needs over against those of others; totally humble, he is totally at one with his fellow-prisoners.

Remembering Bunyan's preoccupation with excremental imagery, we may guess that cummings' interpretation of the *Progress*, for all the affront that it gave to the America of his day, is nearer to the heart of Bunyan's meaning that Shaw's evolutionary zeal. Shaw, as his remarks about St. Paul reveal, sees evolutionary man as 'losing' the parts of him that feel shameful and degrading. cummings suggests the contrary; that it is only by fully admitting 'the dirt' within, that man becomes fully man and so capable of love and being, like his 'Delectable Mountains'. Similarly Bunyan knew that salvation was by way of 'conviction' — that is the discovery of his own filthiness in the Slough of Despond.

NOTES

1 *The Life and Works of Lord Macaulay*, Vol. V (1897).
2 Letter to George Cheyne by Samuel Richardson (1942–3).
3 Boswell, *Life of Dr. Johnson* (1791).

4 *The Life and Works of Lord Macaulay.*

5 Letter to Bernard Barton by Charles Lamb, 11th October 1828.

6 John Bunyan, *A Relation of My Imprisonment.*

7 Matthew Arnold, *Mixed Essays.*

8 David E. Smith, *John Bunyan in America,* Indiana University Press.

9 *Mosses from an Old Manse* (1846).

10 *Sixteen Self Sketches* (New York 1949).

11 *Everybody's Political What's What* (New York 1944).

12 Norbert F. O'Donnell, *Shaw, Bunyan and Puritanism,* Publications of the Modern Language Association, LXXII June 1957.

13 *Preface to Man and Superman* (1903).

14 *Saturday Review* (2nd January, 1897).

15 Preface to *Androcles and the Lion* (1913).

16 G. K. Chesterton, *George Bernard Shaw* (London, 1909).

I O

Puritan's Progress

———

There is real difficulty for us in perceiving the Puritan with clarity, since our minds are so familiar with the caricature and the stereotype that we cannot see beyond their partial truths to other aspects of Puritanism.

The caricature which Ben Jonson sketched of one of the original Puritans, and the many caricatures by other hands which followed, captured a likeness from a particular angle; Mr. Zeale-of-the Land Busy, with his tutting over the permissive society, his self-righteousness, and his compensatory eating had a resemblance to a personality with which no doubt every society is familiar; it also helped to condition people to look for such behaviour in Puritans.

Such caricatures do have a kind of truth, but it is a limited one. In observing nations, or races, we notice what seem to be universal characteristics — we think we know what a typical Englishman, or Frenchman, or negro is 'like'. Yet our certainty begins to fade as soon as our acquaintance is more than superficial; we see that the reality is far more complex, subtle and paradoxical than we had thought, and deeper knowledge supplies more and more profound corrections. Our original observations, however conditioned by prejudices, may not be entirely false. It is rather that we now see them within a much wider landscape in which they appear insignificant beside other features which we had not previously noticed. If we can set our received ideas about the Puritan in a wider landscape we may come to see him rather differently.

The stereotype of the Puritan declares him to be a man who deplores pleasure, more particularly the pleasure of sex. (When Bernard Shaw wished to refute Chesterton's charge that he was a Puritan he did so by saying that he enjoyed sex.) He also tends to disapprove of smoking and drinking alcohol, of the theatre and indeed all devices such as painting or fiction which invite us to take pleasure by living in fantasy.

When we come to examine the Puritan's suspicion of pleasure we find that there is a consistency in his point of view. Pleasure he regards as a sort of confusing tactic, designed to blind him to the reality of existence. What is that reality as he sees it? It is that man lives in a very, very harsh world in which he needs all his wits about him. Like the soldier on the battle-field he cannot afford intoxication, since survival may depend upon being totally in control of oneself.

It is this conviction that he is, all the time, in a desperate situation, that dictates so many of the Puritan's attitudes. He must watch himself constantly so that he does not sink into the torpor which spells death. He must be alert all the time, asking himself questions about what he is doing and why. He must be truthful with himself, forbidding himself comfortable illusions which may lull him into a false sense of security.

In conditions in which a man is principally concerned with survival what matters most to him is practical considerations, and it was on this basis of practicality that so many Puritan attitudes were formed. Smoking, drinking, dancing, theatre-going, reading works of fiction, had no obvious practical usefulness, in fact they all tended to interfere with that eminently practical device — work. Where pleasure is only incidental to a practical purpose — as in the case of sexual intercourse for the purpose of procreation — Puritans did not disapprove of it. Eating was not condemned as a source of enjoyment, as in the case of Jonson's Busy, because eating is an essentially practical activity.

Work, being both practical and often far from enjoyable, was a natural sphere of Puritan activity. It supplies the continual spur, the kind of perpetual discomfort, with which the Puritan was most comfortable. In addition to trying to survive in a harsh world, the Puritan was intensely preoccupied with justification — justification partly of his individual self, whom he seemed to find profoundly unsatisfactory, and of man collectively. Something, he felt, was wrong, both with himself and with all his own kind, and his attempt to put it right drove him in the direction of expiatory rituals, exercises which must not be pleasant since they must draw attention to the tormenting sense of shame. Work, the punishment which, according to Genesis, God had inflicted upon Adam, was the most far-reaching of these expiatory rituals. Of course, expiation produces its own devious kind of pleasure, since there is a lovely moment when the suffering stops, and when the guilt-feeling is removed. Attitudes to work among Puritans, and in particular the tendency to over-work, suggest this covert kind of satisfaction.

He had other compensations too. One of them lay in the 'yon-side' nature of his religion. 'The milk and honey is beyond this wilderness' Bunyan assured his congregation at Bedford. Mankind lives in the unspeakably arid desert to which God consigned Adam. There is no way back into Eden, but for those who are prepared to undertake a certain sort of journey, a journey marked with renunciations of illusory pleasure, there is another Eden to come, one in which the pleasures are no longer illusory.

Yet not all the pleasure is 'yon-side'. The Puritan has one, very genuine, pleasure in this world, and it is the pleasure of watching himself, as the lone hero, setting off into the unknown. It is a deeply Romantic pleasure, quite as Romantic as anything in fiction or drama, yet it is so deeply embedded in his understanding of life and of himself that he cannot perceive it as a fantasy. He is living his fantasy and so choosing to deny its illusory quality. He has made himself the central figure of a drama, and the whole of life has become an enthralling cliff-hanger.

It was this essentially dramatic quality of Puritanism that Shaw admired so deeply, perceiving, probably unconsciously, that it saved a man not only from boredom and a sense of futility, but what was worse, a total and corroding despair. Shakespeare dared to look at the terrible possibility that life might be meaningless, and Shaw could not forgive him for it.

Perhaps if we are to attempt a new definition of Puritanism it should be in terms of its essentially dramatic and purposeful view of the human lot, more especially when it is linked to a reforming zeal. By this definition of Puritanism, Shaw and Solzhenitsyn are Puritans no less than Bunyan.

Bunyan's reforming zeal, it must be admitted, differed considerably from Shaw's. Shaw, the socialist, and neo-Marxist, was interested in reform of this world. The 'progress' that he sought was progress to a better life in this world, a purpose he shared not just with Marxists but with Puritan sects such as the Quakers. Bunyan, on the other hand, did not suppose this world was going to get any better. 'Progress' was in terms of fitting yourself for the Celestial City. But in the end the two groups are not perhaps so different as it appears. Both believe that perfection is possible — they only differ about where and when. Both apply themselves to unceasing work to achieve the desired result, and both share a belief that life is not futile. It is a kind of optimism, though in Bunyan's case profoundly tempered with a pessimism about human nature which the Marxist does not share. The Marxist may thus be seen as within the Puritan tradition, though a naïve exponent of it.

To hold a dramatic view of human existence, with the individual (or the Party members) living out an heroic, and sacrificial life for the sake of 'progress' makes certain implications about life. It suggests that it is, in fact, harsh, and full of painful obstacles to be overcome. It leaves no room for a non-dramatic view of life as pleasant, easy, comfortable, amusing, or trivial.

Our opinion of the Puritan's approach to life must depend to some extent upon whether we believe life to be as harsh and as persecutory as he does. If it is, then his response is not so much paranoid as reasonable and realistic. If it isn't, then he has 'over-reacted'. If a man is being persecuted, whether by a tyrant, or by material hardships, then an attitude, however dramatic and Romantic, that helps him not only to survive but to transform the situation, can be shown to have practical creative value. If he is not being persecuted, but thinks he is, then the belief may be more damaging than it is creative.

The Puritan seems to be at his thriving best when, as in sixteenth- and seventeenth-century England, or New England, his life is attended with hardships and difficulties of all kinds. When life becomes easier, as it did in nineteenth-century America, he seems to search more and more desperately for a cause, and to ride more eccentric hobby-horses, or to become disillusioned as Hawthorne did. What he does not seem to want to consider is that life may not be dramatic, that he may not be called upon to be a hero, or that happiness now, not in some future state, is a proper ambition. In the bad times in human history the Puritan is a useful, indeed an irreplaceable, member of society. In good times, he tends to be a bore. We can neither quite do with him nor without him.

Not, of course, that there is really any choice. Psychological reconstructions suggest that physical type, together with the experiences of the first two years of life, are of crucial importance in determining later patterns in a man's life. Aggressiveness, excessive activity, conscientiousness, tidiness, punctuality, thrift, pedantry, rationality, suspiciousness, melancholia — all traits which a variety of writers, both historical and psychological, have ascribed to the Puritans — are traced, by responsible writers, to their beginnings in the history, and, as it were, the pre-history, of each individual. Very large numbers of people show these characteristics either singly, or, more usually, linked with several others. Some of them are extremely useful — the sheer efficiency of the Puritan can be of the greatest value to others — but useful or not they seem likely to continue, at least in modified form, unless our physique, and our childcare methods, undergo some almost unimaginable change.

Psycho-analysts such as Evans make out a good case for the Puritan as a man fixated at a fairly early stage of infantile development — the anal phase. He exhibits the classic preoccupation with the will, together with parsimony, and a preoccupation with sadistic fantasy, and because his libido has been checked or pruned at the 'pre-genital' stage, he never reaches the 'genital level' which Freud regarded as the final stage of libidinal development. He has paranoid characteristics, tending to use mechanisms of projection and denial. He has many of the signs of the obsessional character, and sometimes the symptoms of obsessional neurosis, and he is much troubled by guilt feelings as a result of unconscious fantasies. Ambivalence, particularly towards the father, and fatherfigures, is central to his character. The internalisation of the stern father, or rather of the child's early picture of him, helps form the 'super-ego', the part of the ego which turns in attack upon the ego as a whole, for failing to live up to impossible expectations.

In addition to his interest and importance socially, as part of, as it were, the ecology of human society — the Puritan is obviously of very great interest as a religious phenomenon.

His religion, like his social stance, is a religion of heroism and of stupendous effort. It is high drama, and the drama is partly one of overcoming seemingly impossible obstacles. Everything 'matters' — every deed, every thought, every event has a significance beyond itself that makes life appear intensely meaningful. Like the hero of adventure stories, the Puritan Christian teeters between life and death.

His religion is an ethical one, one which demands a most elaborate examination and control of conduct. Truthfulness is the key virtue, and is important not only in itself, but also in relation to all the other virtues; whatever a man professes to believe, that he must practice down to the last detail.

It is religion defined by a polarisation of good and evil (unlike, for example, some Eastern schools of religious thought where good and evil are seen as inextricably interwoven), which invites a man to reject what is bad in himself and others and cling only to the good. This emphasis on the division of good and evil is linked to a similar emphasis on being accepted or rejected, saved or damned. It is a religion of inclusion and exclusion, taking man out of his natural context where he is at one with the world about him, and making him acutely and often painfully aware of himself as an individual. It is intensely concerned with 'purity', hence the original nickname, and what this really means is perfection. Whether it is worship, church government, political government, or personal life that is being considered, the classic Puritan believes that perfection is attainable, and that it must be worked towards.

Some of these traits have been found from time to time in Catholicism, but they are much more marked in Protestantism, and the classic statement of them is in Calvinism. The Reformers saw many of their beliefs as a kind of antithesis of religion as practised in Catholic Europe: their strong emphasis on the responsibility of the individual, over against the individual's reliance on the authority of the Church: their emphasis on 'effort' over against the sort of comfortable *laissez-faire* that was represented by such practices as indulgencies; their emphasis on strict truthfulness and the matching of belief and conduct over against the corruption and hypocrisy of the medieval Church. It was a change which gave the 'naughty' side of man much less room to manoeuvre.

There are curious paradoxes at the heart of the Reformation. The Reformers believed that they were releasing men from the tyranny of justification by works and replacing it by justification by grace, yet the sense of 'work', of 'effort' at least in the Calvinist wing of the Reform, was far greater than it had been under Catholicism. At the heart of Protestantism there is an ambivalence about effort. Both Luther and Bunyan (like Augustine before them) carried effort to its furthest extremes, but at the core of their theology is the discovery that beyond a certain point effort is useless, that one must give up, and 'let be'. This is associated with a healing awareness of Christ and opens up a whole new range of possibilities — what Bunyan calls 'the Promise'.

Bunyan, whether looked at from the social, the psychological, or the religious point of view reveals many of the traits associated with Puritanism. He believed in 'progress', of a yon-side kind, and saw man as the lone hero, taking part in the dramatic conflict between good and evil. He believes the world to be a harsh place (and it lived up to his expectations by persecuting him cruelly).

He has many of the psychological traits which psycho-analysis associates with Puritanism — he reveals ambivalence, symptoms of obsessional neurosis and paranoid characteristics. In many respects he could be made out to be an 'anal' character.

Religiously-speaking, he shares the sense of effort and of 'meaningfulness', he is caught up in the battle between good and evil. He is deeply affected by the inclusive/exclusive nature of Christian thought; the issues of salvation and damnation interest him more than anything, at least in his years of crisis. He discovers that the way out of his dilemma is not effort, and more effort, but 'letting be', and he can only 'let be' because he discovers love. 'Thou art my Love, thou art my Love; and nothing shall separate thee from my love.' To this love he gives the name Christ.

Love, or Christ, becomes for him the path of his progress — the 'narrow way', and also the object to be attained at the end of the journey. ('I am going now to see that Head that was Crowned with Thorns, and that face that was spit upon, for me . . .') The journey is marked with signs of Christ's presence, as for instance the Cross where Christian loses his burden, and with tokens of his love — the 'broidered coat', the Roll, the help of Mr. Greatheart. If a pilgrim follows this path as well as he can, is not deceived by malicious wayfarers who give him bad advice, and not deterred by mistakes, accidents, and failures, then he reaches a place which he recognises as a completion, a fulfilment, a rounding-out of his partial experience. He knew the tokens of love. Now he lives with the reality.

Bunyan is describing a healing-process that he had personally experienced, and which he believed was available to others. Like most religious believers of his time he would have believed that he was talking about an experience only available to those who subscribed to the Lutheran Calvinist ideas about justification and salvation. It would not have occurred to him that many similar emotions and experiences might be available to people under very different systems of belief.

With more sociological, anthropological and psychological information at our disposal, we can see that the methods and beliefs of, say, the sect to which Bunyan belonged, were not a *sine qua non* of healing and of psychological growth, but rather a vehicle, or container for a whole range of human emotions which might be classed together under the heading of the 'conversion experience'.

The peculiarity of the conversion experience as experienced by Calvinists and later by Methodists and others was the extreme state of tension that preceded it. Starbuck, in a famous study, said that 'The feelings are reduced to the last degree of tension, and then recoil; are pent up and suddenly burst; life appears to force itself to the farthest extreme in a given direction, and then to break into free activity in another.' The tension arises from strong guilt feelings which gradually intensify, until the state known as 'conviction' is reached. 'The subject,' wrote Starbuck, 'is brought to the last degree of dejection, humility, confusion, uncertainty, sense of sinfulness and the like.' One subject he interviewed said that 'Conviction became so strong that I thought I would die that very summer if I did not get relief.'[1]

For Starbuck's subjects the tension burst like a boil (it seemed to be a slower and more complex process in Bunyan's case) and they enjoyed a reversal of their pre-conversion feelings. Joy, lightness of heart, clarified vision, exultation, and the sense of freedom and harmony with God, filled their minds.

Starbuck noted that among males, the pre-conversion guilt-feelings seemed to be associated with sexual temptation, but also that many who had led perfectly good and pious lives suffered no less a sense of conviction than those who had led wild lives. Writing before Freud's work had proceeded very far, or was at all well known, he commented that the sense of sin seemed to have other causes than the actual bad habits of the subject.

What he was observing, according to psycho-analytic theory, was the emergence of repressed guilt-feelings, an emergence hastened, if not caused, by scolding sermons, and threats of damnation still in vogue in some religious groups at the turn of the century. A later American psychologist thought that the strictness of sexual mores in America magnified the sense of guilt, particularly in young men, who either in fact or in fantasy transgressed the sexual code of their society.[2]

Times have changed, however. 'Hellfire' preaching, together with techniques for arousing guilt, has declined, and sexual experimentation among the young is widely practised in England and America. What has also declined is the number of dramatic 'conversion' experiences, of the classic kind described by Starbuck, in which the subject reached total dejection and then suddenly passed from this into total happiness. We may hypothesise a degree of cause and effect here.

There seems to be gain in this change. No one could wish for another human being the long drawn out agony of spirit which Bunyan so movingly described, nor the utter misery which Starbuck's subjects revealed. 'Before conversion I had not a single happy day, because of dread of the future.' 'I had fear of being lost; was pensive and worried; was greatly depressed and could not sleep.'

On the other hand we may wonder what catharsis people nowadays who are greatly afflicted with guilt-feelings can hope for. The way the old hellfire preachers exacerbated guilt-feelings undoubtedly caused immense suffering, yet converted people might have felt that the suffering was more than matched by the joy that followed. They had felt themselves partaking in high drama. Their lives, however insignificant, humdrum, poverty-stricken, or unimportant in the eyes of the world, had for a time become thrillingly meaningful.

Few people nowadays experience that agony and joy. Guilt-feelings are more likely to give twinges of misery like a grumbling appendix than to become the source of ecstatic joy. The high drama is no longer available to many who may have no other drama in their lives.

It is tempting to speculate how Bunyan would have fared if he had lived today. Drugs would have relieved his terrible depression, and he might have lived out the acute phase of his paranoia in a mental hospital instead of in his own home. He would have been regarded, and so have come to regard himself, as a sick man, even as a mad man.

Whatever other feelings of inferiority Bunyan suffered from, that particular kind did not trouble him. Unselfconsciously he tells us about the tortured workings of his mind, never, it is clear, anticipating any sneer from his audience about his sanity, of which he himself has no fundamental doubt.

As Luther had done before him he found a therapist in the person of a stable father-figure, and a therapy in his mission to counsel and to preach. He suffered his agony to the full, unrelieved by drugs, yet by the sort of reversal, or 'explosive' process Starbuck describes he was then able to experience its opposite, the 'Love' which made him want to preach even to the crows upon the ploughed land and which he would never forget for a lifetime. Above all, the suffering-followed-by-joy, a kind of crucifixion-and-resurrection sequence, branded his imagination so deeply that it became the subject of his art. We must wonder whether our own society could offer a man like Bunyan any vehicle of self-realisation, self-expression, and self-healing half as effective as that he found for himself in his religion, or whether rather it would not have reduced and discredited him.

Puritanism is a desperate remedy, but it seems to have been of value to people who were already desperate, partly because it did not tell them that their fears were groundless, but rather that things were even worse than they feared. In a sense it abolished projection, declaring that the inner and outer state of a man are one. It is a sort of homeopathic remedy — a treating of madness with a mad remedy — yet men such as Bunyan came through it to a calmer and less persecuted state of mind.

We are, perhaps, more the heirs of Puritanism than we sometimes suppose, not least in some of our methods for examining the sicknesses of the personality. Psycho-analysis itself adopted a method, that of introspection, that had been pioneered by the Puritans, and Freud, whose personality left such a lasting mark upon his method, had some of the heroic qualities of the 'lone hero'. Psycho-analysis has an implicit belief, as all would-be healing processes must, in a kind of 'progress', a salvation or redemption.

The intensive self-examination upon which both psycho-analysis and Puritanism rely, derive from a belief that progress, which both of them desire, is dependent upon an increase in consciousness. From studying the self a new awareness emerges, and, it is hoped, a new control. Critics of Puritanism complained that this 'watching' of the self brought about a loss of spontaniety, the child-like quality that can be one of the greatest human charms, yet Puritanism (indeed Protestantism altogether) may have arisen from the discovery that spontaneity no longer wholly worked for mankind, that whether he liked it or not, he could not be unselfconsciously childlike any more. In fact the Reformation may be seen as a kind of adolescence in the history of Europe, the point where men are no longer content to speak as a child, or think as a child, but are trying to put away childish things. Of course, like adolescents, they overdo it. The strange note of caricature which so often seems to mark Puritan behaviour suggests an attempt to be more grown-up than any grown-up tries to be. The Reformation is characterised by exaggeration, yet the things exaggerated — the need for independence of authority, for freedom, for a real inwardness of belief — are of vital importance. Those who were martyrs for it, as Bunyan partially was, knew that it was mankind for which they were laying down their lives or their liberties, and were prepared to suffer accordingly.

Bunyan survived his suffering and, after the manner of great men, went on to achieve inwardly the progress he wanted for mankind. In his maturity he could forego the exaggeration of adolescence — the preoccupation with purity and perfection, the polarisation of good and evil, together with the denial of evil in oneself and the projection of it on others. He could rediscover the body and its pleasures. In a sense he ceased to be a Puritan.

Mankind, at least in Europe and America, has not progressed so far. We still admire most of the Puritan virtues (and some at least of them are well worth having) — hard work, truthfulness, order, conscientiousness, courage, sexual restraint; and we still reveal many of the less attractive traits of the Puritan — prurience, an interest in sadism, a passion for making money, the tendency to project wickedness upon others. The last trait seems to be the most destructive. The confrontation of the 'shadow' (instead of projecting it upon a nation, or race, or group whom we dislike) does, in fact, seem to be the only hope for the continued survival of mankind, and to this end, we must all cease to be Puritans.

Man cannot be pure, or perfect, however much he would like to be, and life, for himself and others, begins afresh when he knows this. For Bunyan this knowledge led to a new peace of mind, a new level of creativity, and a new perception of tenderness and femininity. Woman was no longer the seductress to be shunned or punished, but was recognised as part of himself.

Bunyan moved towards his death, having answered the question 'What shall I do?' and found the liberation of wholeness towards which all men blindly struggle. F. R. Leavis said that the second part of the

Progress, Bunyan's hymn of liberation, finished on a note of 'sustained exaltation'. Apart from the sublime language the most moving thing about the successive deaths is the way one character after another, hitherto shackled by fear, suddenly finds freedom on the shores of the River of Death. Mr. Dispondencie discovers that the fears which have tortured him all his life are insubstantial ghosts. His daughter Much-afraid, to everyone's surprise, goes through the waters singing. Mr. Stand-fast says that though he too, like so many others, has always been frightened of the River, the reality is quite different from the expec-tation. 'Now methinks I stand easie.'

But the most famous end of any of Bunyan's pilgrims is that of Mr. Valiant-for-Truth, the character whom lovers of the Progress have often identified with Bunyan himself. It has all been a terrible and laborious struggle, but he does not regret a moment of it.

Then he said, I am going to my Fathers, and tho with great Difficulty I am got hither, yet now I do not repent me of all the Trouble I have been at to arrive where I am. My Sword, I give to him that shall succeed me in my Pilgrimage, and my Courage and Skill, to him that can get it. My Marks and Scarrs I carry with me, to be a witness for me, that I have fought his Battels, who now will be my Rewarder. When the Day that he must go hence was come, many accompanied him to the River side, into which, as he went, he said, Death, where is thy Sting? And as he went down deeper, he said, Grave where is thy Victory? So he passed over, and the Trumpets sounded for him on the other side.

NOTES

1 E. T. Starbuck, *The Psychology of Religion* (1901).
2 J. B. Pratt, *The Religious Consciousness*, Macmillan, N.Y. (1920).

Bibliography

———

WORKS OF JOHN BUNYAN

Grace Abounding to the Chief of Sinners, ed. Roger Sharrock, Oxford University Press (1966)
The Pilgrim's Progress, Parts I and II
The Holy War, ed. Rev. Williams Landels, James Sangster (1880)
The Life and Death of Mr. Badman, ed. G. B. Harrison, Dent (1928)
Sermons and other writings, *The Works of John Bunyan*, ed. Rev. George Offor (1853)

BOOKS THAT INFLUENCED BUNYAN

The Practice of Piety, Lewis Bayly (1649)
The Plaine Mans Path-way to heaven, Arthur Dent (1601)
Fox's Book of Martyrs
Abstract of a Commentarie by Master Martin Luther upon the Epistle of St. Paul to the Galathians (London, 1635)

BIOGRAPHICAL MATERIAL ABOUT BUNYAN

Charles Doe, *The Struggler* (essay about Bunyan) (1691)
Robert Southey, 'Life of Bunyan': introduction to 1830 edition of *The Pilgrim's Progress*, John Murray

George Offor, 'A Memoir': preface to *The Works of John Bunyan* (*op. cit.*)

John Brown, *John Bunyan: His Life, Times and Work* (1885)

William York Tindall, *John Bunyan, Mechanick Preacher*, Columbia University Press (1934)

Jack Lindsay, John Bunyan, *Maker of Myths*, Methuen (1937)

Henri Talon, *John Bunyan: The Man and His Works*, tr. Barbara Wall, Rockcliff (1951)

Roger Sharrock, *John Bunyan*, Hutchinson (1954)

PURITANISM

William Haller, *The Rise of Puritanism*, Columbia University Press (1938)

R. L. Greaves, *John Bunyan*, Sutton Courtenay Press (1969)

Edmund Gosse, *Father and Son*, Heinemann (1907)

Ben Jonson, *Bartholomew Fair* (1614)

Owen Watkins, *The Puritan Experience*, Routledge and Kegan Paul (1972)

Perry Miller, *The New England Mind: The Seventeenth Century*, Harvard University Press (1954)

François Wendel, *Calvin*, Collins (1963)

Geoffrey F. Nuttall, *The Holy Spirit in Puritan Faith and Experience*, Blackwell (1946)

——, *The Puritan Spirit*, Epworth (1967)

The Journal of George Fox, Ellwood Text

W. N. Wigfield, *Recusancy and Nonconformity in Bedfordshire*, Bedfordshire Historical Record Society, Vol. XX

A Booke containing a record of the Acts of a Congregation of Christ, in and About Bedford (1656–1821)

Larzer Ziff, *Puritanism in America*, Oxford University Press (1974)

HISTORICAL BACKGROUND

Christopher Hill, *Society and Puritanism in Pre-Revolutionary England*, Secker and Warburg (1964)

——, *The World Turned Upside Down*, Temple Smith (1972)

C. V. Wedgwood, *The King's Peace*, Collins (1955)

——, *The Trial of Charles I*, Collins (1964)

W. G. Hoskins, *The Midland Peasant*, Macmillan (1957)

R. H. Tawney, *Religion and the Rise of Capitalism* (1926)

H. G. Tibbutt, *Bedfordshire and the Protectorate*, Elstow Moot Hall pamphlets

——, *Bunyan's Standing Today*, Elstow Moot Hall pamphlets

——, *Bedfordshire and the First Civil War*, Elstow Moot Hall pamphlets

Ernst Gombrich, *The Story of Art*, Phaidon Press (1950)

PSYCHOLOGICAL BACKGROUND

William James, *The Varieties of Religious Experience* (1901)

E. T. Starbuck, *The Psychology of Religion* (1901)

J. B. Pratt, *The Religious Consciousness*, Macmillan, N.Y. (1920)

R. H. Thouless, *The Psychology of Religion*, Cambridge University Press (1923)

W. N. Evans, 'Notes on the Conversion of John Bunyan', *International Journal of Psycho-Analysis*, XXIV (1943)

William H. Sheldon, 'Constitutional Factors in Personality', in *Personality and Behaviour Disorders*, ed. J. McV. Hunt, Ronald (1944)

C. G. Jung, *The Integration of the Personality*, Routledge and Kegan Paul (1940)

Erik Erikson, *Young Man Luther*, Faber (1959)

Norman O. Brown, *Life Against Death — The Psychoanalytical Meaning of History*, Routledge and Kegan Paul (1959)

Jolande Jacobi, *The Way of Individuation*, Hodder and Stoughton (1967)

Charles Rycroft, *A Critical Dictionary of Psychoanalysis*, Nelson (1968)

THE LITERARY INFLUENCE OF BUNYAN

The Life and Works of Lord Macaulay, Vol. V (1897)

Matthew Arnold, *Mixed Essays*

Coleridge's edition of *The Pilgrim's Progress*

David E. Smith, *John Bunyan in America*, Indiana University Press (1966)

Nathaniel Hawthorne, *Mosses from an Old Manse* (1846)

L. M. Alcott, *Little Women* (1868)

Bernard Shaw, '*Review of the Dramatic Presentation of The Pilgrim's Progress*', in *Saturday Review*, 2nd January 1897

——, Preface to *Man and Superman*, Standard Edition (1903)

——, Preface to *Androcles and the Lion*, Standard Edition (1913)

Norbert F. O'Donnell, *Shaw, Bunyan and Puritanism*, publication of the Modern Language association, LXXII, June 1957

J. B. Wharey, *The Sources of Bunyan's Allegories*, J. H. Furst Ltd. (1904)

Charles Firth, *Essays Historical and Literary*, Oxford University Press (1938)

F. R. Leavis, *The Common Pursuit*, Chatto and Windus (1952)

e. e. cummings, *The Enormous Room*, Boni and Livright Inc. (1920)

Index